Unshakable Faith in Almighty God

Jack and Judy Hartman

Lamplight Ministries, Inc.
Dunedin, Florida

DEDICATION

We dedicate this book to Elizabeth Sokolik, Judy Mangle and Gail White.

Elizabeth has been working side by side with us in Lamplight Ministries for twelve years. She is the "glue" that holds Lamplight Ministries together. Elizabeth is responsible for all of our shipping, our bookkeeping and a maze of other intricate details that she handles extremely efficiently. Elizabeth is a treasured friend and coworker.

Judy Mangle has been on our team for eleven years. She types all the research material and each of the multiple drafts of our books and Scripture Meditation Cards. She does all of our preparation for publication including the graphic art work. Judy's desktop publishing skills, her thoughtful editing, her creativity and her delightful spirit are invaluable to us.

Gail White is in her third year as our executive secretary. She has brought many new concepts to Lamplight Ministries. She is extremely efficient. I (Jack) have employed many secretaries during the past forty-five years. Gail is the best secretary I have ever had.

Thank You, Lord, for bringing Elizabeth, Judy and Gail to us. Elizabeth, Judy and Gail, we thank you for your dedication and the joy you bring into our lives as we labor together for the glory of God. We are very grateful to each of you.

FOREWORD

For many years my wife edited my books. When we stopped writing books to devote five years of our lives to writing ten sets of Scripture Meditation Cards, Judy contributed so much that she rightfully was listed as the co-author of each set of Scripture cards.

When we started to write books again, I assumed that Judy would edit the books as she had done previously. Judy made so many changes on each draft of our next book that she changed the book significantly. I concluded at that time that she legitimately should be listed as the co-author of that book. This same situation has occurred in each of our subsequent books.

I have written several portions of this book in the first person because this book is filled with principles I have taught during the past thirty years, but I want to emphasize that Judy definitely is the co-author of this book. I am indebted to Judy for hearing God and for all of the constructive writing and rewriting she has done. Thank you, my dear wife. I believe the readers of this book also will thank you as they read the following pages.

Jack Hartman

I first started using this version of the Bible when I bought a paperback version of *The Amplified New Testament* in 1975 because of the inscription on the cover. This inscription said, "...the best study Testament on the market. It is a magnificent translation. I use it constantly." (Dr. Billy Graham)

As I read about the history of this version of the Bible, I found that a group of qualified Hebrew and Greek scholars had spent more than twenty thousand hours amplifying the Bible. They believed that traditional word-by-word translations often failed to reveal the shades of meaning that are part of the Hebrew and Greek words.

After many years of extensive Bible study I have found that *The Amplified Bible* reveals many spiritual truths I cannot find in other versions of the Bible. Because of this marvelous amplification we now use this version of the Bible exclusively in all of our books and Scripture Meditation Cards.

Please be patient with the brackets and parentheses if you are not familiar with this translation of the Bible. They are used to indicate what has been added in the amplification. The brackets contain words that clarify the meaning. The parentheses contain additional phrases included in the original language. I do not want to bury you under a mass of parentheses and brackets, but I have found that *The Amplified Bible* is filled with specific and practical information that I believe will help *you* to increase your faith in God.

Table of Contents

Introduction

We believe that the first five chapters of this book are extremely important. They are filled with *facts* from the Bible and *facts* about the state of the world today. We tell you what we believe God will do as a result of these facts. We encourage you to read these chapters prayerfully. Then you can decide for yourself how these facts pertain to *you* and the necessity for you to follow God's specific instructions to increase *your* faith in Him.

Do *not* agree with anything we say unless we can back up each point we make with facts from the holy Scriptures or with factual information concerning the world today. We hope you will be willing to change any preconceived opinions you have if your opinions do not concur with facts from the Word of God or with the other specific and undeniable facts we have provided.

In the first five chapters we will give you many specific reasons why we believe that we definitely live in the last days before Jesus returns. The purpose of this book is to show you exactly what the Bible teaches about increasing your faith in God. The brief information in these initial chapters is included solely to help you to see the absolute necessity of increasing your faith in God *now*.

For purposes of simplicity and clarity we often will mention the United States when our comments also could include Canada and many other relatively affluent countries. Many people in Third World countries already are experiencing extremely difficult times. We believe that Christians in the United States and other relatively affluent countries must understand that our grace period from God *is drawing to a close.* We believe that severe adversity is coming into the lives of people in the United States and other countries that currently are enjoying relative prosperity.

Many of us will pay a severe price in the future if we do not know what the Bible teaches about the end times. We must learn and obey the specific scriptural instructions our Father has given us to show us exactly what we should do to increase our faith in Him. "My people are destroyed for lack of knowledge…" (Hosea 4:6).

When God referred to "My people" in this passage of Scripture, He was referring to the Israelites almost 2,800 years ago. We believe this comment from God applies to all Christians today because all of us who have asked Jesus to be our Savior are "God's people." We each become an adopted member of the family of God when we are saved. "…in Christ Jesus you are all sons of God through faith" (Galatians 3:26).

Many of God's children have little or no knowledge of what our Father has told us about the difficult times that lie ahead. Christians have been given the spiritual ability to hear these warnings from God, but many Christians are so preoccupied with other seemingly important activities that they are missing out on what God is saying about the end times.

Many Christians are *not* doing what our Father has instructed us to do to increase our faith in Him. We pray that you will not make this mistake. We hope you will carefully read the initial chapters of this book to see what is taking place in the world today and what inevitably must occur in the future.

We want to emphasize that this book is *not* a book of dread. This book is a book of *hope, faith and encouragement.* If you learn and obey God's specific instructions to increase your faith in Him, your deep, unwavering and unshakable faith in God *will* enable you to adjust to the tremendous changes that will take place in the end times. Because of your faith in God you will be able to receive the wonderful protection your Father wants to give *you* at a time when many other people will experience severe fear and hardship because of their lack of faith in God.

We must not turn our backs on what God is saying to us. "…see to it that you do not reject Him or refuse to listen to and heed Him Who is speaking [to you now]. For if they [the Israelites] did not escape when they refused to listen and heed Him Who warned and divinely instructed them [here] on earth [revealing with heavenly warnings His will], how much less shall we escape if we reject and turn our backs on Him Who cautions and admonishes [us] from heaven?" (Hebrews 12:25).

In the initial chapters of this book we will discuss the complacency and apathy that exists among many people in the United States and other relatively affluent countries. We will carefully examine the moral filth and decadence that is sweeping through the world. This filth is in direct disobedience to specific instructions in the Word of God.

In these initial chapters we will look carefully at the lifestyle of our generation. We believe that Satan and his demons have had a significant effect on the apathy, complacency and moral decay that exists in the world today. Satan and his demons know that they only have a short time remaining before they will begin their eternal suffering in the lake of fire. "…the devil has come down to you in fierce anger (fury), because he knows that he has [only] a short time [left]!" (Revelation 12:12).

Satan and his demons are desperate. We believe that legions of demonic spirits are being unleashed in these last days before Jesus returns. Satan and his demons know that all people who trust Jesus for their eternal salvation will live eternally in the glory of heaven. Satan and his demons know that they will suffer *intolerable anguish* throughout eternity.

Satan does not want us to learn and heed our Father's warnings pertaining to the last days before Jesus returns. Satan wants us to be completely unprepared for what lies ahead. Satan and his demons will do everything they can to take every unbeliever to hell with them. They also will do everything they can to make life miserable for all Christians who will live eternally in heaven.

In the difficult times that lie ahead many Christians will pray asking God to increase their faith in Him. God *already* has provided us with everything we need to increase our faith in Him. Every person who has asked Jesus to be his or her Savior was able to make this decision because of the grace of God. God gave each of us the faith we had to have to receive eternal salvation through Jesus. "…it is by free grace (God's unmerited favor) that you are saved (delivered from judgment and made partakers of Christ's salvation) through [your] faith…" (Ephesians 2:8).

Instead of praying to God for more faith, we should learn and obey the specific instructions our Father has given each of us telling us *how* to increase the initial faith He gave us so that we could be saved. This book is filled with hundreds of specific instructions to show you exactly what our Father wants us to do to increase this faith He has given to each of us.

We want to emphasize at the beginning of this book that *faith is not a formula*. Unwavering faith in God requires such a close and intimate relationship with God that we will trust Him completely at all times because of our wonderful relationship with Him. If you specifically obey these scriptural instructions, you will find that your relationship with God will improve and that you will be able to trust Him completely.

This book is filled with hundreds of specific promises from the Word of God. These promises will help us to improve our relationship with God. "...He has bestowed on us His precious and exceedingly great promises, so that through them you may escape [by flight] from the moral decay (rottenness and corruption) that is in the world because of covetousness (lust and greed), and become sharers (partakers) of the divine nature" (II Peter 1:4).

The promises in the Word of God are "precious and exceedingly great." The promises of God surpass all human greatness. These promises will enable us to "escape from the moral decay, rottenness and corruption" that are sweeping across the world in these last days before Jesus returns.

This passage of Scripture concludes by assuring us that the precious promises of God will enable us to be "sharers and partakers of the divine nature." *You* actually will partake of God's nature if you obey God's instructions, learn these promises and learn how to have absolute faith that our Father will do exactly what He promises to do.

As you read this book you will see that it is simple and easy to understand. So much Scripture is included that you will need to *study* the scriptural facts in this book carefully, thoughtfully and prayerfully. We recommend that you read at least one chapter of this book each morning to begin your day.

We recommend that you read this book with a highlighter or a pen to mark the Scripture references, facts and explanations you would like to retain. Write notes in the margin that will help you to do exactly what the Bible tells you to do to increase your faith in God.

You can finish reading the forty-three chapters in this book in approximately a month and a half if you read one chapter each day. If you read two chapters each day in this manner, you can finish reading this book in approximately three weeks. We suggest that you read the book at least one more time to *meditate* on the Scripture references and the explanation of Scripture you have highlighted or underlined. Your study and meditation on the scriptural facts contained in this book will help you to progressively increase your faith in God.

We realize that some of our books contain a certain amount of content that overlaps with our other books. Each of our books has the same message – "Get into the Word of God and get the Word of God into you." This book is filled with hundreds of specific facts from the holy Scriptures that are not included in any of our other books. We pray that this book will be a great blessing to you and that it will help *you* to significantly increase *your faith* in Almighty God.

Chapter 1

Spiritual Storm Clouds
Are on the Horizon

In these initial chapters you will clearly see that spiritual storm clouds are on the horizon. We can look past these clouds to find God Who *will* bring us safely through the storms that lie ahead of us *according to our faith in Him.* Jesus said, "...According to your faith and trust and reliance [on the power invested in Me] be it done to you" (Matthew 9:29).

We make whatever preparations we can when we see a storm with thunder and lightning approaching. Similar preparations are necessary with these spiritual storm clouds. In the past these storm clouds gathered over groups of countries that were engaged in war or specific countries that were faced with other severe problems. We believe the spiritual storm clouds that are coming will engulf the entire world.

The Bible tells us that circumstances in the world will be so severe during the final days before Jesus returns that some people will pay a severe price because of their fear of what they see coming. The Bible speaks of "...men swooning away or expiring with fear and dread and apprehension and expectation of the things that are coming on the world; for the [very] powers of heaven will be shaken and caused to totter" (Luke 21:26).

Can you even begin to comprehend the magnitude of the problems in the world being *so severe* that people actually will *faint* or even *die* because of their fear of the future? Jesus gave us additional explanation of the difficult times that lie ahead when He said, "...there will be great tribulation (affliction, distress, and oppression) such as has not been from the beginning of the world until now – no, and never will be [again]. And if those days had not been shortened, no human being would endure and survive, but for the sake of the elect (God's chosen ones) those days will be shortened" (Matthew 24:21-22).

These two passages of Scripture refer to the seven years of the Great Tribulation. We can be certain that very difficult times lie ahead. "...in the last days will come (set in) perilous times of great stress and trouble [hard to deal with and hard to bear]" (II Timothy 3:1).

After reading Luke 21:26, Matthew 24:21-22 and II Timothy 3:1, there is no question that very difficult times will come upon the generation living on earth in the final days before Jesus returns. We are now ready to look carefully into the Word of God and also to consider many additional facts about our world. These facts will explain why we believe that our generation definitely is the generation living in the last days before Jesus returns.

The best place to begin our study of what the world will be like in the last days before Jesus returns is with the three verses of Scripture immediately following II Timothy 3:1. "...people will be lovers of self and [utterly] self-centered, lovers of money and aroused by an inordinate [greedy] desire for wealth, proud and arrogant and contemptuous boasters. They will be abusive (blasphemous, scoffing), disobedient to parents, ungrateful, unholy and profane. [They will be] without natural [human] affection (callous and inhuman), relentless (admitting of no truce or appeasement); [they will be] slanderers (false accusers, troublemakers), intemperate and loose in morals and conduct, uncontrolled and fierce, haters of good. [They will be] treacherous [betrayers], rash, [and] inflated with self-conceit. [They will be] lovers of sensual pleasures and vain amusements more than and rather than lovers of God" (II Timothy 3:2-4).

Please take a few minutes to carefully reread and think about this passage of Scripture. Ask yourself if these words that were written almost two thousand years ago accurately describe today's world. In these initial chapters we will look at many facts about the world today that will document the selfishness and self-centeredness we have just read about in II Timothy 3:2-4.

Anyone who takes a careful look at our generation must conclude that selfishness and self-centeredness have increased tremendously in recent years. Our generation first was referred to as the "Me generation" in the 1980s. The description given in this passage of Scripture has become increasingly accurate with each subsequent decade.

Do we see more "proud and arrogant" people today than in the previous generation? Are more children "disobedient to parents and ungrateful?" Do we hear more profanity today than in the past? Do we see more "intemperate troublemakers" who are "loose in morals" in the world today than when our parents and grandparents were our age? Do we see a constantly increasing number of people who love "sensual pleasures and amusements" more than they love God?

The thoughts of many people today are centered around themselves and their selfish desires instead of being centered around God and His plan for their lives. Our newspapers are filled with stories about the acts of selfish people who abuse, rape and murder. We read about a greater variety of selfish and self-centered crimes than what people read about in their newspapers when our parents were our age. There is no question that selfishness, self-centeredness and greediness have increased tremendously in recent years, just as II Timothy 3:2 says.

One of the foremost signs of people who are "lovers of self and utterly self-centered" is the tremendous increase in the number of abortions that have been performed in recent years. The great majority of these abortions have been caused by selfish sexual desires of men and women that resulted in unwanted pregnancies.

Some people say that little babies really are not being killed in an abortion because a fetus is not a human being. *What is God's perspective* on this subject? The psalmist said, "...You did form my inward parts; You did knit me together in my mother's womb. I will confess and praise You for You are fearful and wonderful and for the awful wonder of my birth! Wonderful are Your works, and that my inner self knows right well. My frame was not hidden from You when I was being formed in secret [and] intricately and curiously wrought [as if embroidered with various colors] in the depths of the earth [a region of darkness and mystery]. Your eyes saw my unformed substance, and in Your book all the days [of my life] were written before ever they took shape, when as yet there was none of them" (Psalm 139:13-16).

God "forms and knits together" babies in their mother's womb. These babies who are "formed in secret" are "intricately wrought." God has a specific plan for every day of the life of each "unformed substance." We do *not* believe that God looks at the abortion of these "unformed substances" from the same perspective that many people in the world do.

Each year on Memorial Day people in the United States remember our veterans who have been killed in wars. More than one million Americans have died for our country since the United States was founded in 1776. These valiant Americans are appropriately honored for the sacrifice they have made. However, the approximately *forty million babies* who have been murdered through abortion since the US Supreme Court Roe v Wade decision in 1973 are ignored by many people.

Our generation essentially has declared war on unborn children. Our country has ignored God's perspective on babies being formed in a mother's womb to the extent that abortion on demand is legal in the United States. Millions of men and women have suffered tremendous psychological damage as a result of the abortions that were rooted in their selfish sexual desires.

In the United States almost three thousand babies are *legally murdered* through abortion each day. Approximately sixty percent of the people in the world live in countries that allow abortion while approximately forty percent of the people in the world live in countries where abortion is illegal. The United States leads the world in many positive areas. Our country also leads the world in the number of legal murders of unborn babies.

The United States Supreme Court that has made abortion legal is, in our opinion, part of a widespread movement in the judicial branch of government that has been significantly influenced by Satan. The judicial branch of government has usurped tremendous power in recent years. The United States Supreme Court and many other courts have continually made decisions that are in direct opposition to specific instructions that are given in the Word of God. Legalized abortion violates one of the Ten Commandments that says "You shall not commit murder" (Exodus 20:13).

The irony of the more than forty million abortions that have been performed in the United States is that the very doctors who were trained to preserve life instead are taking millions of lives. These selfish doctors are doing exactly the opposite of what they were trained to do.

Abortions caused by rape, incest, or threat to the health of the mother or the baby account for less than five percent of all abortions. Approximately ninety-five percent of all abortions are performed as a means of birth control for people who do not want to pay any other price for their sexual desires.

Christians in the United States who are opposed to abortion are referred to as "pro-life." The logical opposite of "pro-life" is "pro-death." "Pro-choice" sounds much better than "pro-death" but we believe that, in the eyes of God, all advocates of "pro-choice" actually are advocates of legalized murder.

We believe that all aborted babies will live in the incomprehensible glory of heaven. We do not believe that these aborted babies who have never lived and never sinned will live eternally in the horrible lake of fire. There is no passage of Scripture that gives us an explicit answer on this subject. The Bible does speak many times of God's love, compassion, mercy and grace. The Bible says that God loves children (see Matthew 18:1-6 and Matthew 19:13-15).

Unborn babies in the womb, infants and very young children on earth are too young to know anything about their personal sin. God is eminently fair. He always does what is right. We believe that these babies and other young children who died before they reached an age of accountability will live eternally in heaven.

We represent our loving and forgiving Father. Have you had an abortion? God is faithful to forgive you if admit your sin, truly express your sorrow and ask Him for forgiveness (see I John 1:9). If you know you have been forgiven by God, you should forgive yourself. You can turn to a local Christian pregnancy center for counsel and assistance. Look in the yellow pages of your telephone book under "Pregnancy Counseling" if you are considering abortion or if you have had an abortion.

God has granted favor to the United States for many years because this country was founded as a godly country based on scriptural principles. We believe that the murder of more than forty million unborn children in the United States is an abomination to God. *How much longer* will God continue to grant favor to a country that has *legalized* the widespread murder of more than forty million "unformed substances" for whom He had a detailed and specific plan for every day of their lives?

In this chapter we have read several scriptural facts about the difficult times the world will experience in the last days before Jesus returns. We have discussed widespread abortion which is just one of many signs indicating that our selfish generation lives in the end times. In the next three chapters we will carefully examine many additional specific indications that we live in the last days before Jesus returns.

We want to constantly remind you that the remainder of this book after these initial chapters is *positive, encouraging and uplifting*. We all must understand that we do indeed live in the end times. We *must* make the decision *now* to diligently do exactly what our loving Father has instructed us to do to increase our faith in Him.

Chapter 2

Sexual Degradation That Violates Instructions from God

In the last chapter we saw that the Bible says that "people will be lovers of self and utterly self-centered" in the last days. We examined several specific facts pertaining to the tremendous number of abortions that have been performed because of the selfish sexual desires of people who did not want the responsibility of a baby. In this chapter we will look at many additional selfish sexual desires that have grossly perverted God's wonderful gift of a sexual relationship that was intended to be enjoyed only by husbands and wives.

Our culture has become increasingly sexualized. I believe that the Kinsey report on male and female sexuality that came out in the late 1940s represented the beginning of today's sexual revolution. *Playboy* magazine began publication in the early 1950s. *Playboy* and similar magazines took up where the Kinsey report left off. These magazines have led to a tremendous unscriptural revolution in sexual perception in the United States.

In recent years we have experienced a significant escalation of the gay rights movement. The use of the word "gay" to describe same-sex relationships is scripturally inaccurate. The

Bible refers to these relationships as "… vile affections and degrading passions. For their women exchanged their natural function for an unnatural and abnormal one. And the men also turned from natural relations with women and were set ablaze (burning out, consumed) with lust for one another – men committing shameful acts with men and suffering in their own bodies and personalities the inevitable consequences and penalty of their wrongdoing and going astray, which was [their] fitting retribution" (Romans 1:26-27).

In spite of what homosexuals and lesbians say about themselves, we must know what the Word of God says about their "vile," "degrading" and "abnormal" relationships. The Word of God refers to these relationships as "shameful acts." Romans 1:27 says that homosexuals and lesbians will pay a severe penalty for their ungodly lifestyle. They will "suffer in their bodies and personalities the inevitable penalty of their wrongdoing and going astray." Homosexuals and lesbians will receive "fitting retribution" for their sins.

How can any thinking person believe that God would approve of homosexual or lesbian relationships? Common sense tells us that the anatomy of men and women precludes marriage between members of the same sex. Children obviously cannot be produced from these relationships. Advocates of same sex marriages base their demands on the adoption of children who have been born from a sexual relationship between a man and a woman. This premise makes no sense whatsoever.

We are seeing an increasing wave of open homosexuality. These people either do not know and understand what Romans 1:26-27 says about this lifestyle or they do not care what the Bible says. As this book is written, the demand in the United States for same-sex marriages has escalated tremendously. Officials in some cities have married gay couples in open defiance of the law. Gay clergymen are coming out into the open. Religious denominations are appointing national leaders who are openly gay.

Homosexuality is being perceived as an acceptable lifestyle by an increasing number of people. A recent poll shows that almost fifty percent of all adults and more than eighty percent of all high school seniors consider homosexuality to be an acceptable lifestyle. Some public schools have a curriculum that presents the homosexual lifestyle as normal. Homosexuals are relentless in their desire to receive approval.

We feel great pain for the deception of these people. Christians should pray for homosexuals and lesbians. We should pray for them just as we should pray for anyone who has sinned. The facts we have just read indicate their need for prayer. Only God in His mercy can help these people.

We must state clearly that we do not judge any man or woman. We know that Jesus is the judge. We are filled with sorrow for the deception that can consume a person. The name of this deception is lust. It can be so consuming that a person is totally controlled by it. Our prayer is that every captive will be set free by the resurrection power of Jesus. "Father, You sent Jesus Christ, Your Son, to set the captives free. We pray in Jesus' name, 'Be released' for anyone who is controlled by sexual sin."

Many homosexuals and lesbians will suffer from sexually transmitted disease. AIDS is not exclusively a homosexual disease, but the facts show that homosexuals account for well over fifty percent of the AIDS cases in the United States today. Since homosexuals only represent between one percent to two percent of the population in the United States, this figure of well over fifty percent is a very significant item of concern.

There is no question that much of the misery and death that the AIDS epidemic has brought upon the world is due to the perversion of homosexuality.

Many other sexual relationships indicate that the tremendous increase in sexual sin in our generation is an abomination to God. The sexual relationship between a man and a woman is a gift from God that is meant to be enjoyed between a husband and a wife. People who violate God's instructions in this area are committing adultery if married or fornication if unmarried. These sexual sins specifically disobey one of the Ten Commandments that says, "You shall not commit adultery" (Exodus 20:14).

Sexually transmitted disease is part of the penalty that many adulterers and fornicators pay. At this time there are more than twenty-five different varieties of sexually transmitted disease. More than half of these diseases have been classified as incurable.

We can clearly see the results of the sweeping sexual immorality that has become so commonplace in our generation. The latest United States Census Bureau report indicates that there are more than five million unmarried partner homes in the United States. The number of unmarried couples living together has almost doubled in the last ten years.

These unmarried partner relationships produce many abortions. They also produce many illegitimate babies. In 1960 five percent of all births were conceived by unmarried partners. As this book is written almost forty percent of all births in the United States come from unmarried partners.

In recent years sexual misconduct between clergymen and people in their churches has escalated tremendously. Many unmarried Catholic priests have been exposed and convicted because they have molested children in their churches over a period of many years. Many adults have come forward to testify of the abuse they suffered when they were children.

Sexual sin by Christian leaders continues to stain and cripple the church of Jesus Christ. This behavior mars the lives of people who were betrayed by these leaders. This betrayal often traps these people in a life of fear and sorrow.

We have deep sorrow for the degradation of the precious people that has been perpetuated by people representing the Church of Jesus Christ. Our prayer is that each one be set free by Jesus Who took all sin and shame upon Himself.

Many sexual sins have their root in pornography. In 1973 Americans spent approximately ten million dollars a year on pornography. This figure has risen to more than eight billion dollars today. The multibillion dollar pornography industry has become increasingly graphic. Pornography that previously was perceived as very shocking and gross now has become common and acceptable to many people.

The tremendous growth of the internet in recent years has been both a blessing and a curse. The internet definitely has contributed to increased immorality. A significant increase in online sex has been reported in recent years. Many people in the privacy of their own homes have developed a secret pornography habit or are engaged in other online sexual activity. People who originally came across an online sex site and looked at it for just a few minutes have steadily increased this habit. We recommend an internet filter. An excellent filter is provided free of charge by Rev. Bill Keller at http://www.liveprayer.com.

Many of the pornographic sites on the internet are filled with filth that is beyond the comprehension of many people.

Addicts continually require more and more explicit pornographic material to meet the bondage of their constantly increasing illicit sexual desires.

The widespread sexual degradation that we see in the world today is fed by many of our movies, books, television programs, videotapes and DVDs. High school students today spend more time on the average watching television than they do in the classroom. The moral standards of television and movies are very low. Things that would have seemed shocking a few short years ago are treated casually by many people today. Surveys have shown that more than two-thirds of all programs on American television contain sexual content.

Television viewers are subjected to a wide variety of sexually suggestive commercials. Any child who watches television to any extent is subconsciously influenced by many of these sexual implications. Some television programs are so filled with sex, violence and profanity that they have been labeled as programs that should be watched only by "mature" adults. The words "adult" and "for mature viewers only" in this context actually means "open to the influence of Satan." The violence in our movies, television programs, videotapes and DVDs is a primary cause of the tremendous increase of violence in the United States in recent years.

Our bookstores and our libraries are filled with books that describe sex in terms that would have been unthinkable just a few short years ago. Movies that are rated R, PG and PG13 are filled with sex, profanity and violence. Many businesses that rent or sell videotapes and DVDs overflow with a wide variety of hardcore products. The percentage of the sale of hardcore videos and DVDs has increased by almost one thousand percent in the last ten years.

Sexually oriented businesses such as strip clubs and massage parlors are flourishing. The United States has the highest rate of sales of sexually explicit materials of any country in the world. Pornography in our sexually oriented culture has caused violence against women to increase rapidly in recent years.

Sexual abuse of children has increased tremendously. Recent surveys estimate that one out of every four girls and one out of every six boys in the United States will be sexually molested before their eighteenth birthday. Most of these children never report this abuse. Many families live with the tragedy of a child who has been violated inhumanely by sexual molestation. Our desire is for all captives to be set free in the name and power of Jesus Who came to set the captives free.

Chapter 3

Additional Violation
of Instructions from God

We have seen that people in the end times will be "...lovers of sensual pleasures and vain amusements more than and rather than lovers of God." We live in a hedonistic world where the pursuit of pleasure is the primary goal of many people.

Our culture gives tremendous honor to sports celebrities, movie stars and other entertainers. The honor and the enormous financial income we give to these people is idolatrous. This recognition speaks loudly about the value system of our culture. There is no question that hundreds of millions of people in the world today love the pursuit of pleasure much more than they love God Who says, "You shall have no other gods before or besides Me" (Exodus 20:3).

We believe that the tremendous increase in alcoholic consumption is another sign that we live in the end times. The abuse of alcohol is not new, but the number of people who are adversely affected by alcohol has increased significantly in recent years. More and more people are attempting to escape the reality of life by drowning their problems in alcohol.

People drink alcoholic beverages for many reasons, but one of the primary reasons is an attempt to escape from problems that are caused by stressful situations. Alcohol quickly dulls peoples' reactions to their problems. Alcohol can provide temporary relief, but dependence on alcohol inevitably creates even more problems. The Bible tells us that we make a mistake if we overindulge in this area. "Wine is a mocker, strong drink a riotous brawler; and whoever errs or reels because of it is not wise" (Proverbs 20:1).

Why would any Christian want to be "not wise" from God's perspective? The Word of God warns us against overindulging in "strong drink" that can cause us to "reel." Alcoholics are consumed throughout the day and night by their bondage. "Woe unto those who rise early in the morning, that they may pursue strong drink, who tarry late into the night till wine inflames them!" (Isaiah 5:11).

The Bible spells out the symptoms and consequences of drunkenness. "Who has woe? Who has sorrow? Who has strife? Who has complaining? Who has wounds without cause? Who has redness and dimness of eyes? Those who tarry long at the wine, those who go to seek and try mixed wine" (Proverbs 23:29-30).

The Bible tells us that "woe" and "sorrow" will come to many people who drink alcoholic beverages. We are told that the strong drink that looks, tastes and feels good to these people eventually will "bite" them and "sting" them. "Do not look at wine when it is red, when it sparkles in the wineglass, when it goes down smoothly. At the last it bites like a serpent and stings like an adder" (Proverbs 23:31-32).

The Bible is very specific about the things people do when they are drunk and about the consequences they ultimately will pay. "[Under the influence of wine] your eyes will behold strange things [and loose women] and your mind will utter things turned the wrong way [untrue, incorrect, and petulant]. Yes, you will be [as unsteady] as he who lies down in the midst of the sea, and [as open to disaster] as he who lies upon the top of a mast" (Proverbs 23:33-34).

Many Christians do not know what the Bible says about overindulgence in alcohol. Recent studies show that almost fourteen million Americans abuse alcohol or are alcoholics. Approximately fifty percent of all adults in the United States have a parent, child, sibling or spouse who is or was an alcoholic.

Two-thirds of all adults in our country consume alcohol, but ten percent of this group of people drinks more than fifty percent of all alcohol that is consumed. One-half of all traffic fatalities and one-third of all traffic injuries are alcohol related. Alcohol contributes to more than one hundred thousand deaths annually. This statistic makes alcoholic consumption the third leading cause of preventable death in the United States. Studies of suicide victims in this country show that approximately twenty percent of the people who commit suicide are alcoholics.

The use of illicit drugs also has increased significantly in recent years. An estimated sixteen million adult Americans currently use illicit drugs. Many people also have become addicted to prescribed drugs such as pain relievers and tranquilizers.

We believe that the increase of sickness and premature death that has been caused by the use of tobacco is another sign that we live in the end times. More than sixty million people in the United States smoke cigarettes. More than ninety percent of all lung cancer deaths are caused by cigarette smoking.

Cigarette smoking also is associated with coronary heart disease, strokes, ulcers, increased respiratory infections and cancers of the larynx, esophagus, bladder, kidney, pancreas, stomach and uterus. Cigarette smoking causes an average man to lose more than thirteen years of life expectancy and an average woman to lose approximately fifteen years of life expectancy.

All fifty state governments have settled law suits against tobacco companies to recover tobacco related health costs. These settlements required tobacco companies to make a total payment of 246 billion dollars to fifty states over a period of twenty-five years.

Tobacco companies have passed the majority of this cost on to tobacco consumers with substantially increased prices for tobacco products. Under terms of the agreement with the tobacco companies, states supposedly were to use a significant percentage of this money on smoking cessation programs. These programs were intended primarily to reduce the effect of tobacco on children. Most states have failed to keep this promise. They have used this annual "windfall" of money to help balance their deficient state budgets.

We believe another sign that we live in the end times is the tremendous change that has taken place in our music in recent years. We believe that the rock and roll music that began in the 1950s with Elvis Presley and the Beatles has progressed to the point where much of the so called music of our generation is an insult to God. Deranged heavy metal music is not even remotely similar to the beautiful Christian music the Bible speaks of. "Speak out to one another in psalms and hymns and spiritual songs, offering praise with voices [and instruments] and making melody with all your heart to the Lord" (Ephesians 5:19).

Much of the loud music we hear today could not be further from beautiful spiritual music that is intended to "make melody to the Lord." Much of the music that God meant to be beautiful has become very ugly. Many songs are filled with profanity and vulgarity. The writhing of many musicians is sexually explicit.

Satan knows the power of music. Satan was an archangel in heaven named Lucifer before he fell. He constantly observed the wonderful praise and worship music that resounds throughout heaven. Satan does not want the power of music to be released for God's purpose here on earth. Satan and his demons have worked diligently in the last fifty years in an attempt to pervert the beauty of music from what God intended it to be to the travesty that people call music today.

We saw in II Timothy 3:2 that many people in the end times will be "ungrateful, unholy and profane." Many people today are self centered, hard and unloving. Profanity continually flows out of their mouths. The profanity that is so commonplace in daily conversation today and in movies, television programs, books, videotapes and DVDs is a definite indication that we live in the last days before Jesus returns. In recent years many more women have joined men in speaking vulgarity. People paint a picture of themselves with their words. Who would want a self portrait of profanity?

I shudder when I hear people using the name of Jesus Christ in vain. The context in which many people use this precious name is incomprehensible. I often wonder if people who use the words "hell" and "damn" as part of their everyday vocabulary have any concept whatsoever that these words they speak so often are derived from eternal damnation in the horrible place where all unbelievers will spend eternity.

These people actually are speaking death. They have no concept of the spirit world or their participation on the evil side. The profanity that continually flows out of their mouths is a clear indication that they have not been born of the Spirit by asking Jesus to be their Savior and Lord.

The name of our precious Lord is sacred. His name yields enormous power. People who use His name "profanely or frivolously" violate specific instructions in the Word of God. "You shall not use or repeat the name of the Lord your God in vain [that is, lightly or frivolously, in false affirmations or profanely]; for the Lord will not hold him guiltless who takes His name in vain" (Exodus 20:7).

We believe the rapid escalation of the divorce rate in recent years is another sign that we live in the end times. Marriage was designed by God to be a lifetime relationship between a man and a woman. Divorce, which was the exception in the 1950s, has become commonplace today. Increased selfishness and the no-fault divorce laws that were adopted in the 1970s have made it easy to end a marriage.

The divorce rate in the United States has increased from approximately five percent in 1950 to almost fifty percent today. This increase is not pleasing to God. "...the Lord, the God of Israel, says; I hate divorce and marital separation..." (Malachi 2:16).

Another sign of the end times is the tremendous change that is taking place in children today and in the schools they attend. Many children grow up in families that have no knowledge of God, salvation through Jesus, the divine inspiration of the Word of God and the guidance and strengthening that is available to us from the indwelling Holy Spirit. We see the results of godless families in these children and in the schools they attend.

When I was in grammar school and junior high school (called middle school today) children were punished for things such as chewing gum and talking in class. Today children in the same age bracket are punished for bringing knives and guns to school, for using alcohol and drugs, for sexual immorality and even murder on the school grounds. We have experienced an epidemic of school shootings in recent years.

Surveys have shown that many grammar school students engage in sexual intercourse. Some schools issue condoms to children because they say that these condoms encourage "safe sex." Teenage pregnancies have increased at an alarming rate. The United States has the highest rate of teenage pregnancy in the world. Teenage abortions without parental consent are currently allowed in twenty-nine states, even though each of these states that do not require parental notification has shown an increase in the percentage of teenage abortions.

Lying and cheating have increased significantly in our schools, colleges and universities. A recent survey indicated that eighty-four percent of college students believe that cheating is necessary to get ahead in the world. The lying and cheating that is increasingly prevalent in our schools and in society in general gives clear indication of the influence of Satan in the world today. Jesus said that Satan "...does not stand in the truth, because there is no truth in him. When he speaks a falsehood, he speaks what is natural to him, for he is a liar [himself] and the father of lies and of all that is false" (John 8:44).

This passage of Scripture says that *all* lies come from the influence of Satan. There is no doubt that many of the problems we see in the world during these last days before Jesus returns are caused by the influence of Satan and his demons. People who have not asked Jesus to be their Savior and have not been thoroughly instructed in and transformed by the Word of God are easy prey for Satan.

Many of our children are adversely influenced by television, books, magazines, the internet, advertising and peer pressure. Many parents are not even remotely aware of what their children are exposed to in the books they read, the movies they attend, the videos and DVDs they watch, the music they listen to, the internet and the influence of their friends.

Even the checkout lanes in our supermarkets have a negative effect on many children. The tabloid newspapers and magazines that people scan while they are waiting to check out are filled with lurid headlines. This situation has become so bad that some concerned parents have gone to the management of these supermarkets to request generic checkout lanes that do not have these lurid details for their impressionable children to read.

The use of alcohol and drugs among children has increased significantly in recent years. More than sixty percent of all high school seniors report that they have been intoxicated. More than thirty percent of these high school seniors say that they have had five or more drinks at one time during the preceding two weeks.

Alcoholic consumption by children has been tremendously influenced by advertising. Children today are exposed to a great deal of peer pressure to drink alcohol, to take drugs and to smoke cigarettes. A current study shows that eighty percent of all high school seniors have used alcohol, more than sixty percent have smoked cigarettes and almost fifty percent have used marijuana. Many students obviously are able to obtain alcoholic beverages even though the purchase and possession of alcohol by minors is illegal in all fifty states.

Another sign of the end times is the increasing focus on astrology and psychics. Many newspapers contain astrology columns. Readers faithfully look under their birth sign each day to see what supposedly is in store for them that day. Sometimes psychics are called upon to provide information in courts of law. "There shall not be found among you anyone who makes his son or daughter pass through the fire, or who uses divination, or is a soothsayer, or an augur, or a sorcerer, or a charmer, or a medium, or a wizard, or a necromancer. For all who do these things are an abomination to the Lord…" (Deuteronomy 18:10-12).

Divination refers to an attempt to foretell the future through occult means. Soothsayers are people who claim to predict the future. Augurs are fortune tellers. Sorcerers are people who engage in witchcraft and magic. A medium is a person who says that he or she can communicate with spirits of dead people. Wizards are magicians and sorcerers who often practice witchcraft. Necromancers are people who attempt to tell the future by their so called communication with the dead.

This passage of Scripture clearly tells us that our Father does not want us to use the astrologers, fortune tellers and psychics that are so prevalent in the world today. I looked in our local telephone yellow pages and found more than thirty advertisements from people who promise spirit readings from palms, tarot cards and psychic reading. Deuteronomy 18:12 says that these things "are an abomination to the Lord."

We have seen that II Timothy 3:3 says that people in the end times will be "intemperate and loose in morals and conduct, uncontrolled and fierce, haters of good." In these initial chapters we have read numerous illustrations of the significant decay in our moral climate today. Many people are not fully aware of these facts. They are so preoccupied with their personal goals and the pursuit of pleasure that they have given little or no thought to all of these facts that clearly indicate we live in the end times.

Jesus explained that many people in the end times will be partying and carrying on just as they did before Noah, his family and a large number of animals went into the ark just before God destroyed the world in a massive flood. Jesus said, "As were the days of Noah, so will be the coming of the Son of Man. For just as in those days before the flood they were eating and drinking, [men] marrying and [women] being given in marriage, until the [very] day when Noah went into the ark. And they did not know or understand until the flood came and swept them all away – so will be the coming of the Son of Man" (Matthew 24:37-39).

God reached the end of His patience with the world during the time when Noah lived. The moral climate in our generation today is similar to the moral climate that existed before God destroyed mankind leaving only Noah, his family and a large number of animals to start over again. "The Lord saw that the wickedness of man was great in the earth, and that every imagination and intention of all human thinking was only evil continually" (Genesis 6:5).

The moral climate of our generation today also is quite similar to the climate that existed in Sodom, Gomorrah and other cities that God destroyed because of their wickedness. These cities originally were good and prosperous before they became increasingly wicked. "…Before the Lord destroyed Sodom and Gomorrah, it was all like the garden of the Lord…" (Genesis 13:10).

Another area that could indicate the return of Jesus is near is our financial economy. All of the information in these initial chapters is essentially negative. The Bible does not say a lot about the finances of the world during the end times. We want to present *both* a positive look at current financial trends and also to express our concern about some of the financial implications in our economy today.

The stock market in the United States has been in existence for approximately one hundred fifty years. There never has been a prolonged downtrend during this lengthy period of time. Every time the market has gone down significantly, it always has bounced back.

The worst collapse of the stock market took place in the depression years from 1929 to 1933 when there was approximately a ninety percent decline in the Dow Jones Industrial Average. Financial panic set in. Some investors committed suicide. Nevertheless, the stock market ultimately rebounded.

Some investors panic over market fluctuations. Seasoned investors have learned to wait out these fluctuations. History has shown consistent rallies in the stock market after abrupt declines.

Other good economic indicators are the low interest rates and the low rate of inflation that exist as this book is written. Interest rates during the early 1980s exceeded twenty percent. We have enjoyed a relatively low rate of inflation since that time.

As this book is written, we are currently enjoying an upturn in our economy. The Dow Jones average has rebounded by almost twenty-five hundred points in the past two years. Perhaps the market may have gone the other way when you read this book. We do want to emphasize that, in a period of more than one hundred and fifty years, the stock market *has* adjusted positively after every downtrend.

Now that we have made these positive statements, we want to take a careful look at some potential negative financial concerns. We are concerned because our federal, state and local governments operate under a staggering debt load. Our entire economy is fueled by borrowed money.

All of this borrowing is in direct disobedience to the Word of God. "Keep out of debt and owe no man anything, except to love one another…" (Romans 13:8). We give the lender power over us when we borrow money. The lender is the master. We are "servants to the lender." "…the borrower is servant to the lender" (Proverbs 22:7).

Our national debt is more than seven trillion dollars as this book is written. The United States government currently is paying more than three hundred billion dollars a month in interest on the national debt. Our national debt will increase even more rapidly if interest rates should increase significantly.

As this book is written, the United States government is operating at a budget deficit of almost four hundred billion dollars for the current fiscal year. Projections show that this budget deficit could exceed five hundred billion dollars in the not too distant future.

Some financial experts are very concerned about the value of the United States dollar. After the 1929 depression the United States government under President Franklin Delano Roosevelt abandoned the gold standard in 1933. Since that time the value of the United States dollar has been backed solely by Federal Reserve notes instead of every dollar of paper money being backed by one dollar in gold or silver. The words "good as gold" no longer can be used to describe the value of our current dollars. Some financial experts are concerned about the long term prognosis for this paper based economy.

Another area of increasing financial concern is a rapidly increasing business practice that is called outsourcing. Outsourcing consists of sending jobs that previously were performed by people in the United States to foreign countries where wage earners work for as little as five to ten percent of what workers in the United States would be paid to do the same job.

Outsourcing which began as a mere trickle in the early 1990s has become a torrent in recent years. Many businesses that face a tight market and decreasing profits are turning to outsourcing in an attempt to decrease their production costs so they can be competitive in the marketplace.

Outsourcing, which once consisted almost entirely of low income workers performing menial tasks, is rapidly expanding to include technical workers who work for much less than their high salaried counterparts in the United States. This outsourcing now is expanding as many United States manufacturers are erecting buildings in foreign countries with much lower land costs, construction costs and labor costs.

We probably will see a tremendous increase in outsourcing if our economy does become worse. Competitive pressure and labor profits will force many businesses to look into outsourcing as a means of cutting costs to remain competitive.

This trend is becoming a major concern as this book is written. The number of people in the United States currently receiving unemployment benefits is the highest in twenty years. Labor unions and other organizations who already are concerned about our trade deficit are lobbying Congress in an attempt to stop or at least significantly reduce outsourcing and offshore companies.

Our federal government also is under great financial pressure because the cost of the welfare state has increased rapidly in recent years. Another cause for concern is the rapidly increasing cost of operating our prisons and jails. Almost seven million people are incarcerated in prisons and jails at the time this book is written. The cost for our correctional population will be a tremendous financial burden if our economy becomes worse.

Our federal government is no different than individuals. Each must increase revenue to offset increased spending. Many politicians have not learned this lesson. Because of their desire to be reelected, they make continued promises to give money to their constituents that our government does not have.

The federal government has the ability to regulate the money supply. Government officials often make short term decisions, particularly during an election year, that ultimately inhibit the free market system. Short term decisions that are made for purposes of political expediency often cause significant long term problems.

Many state and local governments also are experiencing financial concerns. Some state and municipal governments are under severe financial pressure. Many cities look for help in state aid. Many states look for federal aid.

Forty-nine of our fifty states are required by law to balance their budgets each year. Some states have balanced their budgets by borrowing money to offset their budget deficit. Borrowing to balance a budget is just as dangerous for state and local governments as it is for individuals. If this trend continues, state and local governments and the federal government will experience the same penalties that individuals experience when they make this mistake.

Many state and local governments are laying off employees. Some of them offer early retirement in an attempt to partially balance their budgets. Some local governments have laid off teachers and increased class sizes. Many state and local governments have cut their budgets to the bone in an attempt to be fiscally responsible.

The debt problems that our federal, state and local governments are experiencing also are occurring with individuals. Easy credit has led tens of millions of people to be heavily in debt because they borrowed money for purchases they did not need and could not afford. The average personal debt of a family in the United States has increased by almost one hundred percent during the past ten years. The average household credit card balance in the United States has more than doubled in the past ten years.

Many people are struggling under the pressure of large student loans because they borrowed money to finance college education. Americans are constantly barraged with advertisements for debt consolidation loans to combine all of their loans into "one easy monthly payment." Homeowners are encouraged to make loans on the equity in their homes to provide money for debts they have incurred by living above their means.

A current financial report from General Motors clearly indicates the prevalence of debt in our country today. Would you think that most of the profits of this large automobile manufacturer would come from selling the automobiles they manufacture? The truth is that General Motors currently earns approximately two thirds of its profit from loans to people who buy their automobiles and one third from the sale of their vehicles.

At the time this book is written, real estate prices have skyrocketed primarily because of cheap credit caused by low interest rates. Because of the lower cost of credit many Americans are buying much more expensive homes than they could have purchased in the past. Because of the low credit rates people are borrowing more against their homes than they borrowed previously. In the ten years before this book was written the equity of homeowners has decreased from sixty-one percent of the home value to fifty-five percent of the home value.

Many people have refinanced their mortgages because financing is so attractive due to low interest rates. Some people have refinanced their mortgage several times. Most of these people are only concerned with the amount of their monthly payment. They ignore the increasing number of years of indebtedness. They have no concept of God's instructions to be free of debt.

The long term amount of interest that people will pay because of constant refinancing of mortgages is almost inconceivable. Many people do not even begin to understand how much money will be required to pay off their mortgage during the mortgage period. When difficult times come, how will these people be able to meet these extended payments for so many years in the future? What will happen to our economy that is so dependent upon large amounts of borrowed money?

People in the United States today have been exposed to the moral decline, the financial crisis and all of the other things we have mentioned in these chapters. Many people look at our current depraved and debt-ridden society as normal. They do not even begin to understand how abnormal our lifestyle is from God's perspective.

God has set in place natural consequences that ultimately must take place when His laws are ignored. We are facing these consequences today in each of the areas we have mentioned. God's laws are for our protection. We are writing this book to inform people of the consequences of ignoring God. We want to ignite people to obey scriptural instructions to increase their ability to trust God.

The initial chapters of this book are filled with sobering facts. Once again we must emphasize that our purpose is *not* to cause fear and worry. Our purpose is to give you these facts so that hopefully *you* will be motivated to follow specific biblical instructions to increase *your* faith in God instead of looking to federal, state and local governments, to employers and to other external sources for security.

Chapter 4

Complacency and Apathy Must Cease

Many Americans are complacent and apathetic. Their lives have been relatively easy. They are not concerned about the end times. They have no comprehension of the sweeping changes that are about to take place in the world.

Our generation has been relatively secure. I was born in 1931. The 1929 Depression was two years old. Many people committed suicide during that depression because they lost their external sources of security. My parents had to go through some difficult times during that depression, but I was too young to know anything about it.

I was ten years old when World War II began in 1941. I was fifteen years old when it ended. I was too young to be in the military to fight in that war, although I did serve in the Army at a later time.

Our country has enjoyed relatively good times since the 1929 Depression and World War II from 1941 to 1946. Many people who were born since I was born *have not known really hard times*. Our generation could be the most pampered generation in the history of the world. Many people have experienced difficult individual problems, but our generation has not experienced a significant amount of collective hardship.

The terrorist attacks against the United States on September 11, 2001 caused great concern for all Americans. Many people turned toward God because of the shock they had experienced. Church attendance increased tremendously for approximately three months after these attacks. By early 2002 church attendance was back to where it was before September 11th. Many people had become relatively complacent once again.

We believe these terrorist attacks were another indication that we live in the end times. Jesus said, "…you will hear of wars and rumors of wars; see that you are not frightened or troubled, for this must take place, but the end is not yet. For nation will rise against nation, and kingdom against kingdom, and there will be famines and earthquakes in place after place; all this is but the beginning [the early pains] of the birth pangs [of the intolerable anguish]" (Matthew 24:6-8).

We now are ready to look at facts about what is taking place in the world today in regard to wars, famine and earthquakes. Terrorist attacks and suicide bombings have increased significantly in recent years. The threat of biological and chemical warfare and weapons of mass destruction is very real. Some countries have stockpiled nuclear weapons. Only God knows when and if these horrible weapons will produce the dire consequences they are capable of producing.

We cannot look at everything from the perspective of the United States. Although we actually have been at war since the terrorist attacks, we must understand that Israel has been in a constant state of war for many years. The end times prophecy of Jesus pertaining to wars and rumors of wars definitely is taking place.

People in Third World countries are *not* complacent. They face severe hardship every day of their lives. Each year we give many books free of charge to people in Third World countries. We receive many grateful letters from these people who have virtually no external sources of security. Many people in the United States will have to "unlearn" their deeply ingrained habit of turning to external sources for security. These people *must* learn how to increase their faith in God.

Jesus told us in Matthew 24:7 that many people will experience famine before He returns. Nothing seems more remote than famine to the complacent, satisfied and well fed people in the United States who continually partake of an abundance of food. Even the homeless people and people on welfare in our country are fed much better than more than *eight hundred million people* in the world who go to bed hungry every night because of the tremendous famine that exists in their countries.

The United Nations Food and Agriculture Organization estimates that approximately eight hundred and fifteen million people are chronically malnourished. Many poor countries currently are experiencing severe famine even though rich countries have an abundance of food. Most Americans cannot comprehend how quickly this famine could increase in many countries if successive droughts occur and if very cold winters have a widespread effect on crops.

Jesus also said that earthquakes would occur "in place after place" during the end times. Recent studies have shown that earthquakes rated at 6.0 or less on the Richter scale have increased steadily with each passing decade. Many smaller earthquakes now are being recorded throughout the world.

A comparison of earthquakes at present and earthquakes in the past is quite difficult. Many countries have more sophisticated equipment to record earthquakes today than they had in the past. With more than two hundred very large earthquakes taking place in the last decade, there is no question that what Jesus said would occur actually is occurring.

Another passage of Scripture gives us additional information about what Jesus said will occur in the last days before He returns. Jesus said, "There will be mighty and violent earthquakes, and in various places famines and pestilences (plagues: malignant and contagious or infectious epidemic diseases which are deadly and devastating); and there will be sights of terror and great signs from heaven" (Luke 21:11).

This passage of Scripture gives warnings in addition to the comments concerning earthquakes and terror that we read about in Matthew 24:6-8. Jesus warns of "pestilence" which the amplification refers to as "malignant and contagious or infectious epidemic diseases which are deadly and devastating." This description could refer to the AIDS epidemic and the widespread escalation of sexually transmitted disease that we discussed in Chapter Two.

Jesus also spoke of "sights of terror." These words could refer to the terrorist attacks, school shootings and mass murders that have occurred during recent years. Do you believe these events indicate that we definitely live in the last days before the return of Jesus?

Jesus told us that another sign of the end times would be that the gospel of eternal salvation through Jesus will be preached throughout the world. Jesus said, "And this good news of the kingdom (the Gospel) will be preached throughout the whole world as a testimony to all the nations, and then will come the end" (Matthew 24:14).

The Gospel is being preached today in an increasing number of nations. The International Bible Society and Wycliffe

Bible Translators have translated the New Testament into well over one thousand languages and dialects. Missionaries are constantly going into areas of the world that have not previously heard the message of eternal salvation through Jesus.

We are blessed personally by the joy of seeing the results of lives changed through the translation of our books into Russian, German, Danish, Spanish, Armenian, Portuguese, Norwegian, Korean, Hebrew, Greek and the Tamil dialect in India. Judy travels to some of the countries where pastors and leaders use our books, sometimes as their only source of Bible instruction. Judy currently is traveling to India each year where we team with Rev. Moses Ebenezer and his wife, Dr. Helen, for the spread of the gospel in India through India Gospel Fellowship. We have close bonds with pastors and evangelists in Zambia, Israel, the Philippines and many other nations.

One of our missions is for our publications to be made available in every known language. We know that the conversational style of writing and the simple explanation of Scripture is a lifeline to each language group who now has a translation of one of our books. This might be an area where God would touch your heart to partner with us in some way.

We can see additional signs that we live in the end times by looking carefully at the Christian church in the United States today. Many people reading this book are active in their own churches and have very little comprehension of what is going on in many other churches.

Many seemingly religious people who attend church faithfully each week have little or no knowledge of the absolute necessity to receive salvation through Jesus. They know little or nothing about continually filling their minds and their hearts with the supernatural power of the living Word of God. They have no experience whatsoever with the indwelling presence of the Holy Spirit.

Religion and Christianity are very different. *Religion is man reaching up to God. Christianity is God reaching down to man.* Many religious people will *not* live in heaven unless they change their beliefs. Many religious people believe that their good lives will get them to heaven even though the Bible says that "…None is righteous, just and truthful and upright and conscientious, no, not one" (Romans 3:10).

Living what you think is a good life is *not* God's plan for salvation. The Bible teaches that the only people who will live eternally in heaven are those people who admit they are sinners, sincerely repent of their sins and believe in their hearts and confess with their mouths their faith in Jesus. Please see the Appendix at the end of this book for more information on these facts.

Many churches today are merely social meeting places. The doctrine of eternal salvation through Jesus is not taught and the Word of God is not preached under the anointing of the Holy Spirit. These carefully programmed church services stick to a rigid schedule that may not include the anointing and guidance of the Holy Spirit.

There is no question that we live in a lost and dying world. Many religious people and all unbelievers reject the doctrine of eternal salvation through Jesus and the inerrancy of the holy Bible. Some unbelievers become angry when they hear Christians reverently speaking the name of Jesus and speaking facts from the Word of God.

The United States at this time is not the Christian nation some people think it is. The American Civil Liberties Union and similar organizations work constantly to remove anything pertaining to God from our government. The doctrine of separation of church and state is unscriptural.

In the early generations of people in the United States, most people honored God and believed in Jesus as their Lord and Savior. They did their very best to obey the instructions and trust completely in the promises of the holy Bible. Our country has changed greatly since its inception. Tens of millions of Americans have rejected Christianity. A higher percentage of children are being brought up in godless families today than at any time in the past.

Jesus prophesied that many people who once were believers would turn away from Him and from other Christians during the last days. He said, "...many will be offended and repelled and will begin to distrust and desert [Him Whom they ought to trust and obey] and will stumble and fall away and betray one another and pursue one another with hatred" (Matthew 24:10).

The complacency and apathy in America today has lulled many people into a false sense of security. Many of these people are sitting ducks for the various cults that have sprung up in these last days before Jesus returns. "...the time is coming when [people] will not tolerate (endure) sound and wholesome instruction, but, having ears itching [for something pleasing and gratifying], they will gather to themselves one teacher after another to a considerable number, chosen to satisfy their own liking and to foster the errors they hold, and will turn aside from hearing the truth and wander off into myths and man-made fictions" (II Timothy 4:3-4).

Many people in the United States do not want to hear about eternal salvation through Jesus. They do not want to hear that every word in the holy Bible is inspired by God. These people are easy prey for teachers from false religions. They choose teachers "to satisfy their own liking and to foster the errors they hold." These people "turn aside from hearing the truth and wander off into myths and man-made fictions."

God has blessed the United States of America abundantly. His hand has guided this nation to become extremely powerful and prosperous. God has blessed our country since its inception. Many founders of our nation were Christians who established the United States as a godly nation based on godly principles from the holy Bible.

In the last four chapters we have read numerous facts that clearly indicate that many Americans are turning away from God and the principles this country was founded upon. Jesus said that the things we have mentioned in these chapters will take place during the lives of one generation of people. We believe our generation is that generation. Jesus said, "Surely I say to you, this generation (the whole multitude of people living at that one time) positively will not perish or pass away before all these things take place" (Mark 13:30).

How much longer will God continue to bless our country when so many people completely disregard the eternal salvation He has provided through the shed blood of Jesus? How much longer will God endure tens of millions of people in our nation ignoring the specific instructions He has given us in the Bible? Why has God delayed? "The Lord does not delay and is not tardy or slow about what He promises, according to some people's conception of slowness, but He is long-suffering (extraordinarily patient) toward you, not desiring that any should perish, but that all should turn to repentance" (II Peter 3:9).

God has patiently put up with sin and obedience because He does not want anyone to suffer eternally in the horrible lake of fire (hell). We believe that God is waiting for Christians to share Jesus with unbelievers. We must share Christ boldly today.

The moral fiber of our country has deteriorated rapidly. The moral decay we have read about in the last four chapters is almost incomprehensible. The United States has become the world's leading moral polluter through the export of our sleazy television programs, our filthy and violent movies, our satanically inspired "music" and our degrading pornography. Our country has become a moral cesspool.

Our only hope is to do what God instructed the Israelites to do when He said, "If My people, who are called by My name, shall humble themselves, pray, seek, crave, and require of necessity My face and turn from their wicked ways, then will I hear from heaven, forgive their sin, and heal their land" (II Chronicles 7:14).

When God refers to "My people" He refers to every member of His family. Are you a Christian? Have *you* humbled yourself before God and prayed for forgiveness of your sins and all of the sin in the United States? Are you seeking God's face continually? Do you yearn for a close and intimate personal relationship with God? Do you constantly intercede for God's mercy for the United States and for the world?

God will only forgive our sins and heal our land *if* we obey these instructions. We believe that Christians in the United States must fast, pray and repent on behalf of our nation. We must cry out to God for His mercy.

If our nation does not repent, we must prepare ourselves for the difficult times that are ahead of us. "Look carefully then how you walk! Live purposefully and worthily and accurately, not as the unwise and witless, but as wise (sensible, intelligent people), making the very most of the time [buying up each opportunity], because the days are evil. Therefore do not be vague and thoughtless and foolish…" (Ephesians 5:15-17).

Many "unwise and witless" people today are "vague and thoughtless and foolish." They are so busy pursuing their selfish goals and their desire for pleasure that they do not even begin to live the way God has instructed us to live.

We live in an "instant gratification" society. Many people want what they want *now*. They have little or no comprehension of the facts we have discussed in the first four chapters of this book. Most Americans could not be more ill prepared for what lies ahead. Many Christians are no better prepared for the end times than unbelievers are.

Unbelievers have a great deal to fear in these last days before Jesus returns. People who have not asked Jesus to be their Savior are missing a relationship with God. They have no alternative except to trust in their limited human abilities or in various external forms of security that will rapidly disappear.

Christians *do* have hope for the future in spite of the dire warnings we have read about in these four chapters. The last days of human history are fast approaching. We cannot tell when the end will come. It could come in the next year or two. It could come in five or ten years and possibly even as long as twenty years from now.

The world will change in a way that most people cannot even begin to comprehend. The signs are all around us. If there ever has been a time when we need to learn how to increase our faith in God, we live in that time. We must have a close relationship with the eternal and unchanging God and know His eternal and unchanging Word to survive during the difficult days that are ahead of us.

The final thirty-eight chapters of this book will give you a detailed scriptural explanation of how to progressively increase your faith in God instead of attempting to depend on external sources of security that will rapidly erode. Before we begin this scriptural study, we want to devote one chapter to a basic overview of what the Bible says will take place during the rapture of the church, the return of Jesus Christ and after Jesus returns. We believe this chapter is necessary because we do not want anyone to be confused about what lies ahead. We do not want one person who reads this book, or your family and loved ones, to miss eternity with Jesus.

Chapter 5

The Return of Jesus Christ

The scriptural facts we are sharing in this chapter could be so detailed that they would fill an entire book. Our goal is to give you *a brief overview* of what the Bible says will take place during the end times. In order to keep this material brief, we often will not give the complete Scripture reference for each point we make. We will give you the chapter and verse of each Scripture reference so that you can look it up if you desire. If you do look up any of these Scripture references, we want to point out that our comments are based on *The Amplified Bible* which usually will give a fuller explanation than other Bibles.

We believe that the content of this chapter is absolutely necessary to cause you to come to the conclusion that *you* must increase your faith in God. Bible prophecy is not an exact science. Some of the facts we refer to are obvious and clear. Others are open to personal interpretation.

We previously have explained that God has set all of these final end time events into motion. He does not want anyone on earth to live eternally in everlasting torment in the lake of fire (see II Peter 3:9). Nevertheless, we believe that God ultimately will come to the point where enough is enough.

We will begin this brief survey of the end times by looking at a seven year period that most Bible scholars refer to as the Great Tribulation. We have seen in Luke 21:26 that Jesus said people would die because of their fear and apprehension of what was about to take place in the world. We saw in Matthew 24:21 that Jesus spoke of tribulation that will be much greater than anything the world has experienced. We saw that II Timothy 3:1 says, "…in the last days will come (set in) perilous times of great stress and trouble [hard to deal with and hard to bear]."

Revelation 11:2-3 explains that the Great Tribulation will be broken into two separate periods of three and a half years each. We will not explain in detail the horrible ordeals that will take place during this Great Tribulation. You can see what the Bible says about these events if you read from the sixth chapter of Revelation through the eighteenth chapter of Revelation. The Book of Revelation is not easy reading. Our goal is to give you enough of an overview of this seven year period to motivate *you* to follow scriptural instructions to increase *your* faith in God.

The sixth chapter of Revelation speaks of men slaughtering each other, of a severe food shortage with exorbitant food prices and many people dying from famine and disease. This chapter speaks of a great earthquake, the sun turning black, the moon becoming red like blood, stars falling out of the sky and of mountains and islands being dislodged. It speaks of people hiding in caves in mountains and calling on these mountains to fall on them to hide them from the wrath of God.

The seventh chapter of Revelation contains facts pertaining to the Antichrist that we will study in more detail after we finish this overview of the Great Tribulation. The eighth chapter speaks of fire sweeping the earth, loud thunderstorms, lightning, a gigantic earthquake, a storm of hail and one third of the earth being burned up. It speaks of a great mountain that will cause many people to die and many ships to be destroyed when it is cast into the sea. It speaks of a huge star dropping from the sky that will cause water to become bitter and many people to die. It speaks of darkness coming over the earth because the light from the sun, the moon and the stars will be decreased.

The eighth and ninth chapters of Revelation speak of dark smoke covering the earth with gigantic locusts coming forth out of the smoke to torment human beings but not to kill them. The state of the world will be so bad during this portion of the Great Tribulation that Revelation 9:6 says many people will want to die, but they will not be able to die. One third of all people on the earth ultimately will be killed by fire, smoke and brimstone.

The tenth and eleventh chapters of Revelation state that no rain will fall upon the earth and that water will be turned into blood. Chapter Eleven speaks of many dead bodies lying exposed in open streets and a tremendous earthquake that will kill many people.

We will not go into more detail. There is no question that the Book of Revelation says that people who are alive during the Great Tribulation will face an *excruciating ordeal*. Even though the Book of Revelation tells us of many additional gruesome facts, we will not examine them here. The Bible says that the first three and a half years of the Great Tribulation will be very difficult and that the second three and a half years will be even worse.

The Bible also gives us many facts about the Antichrist who also is referred to as "the beast," "the man of lawlessness" and "the false leader." The prefix "anti" means "against." Everything the Antichrist does is against Jesus Christ.

II Thessalonians 2:9 explains that the Antichrist will come from the influence of Satan and that he will seem to perform miracles. Revelation 13:13 says that he will cause fire to fall from the sky while many people watch.

Most Bible scholars believe the Antichrist will manifest himself during the first portion of the Great Tribulation. The world will be in a state of chaos. People all over the world will be looking for a leader who can lead them out of the difficult problems in the world. Many people will believe the Antichrist is that leader.

Revelation 13:2-5 speaks of the power and authority the Antichrist will receive from Satan to influence people on earth. Many people will praise and worship the Antichrist even though he will speak against God. Revelation 13:3 says that many people in the world will look at the Antichrist "in amazement and admiration."

The Antichrist's proposals for world peace will make sense to many people who will be mesmerized by his glibness. Some Bible scholars believe that the Antichrist will lead a new one world government. Some people believe the New World Order that has been planned for many years by a group of wealthy people will come into manifestation with the Antichrist at its head.

Daniel 8:23-25 speaks of the craftiness and the mighty power of the Antichrist. This passage of Scripture goes on to explain that he ultimately will bring great problems upon the world. II Thessalonians 2:3-4 says that the Antichrist will exalt himself by actually claiming that he is God.

The Antichrist will have a tremendous influence on the world during the first three and a half years of the Great Tribulation. He will seem to solve many of the world's problems. He will be widely praised for his accomplishments. Many people will follow him blindly.

Everything will begin to fall apart halfway through the Great Tribulation. God's wrath will be poured out on the earth during the second three and a half years of the Great Tribulation. The Scripture references in the beginning of this chapter refer to this last half of the Great Tribulation.

We now are ready to look at what the Bible says about the rapture of the church. We believe our generation is the generation that will live in the narrow time frame during which the rapture of the church and the second coming of Jesus will occur. We believe that many Christians who live today will *not* experience natural death because they will be raptured before they die. We will go directly into the presence of God.

You may have some doubt about the statement that some Christians actually will leave the world without experiencing natural death. I Corinthians 15:51 speaks of one generation of people who will not experience death. These people will be transformed.

The word "rapture" comes from the Latin word "raper" that means "to be caught up or to be transported from one place to another." Although the word "rapture" is not used in the Bible, the following passage of Scripture tells us exactly what will happen during the blessed event that often is referred to as the rapture of the church. "...we who are alive and remain until the coming of the Lord shall in no way precede [into His presence] or have any advantage at all over those who have previously fallen asleep [in Him in death]. For the Lord Himself will descend from heaven with a loud cry of summons, with the shout of an archangel, and with the blast of the trumpet of God. And those who have departed this life in Christ will rise first. Then we, the living ones who remain [on the earth], shall simultaneously be caught up along with [the resurrected dead] in the clouds to meet the Lord in the air; and so always (through the eternity of the eternities) we shall be with the Lord!" (I Thessalonians 4:15-18).

On the glorious day of the rapture of the church, Jesus will descend from heaven with a loud cry and a trumpet blast. Some people believe that I Thessalonians 4:15-18 refers to the second coming of Jesus. We do not believe this passage of Scripture refers to the return of Jesus to earth because I Thessalonians 4:17 says that Jesus will come for Christians *in the air*. Jesus will physically descend *to the earth* at a later time.

I Corinthians 15:52 explains that Christians who died before the rapture will precede Christians who are alive on earth at the time of the rapture. The dead in Christ will be caught up into the air to meet Jesus.

We know we are talking about things in this chapter that may sound *very extreme* to some people. Every point we make is backed up by specific facts from the Word of God. We have seen in the first four chapters of this book that we live in unusual times. The facts that are explained in these four chapters clearly indicate that our generation is headed toward many events that are very different from anything the world has experienced in the past.

Graves all over the world will open to release the dead in Christ as Jesus descends from heaven on the day of the rapture of the church. Most Christians who have died will rise out of the ground where they were buried, but some Christians will rise from oceans, lakes and rivers where they drowned. Other Christians who were cremated, burned to death, blown up in an explosion or whose bodies were destroyed in other ways will rise from the dead.

None of these circumstances pose a problem to God because Matthew 19:26 says that *all things* are possible for God. God knows where every dead Christian is. Daniel 12:1-2 explains that the Old Testament saints will be resurrected at the end of the Great Tribulation.

Christians who are alive on earth at the time of the rapture of the church will join the resurrected dead to meet Jesus in the air. We will experience an amazing sight on this glorious day as we are lifted up into the sky and look around to see many other Christians who are joyfully ascending with us. Everyone's body will glow brightly in the sky as we shoot up into the clouds. Suddenly we will see the King of kings and the Lord of lords, Jesus Christ, face to face in all of His glory. His appearance will be much more magnificent than anything we can possibly imagine.

The rapture of the church will occur at different times of the day in different parts of the world because of the difference in time zones. In some places the rapture will take place at night when Christians will be sleeping. I believe that these Christians suddenly will disappear leaving empty pajamas or nightgowns behind. If one spouse is a Christian and the other is not, one set of nightclothes will remain in the bed while the other person remains on earth.

In other parts of the world, Christians who are working at their places of employment will disappear in the middle of their work day. Many of their fellow workers will be perplexed. They will wonder what has taken place. Numerous automobile accidents probably will occur during the rapture of the church. Christians who are driving automobiles suddenly will be caught up into the air.

Life on earth will be chaotic after the rapture of the church. The spiritual glue that currently holds this lost and dying world together suddenly will be gone. Born again Christians from all over the world will disappear from the earth.

The President of the United States, or the acting president if our president, vice president and other officials in the line of succession are Christians, probably will declare a state of emergency. The United Nations undoubtedly will be called into emergency session.

Many of the services we now take for granted will not be available immediately after the rapture. People who remain on earth probably will not have lights, heat, air conditioning or telephone service at least for a time. Many industries, businesses and stores will be closed. Crime will increase. There probably will be an epidemic of riots and looting. Radio stations will broadcast on an emergency frequency to people who have batteries for their radios. Newspapers will not be able to print the shocking news shortly after the rapture of the church because of the many problems that will be caused by the rapture.

Billions of people all over the world who are left behind on earth will be surprised and terrified because of the disappearance of some of their friends and loved ones. Many people will crowd into churches because of the shocking events caused by the rapture of the church. All pastors who received Jesus as their Savior will have disappeared. Pastors who were not born again will remain. They will have to attempt to answer many difficult questions.

Many people will ask these members of the clergy why they were not taught the facts from the Bible pertaining to all of the people who were raptured. How will these pastors reply? The content of the initial sermons after the rapture of the church will be very interesting.

As we grow and mature in the Lord, we will look forward to the glorious rapture of the church with eager anticipation. The rapture will be a spectacular event. Mature Christians will have no remorse about leaving the earth and everything on earth that is familiar to them. They will have great sorrow for those people who were left behind.

The Bible does not say exactly when the rapture will take place. Many Bible scholars believe that the rapture will occur before the beginning of the Great Tribulation. Other Bible scholars believe the rapture will take place immediately after the first three and a half years of the Great Tribulation. Some Bible scholars believe the rapture will not take place until the end of the Great Tribulation.

The Bible explains that all unbelievers who remain on earth after the rapture will experience severe trials during the Great Tribulation. Romans 2:9 says that "…there will be tribulation and anguish and calamity and constraint for every soul of man who [habitually] does evil…"

We believe the church will be raptured before the Great Tribulation. In Luke 21:36 Jesus spoke of people who will escape all of the things that will take place. Romans 5:9 speaks of being saved from God's wrath. I Thessalonians 1:10 says that Jesus personally will rescue us from the wrath of God. Revelation 3:10 says that Jesus will keep Christians safe from the trials and tribulations that are coming upon the earth.

Advocates of the pretribulation rapture stand on these passages of Scripture. Advocates of the midtribulation rapture believe that Christians will go through the first three and a half years of the Great Tribulation when the Antichrist comes into power. Some Scripture could be interpreted to support this premise. We can be certain that the rapture of the church *will* take place, but we cannot be certain *when* the rapture will occur.

We should stop here to examine *why* God will pour out His wrath on the earth during the last three and a half years of the Great Tribulation. After being extraordinarily patient for a long time, God finally will pour out His wrath upon all of the people who have completely ignored the enormous price His beloved Son paid for their eternal salvation. He will pour out His wrath on people who have completely ignored His Book of Instructions by absolutely refusing to learn how He has instructed them to live their lives.

Why is it necessary to increase our faith in God *if* the rapture of the church should occur *before* the Great Tribulation? Very difficult circumstances will take place in the world *before* this time. We have learned that the Antichrist will be elevated into a position of world leadership because of the many problems that will occur before the seven year Great Tribulation begins. We believe that all people who are alive at that time will face significant adversity before the Great Tribulation begins. Another reason to increase our faith in God is that we cannot be absolutely certain the rapture of the church will take place before the Great Tribulation.

There is *no question* that difficult times lie ahead of us. We must prepare for these difficult times. We have not written this book with the purpose of giving you a detailed study of the end times. We have written this book to tell you exactly what the holy Scriptures instruct each of us to do to increase our faith in God for the difficult times that are coming.

Now that we have given you a brief overview of what will take place up to the rapture of the church, we are ready to look into the Word of God for facts about the second coming of

Jesus. Acts 1:11 says that Jesus will return to earth the same way He ascended into heaven.

Jesus ascended into heaven from the Mount of Olives. Zechariah 14:4 says that Jesus will return to earth upon the Mount of Olives. We believe that the feet of Jesus will touch the earth on His return in the very same place on the Mount of Olives where His feet were before He ascended into heaven. This passage of Scripture says that the power of the return of Jesus will be so great that the Mount of Olives will be split in half by a great valley. Half of this mountain will be moved to the north and the other half will be moved to the south.

The nineteenth and twentieth chapters of Revelation tell us what will happen when Jesus returns to earth. Revelation 19:14 says that Jesus will be followed to earth by heavenly armies. All Christians who went to heaven with Jesus at the time of the rapture of the church will return to earth with Him. We will be members of His heavenly army.

Revelation 19:16 says that Jesus will wear a robe that will be inscribed "King of kings and Lord of lords." Revelation 19:19-20 says that Jesus will overcome the Antichrist and his army. Revelation 19:20 says that the Antichrist and his assistant who is called The False Prophet will be "hurled alive into the fiery lake that burns and blazes with brimstone."

Revelation 16:16 says that a battle will be fought at a place called Armageddon. The word "Armageddon" comes from two Hebrew words – "har" which means mountains or hills and "megiddo" which refers to the hill of Megiddo near the Carmel Mountain. This place is a battlefield where many battles have been fought. This final battle between Jesus and His angels and Satan and his followers will be fought at Armageddon. This battle will not last long. The Battle of Armageddon will begin and end in one day. All of the armies of the earth will be destroyed quickly.

Revelation 16:18 speaks of lightning, thunder and a tremendous earthquake that is greater than any earthquake that ever has taken place on earth. Revelation 16:21 tells about terrible hailstorms where individual hailstones that weigh more than fifty pounds will fall from the sky.

After the battle of Armageddon, Revelation 20:2 says that a period will begin where Satan is imprisoned for a thousand years. This period of time is referred to as the Millennium. The word "millennium" is a Latin word meaning one thousand years. The words "one thousand years" are mentioned six times in the twentieth chapter of Revelation.

Revelation 20:3 says that Satan will be put into a bottomless pit for one thousand years. He no longer will be able to influence anyone on the earth. During this one thousand year period, all Christians who returned with Jesus will rule and reign with Him.

Revelation 21:1 says that the earth where we live today will vanish. Revelation 21:2 says that the heavenly city of New Jerusalem will descend. Christians will spend eternity in the heavenly city of New Jerusalem in the presence of God and Jesus. We will experience wonderful heavenly joy throughout eternity. All problems will disappear forever. "...the ransomed of the Lord shall return and come to Zion with singing, and everlasting joy shall be upon their heads; they shall obtain joy and gladness, and sorrow and sighing shall flee away" (Isaiah 35:10).

Our eternal lives in the heavenly city of New Jerusalem will be much more wonderful than we can possibly comprehend. "...the abode of God is with men, and He will live (encamp, tent) among them; and they shall be His people, and God shall personally be with them and be their God. God will wipe away every tear from their eyes; and death shall be no more, neither shall there be anguish (sorrow and mourning) nor grief nor pain any more, for the old conditions and the former order of things have passed away" (Revelation 21:3-4).

There are no tears in heaven. Death has no power. There is no sorrow or pain in heaven. The Appendix at the end of this book explains exactly what each person must do to receive eternal salvation through Jesus. Every person who has received Jesus as his or her Savior can look forward to this glorious eternal life in heaven. Much more information is contained in our book *What Will Heaven Be Like?*.

Although unbelievers have good reason to fear the difficult times that will come between now and the return of Jesus, Christians *definitely have reason for optimism* in the years ahead. The *bad news* portion of this book now is *complete*. The remainder of this book will be *filled with encouraging facts*.

In the next chapter we will study many promises from God pertaining to His protection of His children during the last days before Jesus returns. The remaining chapters of this book are filled with hundreds of Scripture references that will explain how we can walk in manifestation of the victory of Jesus, regardless of circumstances that are taking place in the world.

We pray that the positive and uplifting facts in the remainder of this book will encourage you so much that *you* will make the decision to devote large amounts of time from this day forward to consistently improve *your* relationship with God and your faith in God. We pray that your faith in God will develop to the point where you will be able to receive the blessings during the last days that our Father will give to each of

His children who has deep, strong, unwavering and unshakable faith in Him.

We must understand that we do not have in our human abilities what will be required to deal with the difficult times that are coming. Only through God can we deal with the problems that are ahead of us. God is our only hope. Our faith in God must be deep, strong and unshakable.

Chapter 6

God Wants to Help Us During the End Times

Have you asked Jesus to be your Savior? If you have made this decision, you can believe that your loving Father *will* bring you safely through every situation you will face. We must not believe that the situation is hopeless because of the facts we have read about the end times. Our Father wants us to steadily increase our faith in Him.

In the first five chapters we talked about the great move of Satan that is taking place in the world today. We must understand that an *even greater move* of the Holy Spirit is taking place and will continue to take place right up until Jesus returns. "...it shall come to pass in the last days, God declares, that I will pour out of My Spirit upon all mankind..." (Acts 2:17).

Please highlight or underline the words "all mankind" in this passage of Scripture. These words include *you*. The Holy Spirit lives in the heart of every born again believer. You can develop your relationship with God and your faith in God so that you will be certain *you* will partake of the mighty outpouring of the Holy Spirit in these last days before Jesus returns.

In spite of the negative facts we have read about, we actually live in wonderful, exciting times. No other generation has had the privilege of living in these glorified times. Instead of being preoccupied with all of the things that are going wrong around us, we can be in the center of the mighty move of the Holy Spirit.

We believe that this move of the Holy Spirit will increase significantly between now and the time Jesus returns. Christians who consistently set aside significant amounts of time to develop a close personal relationship with the Lord will be the Christians who will partake of this great move of the Holy Spirit. We should draw so close to the Lord and stay so close to Him that we will partake of this mighty move of the Holy Spirit and be vessels of God's glory until Jesus returns.

We have learned about the tremendous apprehension Satan and his demons have because they know that they soon will be living eternally in the lake of fire. We have carefully examined the tremendous increase of sin that has taken place in the world during recent years. Even though sin is rampant in the world today, we should look to God with absolute faith. He is much greater and much more powerful than all of the sin in the world. "…where sin increased and abounded, grace (God's unmerited favor) has surpassed it and increased the more and superabounded" (Romans 5:20).

God's wonderful grace and favor "surpass" all of the sin we have read about. God's grace will "superabound" during these last days before Jesus returns. Our Father wants each of His beloved children to receive the grace He is pouring out.

We must trust God completely during the difficult times that lie ahead of us. We can be absolutely certain that Jesus *will* be with us throughout every minute of every hour of every day right up until the end. Jesus said, "…I am with you all the days (perpetually, uniformly, and on every occasion), to the [very] close and consummation of the age…" (Matthew 28:20).

Please highlight or underline the word "you" in this passage of Scripture. You can be certain that the same Jesus Who died for you at Calvary will be with *you* "perpetually, uniformly and on every occasion" until the end of this age.

Refuse to focus on all that is wrong in the world. Focus instead on the indwelling presence of Jesus. "I have been crucified with Christ [in Him I have shared His crucifixion]; it is no longer I who live, but Christ (the Messiah) lives in me; and the life I now live in the body I live by faith in (by adherence to and reliance on and complete trust in) the Son of God, Who loved me and gave Himself up for me" (Galatians 2:20).

Jesus lives in the heart of every born again believer. He wants us to "share His crucifixion" by yielding every aspect of our lives to Him. He wants us to gladly allow Him to live His life in us and through us. He wants us to have absolute faith, trust and confidence in Him and His great love for us.

Our loving Father has done everything that can be done to prepare us for the difficult times that are ahead of us. He has given us specific instructions in His Word concerning the signs of the end times. He has sent His beloved Son to earth to pay the price for all of our sins. Our Father has provided each of His children with the supernatural power of His living Word. He has sent the Holy Spirit to live in us. He has filled the atmosphere around us with mighty and powerful angels to minister to us and protect us.

We will need deep, strong and unwavering faith in God during these last days. Every child of God should *turn away* from preoccupation with the problems in the world to continually increase his or her faith in God. How will Jesus find your faith when He comes? "…when the Son of Man comes, will He find [persistence in] faith on the earth?" (Luke 18:8).

When Jesus comes He should see that we have remained calm, quiet and confident in Him throughout the difficult times. He should see our deep and unwavering faith in Him. We each should "…be eager to be found by Him [at His coming] without spot or blemish and at peace [in serene confidence, free from fears and agitating passions and moral conflicts]" (II Peter 3:14).

We *can* receive *by faith* the wonderful protection our Father has made available to us. Unfortunately, because of ignorance, doubt and unbelief, some Christians who do not have strong faith in God will not do what they should do to progressively increase their faith in God.

The Bible tells us that opportunities to receive knowledge from God will increase substantially during the last days before Jesus returns. The prophet Daniel prophesied that during the end times "…many shall run to and fro and search anxiously [through the Book], and knowledge [of God's purposes as revealed by His prophets] shall be increased and become great" (Daniel 12:4).

Today we are experiencing greater understanding of prophecy that has been given by the Holy Spirit. Prophecies that previously did not make sense to many people now are unfolding before our eyes. God's plan that was written long ago is coming to pass today. "…in the latter days it shall come to pass that the mountain of the house of the Lord shall be established as the highest of the mountains; and it shall be exalted above the hills, and peoples shall flow to it. And many nations shall come and say, Come, let us go up to the mountain of the Lord, to the house of the God of Jacob, that He may teach us His ways, and we may walk in His paths…" (Micah 4:1-2).

Because of the imminent return of Jesus, many people from all over the world will ask Jesus to be their Savior. This passage of Scripture speaks of the "mountain of the Lord" where people from many nations will come to learn God's ways. The door to eternal salvation through Jesus is not yet closed. One day it will be. We must understand the seriousness of the times. We need to walk closely with our Lord Jesus. We need to share Him with anyone who does not know Him.

The world is changing today at a very rapid rate and it will change even more rapidly during the years ahead. Some people live as if they were the center of the universe. They are gods unto themselves. They have a set pattern of life and they do not like change. We should focus continually on our precious Lord Who never changes instead of focusing on ourselves and all of the changes that will be taking place. "…I am the Lord, I do not change…" (Malachi 3:6).

We *will* be able to flow with the rapid changes that are taking place in the world today *if* God is the absolute center of our lives. We will be able to see that what was prophesied long ago is taking place. We are living the plan of the Bible. God can and will lead us and guide us through every situation. We must listen to Him and obey Him.

Jesus has not changed. He is the same Jesus Christ Who performed all of the great miracles we read about in the Bible. He is the same Jesus Christ Who won a total, complete and absolute victory at Calvary. "Jesus Christ (the Messiah) is [always] the same, yesterday, today, [yes] and forever (to the ages)" (Hebrews 13:8).

Our generation must trust Jesus completely. Jesus is our Shepherd. We are His sheep. Jesus wants us to be absolutely certain that He is with us at all times. He wants us to trust Him completely during the difficult times that lie ahead. Jesus said, "I am the Good Shepherd; and I know and recognize My own, and My own know and recognize Me..." (John 10:14).

Jesus is speaking here *of those who trust Him*. When the Israelites were in the wilderness, God knew every person and understood each one. He knew how much each Israelite trusted Him. He knows exactly how much each person in the world today trusts Him. "...He knows (recognizes, has knowledge of, and understands) those who take refuge and trust in Him" (Nahum 1:7).

The Bible explains that different people have differing degrees of faith in God. The following Scripture references will give you an indication of the degrees of faith that people have in God:

- "no faith" (Mark 4:40).
- "little faith" (Matthew 6:30).
- "weak faith" (Romans 14:1).
- "steadfast faith" (Colossians 2:5).
- "rich in faith" (James 2:5).
- "exceedingly growing faith" (II Thessalonians 1:3).
- "full of faith" (Acts 6:5).
- "completed faith" (James 2:22).

These degrees of faith clearly indicate that we *can* steadily increase our faith in God. We must learn and obey our Father's specific instructions to increase our faith in Him. We want to continually emphasize that faith is *not* a formula. Faith is much more than the sum of its parts. Our faith in God must be solidly anchored on a close personal relationship with God. Our faith in God should be spontaneous and instinctive. Faith will not work if we attempt to mechanically use the scriptural principles in this book.

Your faith in God will work effectively if you learn to fit scriptural principles into your life so that they are part of your innermost being. Your faith in God will be natural and spontaneous. This faith will be much more than an intellectual formula you are attempting to follow.

Please approach each of these chapters with an *open mind.* Please do not say or think, "I already know that." Please invite the Holy Spirit to guide you and to give you revelation as you study and meditate on the Word of God to increase your faith in God. Be determined to increase your faith in God. Persevere in faith so that you will be a strong rock for others in the storms of life that lie ahead of us.

Christians should *look forward* to the coming of Jesus. We can and should trust Him completely to keep us safe during these last days. We should "…wait and watch [constantly living in hope] for the coming of our Lord Jesus Christ and [His] being made visible to all. And He will establish you to the end [keep you steadfast, give you strength, and guarantee your vindication; He will be your warrant against all accusation or indictment so that you will be] guiltless and irreproachable in the day of our Lord Jesus Christ (the Messiah)" (I Corinthians 1:7-8).

We should not be apprehensive. We should "constantly live in hope" regarding the return of Jesus. He *will* "establish" each of us right up until the end according to our faith in Him. He will "keep us steadfast." He promises to give each of us the strength we need according to our faith in Him.

Committed Christians should sing and praise the Lord and worship Him as the end of the world approaches. Words of faith should pour out of our mouths because our hearts are filled with the mighty power of God's supernatural Word. You have seen that God will protect you during the end times. Now we are ready to begin our study of hundreds of specific instructions from the Word of God that will tell *you* exactly what to do to continually increase *your* faith in God.

Chapter 7

What is God's Definition of Faith?

The best place to begin our scriptural study of faith in God is to accurately define what faith in God actually is. *Webster's New World Dictionary* says that faith is "unquestioning belief that does not require proof or evidence." Is *your* unquestioning belief in God *so strong* that it does *not* require proof or evidence?

This definition of faith from a dictionary is similar to the biblical definition of faith. "…faith is the assurance (the confirmation, the title deed) of the things [we] hope for, being the proof of things [we] do not see and the conviction of their reality [faith perceiving as real fact what is not revealed to the senses]" (Hebrews 11:1).

This definition says that our faith is "assurance." We are absolutely certain whenever we are assured of something. The amplification of this passage of Scripture says that assurance is "the confirmation, the title deed." Unbelievers need something tangible to confirm that what they are trusting in is real. Christians do *not* need sensual confirmation. Our faith in God should be so deep, strong and unshakable that the Word of God is all the confirmation we need.

What does this amplification mean when it refers to assurance as a "title deed?" A title deed to a piece of property is absolute proof of ownership of that property. The owner can show the title deed to anyone who ever questions ownership. The Word of God is *our title deed*. It is the absolute assurance that enables us to believe God.

This definition of faith goes on to say that faith is the assurance "of the things we hope for." We will carefully study the biblical definition of hope in a subsequent chapter. We will learn that scriptural hope is very different from the way the word "hope" is used in the world today. People today use this word with wishful thinking when they say "I hope so." Our faith in God is "the *proof* of things we do not see."

Our faith in God gives us *absolute assurance* even though we *cannot see* what we are trusting God for. We can clearly see the difference between the worldly faith of unbelievers and what a Christian's faith in God should be. Our faith in God brings the reality of God to earth. Faith in God does not require any tangible evidence.

This passage of Scripture goes on to say that we should be absolutely convinced of the "reality" of whatever we are trusting God for. Our faith in God should be just as real, just as tangible, just as solid and just as concrete as the faith that unbelievers have when they have something that is very tangible to base their faith on.

Next we will look at an amplification of the definition of faith from *The Amplified Bible*. This amplification gives us additional knowledge of what the faith of a Christian should be. Faith in God is "…(that leaning of the whole human personality on God in absolute trust and confidence in His power, wisdom, and goodness)…" (II Thessalonians 1:11).

This amplification is used in many passages of Scripture in *The Amplified Bible* to explain what faith is. How do these words of explanation pertaining to faith in God apply to you? What does it mean to "lean the whole human personality on God?"

A good way to explain what it means to lean entirely on God is to visualize a severely injured football player who cannot put any weight on his injured leg. He has to be helped off the playing field by two people. The athlete puts his arms across their shoulders and puts all of his weight on them. He cannot bear any weight on the injured part of his body. *Our Father wants us to lean on Him in the same way.* He wants us to lean totally, completely and absolutely on Him because of our unwavering and unshakable faith in His "power, wisdom and goodness."

Our Father does *not* need a helping hand from us. Some Christians try to help God out when they face a difficult circumstance. Our Father wants us to trust Him completely. He does not want us to strain, struggle and strive trying to make something happen. Our Father wants us to *let go* of our burdens because we trust Him completely. "Cast your burden on the Lord [releasing the weight of it] and He will sustain you; He will never allow the [consistently] righteous to be moved (made to slip, fall, or fail)" (Psalm 55:22).

The amplification of this passage of Scripture tells us that we should "release the weight" of every burden when we "cast this burden on the Lord." When we cast something, we actually *throw* it. Our Father wants us to throw our seemingly heavy burdens to Him because we are absolutely certain that "He will sustain us."

The Hebrew word "kuwl" that is translated as "sustain" in this passage of Scripture means "to keep, to maintain and to make provision." Our loving Father will keep us, maintain us and make provision for us *if* we will release the weight of our burdens by giving them to Him and leaving them with Him.

Two Christians can hear the same message of faith. One person can step out in absolute faith and receive enormous manifestation of his or her faith in God, while the other Christian receives nothing at all. How can there be such a great divergence between two Christians who have heard the same anointed message from God? "...the message they heard did not benefit them, because it was not mixed with faith (with the leaning of the entire personality on God in absolute trust and confidence in His power, wisdom, and goodness) by those who heard it; neither were they united in faith with the ones [Joshua and Caleb] who heard (did believe)" (Hebrews 4:2).

This passage of Scripture refers to the Israelites who heard the good news of deliverance from bondage when they were in the wilderness. The Israelites heard this message, but they did not place their faith in God. Joshua and Caleb were the only Israelites who heard this message, believed God and acted on their trust in God. Joshua and Caleb were the only Israelites who were allowed to enter into the promised land because of their unwavering faith in God.

We cannot receive what God says He will give us unless this promise from God is "mixed with faith." Once again we see that our faith in God should grow and mature constantly so that we will be able to "lean our entire personality on God." We must have total, absolute and complete faith in "His power, wisdom and goodness."

Our loving Father wants us to trust Him *so much* that we always will step out on our absolute and unconditional faith in Him. "Let us all come forward and draw near with true (honest and sincere) hearts in unqualified assurance and absolute conviction engendered by faith (by that leaning of the entire human personality on God in absolute trust and confidence in His power, wisdom, and goodness)…" (Hebrews 10:22).

Please highlight or underline the word "all" in this passage of Scripture. This word includes *you*. Your loving Father wants you to constantly "draw near" to Him. *All Christians are as close to God as they really want to be.* God will not hold any of us back. "Come close to God and He will come close to you…" (James 4:8).

This passage of Scripture instructs us to initiate contact with God. Each day of our lives we should set aside a period of quality time to "come close" to God. Our loving Father promises that *He will come close to each of us* if we yearn for a closer relationship with Him.

Hebrews 10:22 instructs us to "come forward and draw near with true, honest and sincere hearts." We will develop "unqualified assurance" and "absolute conviction" in God *if* we continually develop a closer relationship with Him. *God is all that we need.*

Our Father wants us to develop our faith in Him so that we will step out on this faith with absolute conviction regardless of the circumstances we face. Here in the United States many people allow external sources of security to comfort them. Many Christians have not paid the price of developing deep faith in god because they have never felt completely insecure.

The amplification of Hebrews 10:22 tells us that we must have "absolute trust and confidence in God's power, wisdom and goodness." Our Father wants each of us to have such a close relationship with Him that we will trust Him completely.

Hebrews 10:22 instructs us to trust in the *wisdom* of God. Believers have the mind of Christ (see I Corinthians 2:16) and can receive the wisdom of God. Unbelievers are limited to human wisdom that cannot even begin to solve the severe problems we will face in the last days before Jesus returns. Our Father explains the sad lot of unbelievers. "…this world's wisdom is foolishness (absurdity and stupidity) with God…" (I Corinthians 3:19).

We will receive the wisdom of God if we consistently spend quality time alone with Him silently listening to Him, praising Him, singing to Him, thanking Him, asking His forgiveness, praying for others and studying and meditating on His Word. We develop God's nature when we consistently spend time with Him. We cannot live effectively in the difficult days that lie ahead of us without the wisdom of God. There is no shortcut to receiving the wisdom of God. There is a price to pay. The price is time with God Himself.

We recommend that you carefully study our book titled *God's Wisdom is Available to You*. This book is solidly anchored on 501 Scripture references that explain exactly what our loving Father wants us to do to receive His wisdom. "If any of you is deficient in wisdom, let him ask of the giving God [Who gives] to everyone liberally and ungrudgingly, without reproaching or faultfinding, and it will be given him" (James 1:5).

The amplification of Hebrews 10:22 also tells us that we should lean completely on the *goodness* of God. You can order our Scripture Meditation Cards entitled *Our Father's Wonderful Love* for a beautiful experience in the goodness and love of God. This set of Scripture cards contains more than eighty Scripture references that thoroughly describe the love of God and explain how God's love can be manifested in our lives. Any person who continually meditates on these facts from the holy Scriptures will be able to trust in the goodness and love of God.

We must know and be certain of our Father's love before we can trust Him completely. Deep, strong, unwavering and unshakable faith in God will be essential in the last days before Jesus returns. This faith must be solidly anchored on our absolute certainty of God's goodness and His marvelous unconditional love for each of us.

Now that we have defined faith in God, we are ready to move forward one step at a time to learn exactly what the holy Scriptures instruct us to do to develop deep, strong, absolute, unwavering and unshakable faith in God. As this book unfolds you will see that it overflows with hundreds of Scripture references that will help *you* to lean totally and completely on God, regardless of the seeming severity of the problems you face.

Chapter 8

How Much Do You Want to Please God?

The title of this chapter asks how much you want to please God. The answer, of course, is that all Christians want to please God. However, even though we all say that we want to please God, we need to learn exactly what the Bible tells us to *do* to please God. "…without faith it is impossible to please and be satisfactory to Him. For whoever would come near to God must [necessarily] believe that God exists and that He is the rewarder of those who earnestly and diligently seek Him [out]" (Hebrews 11:6).

Please highlight or underline the word "impossible" in this passage of Scripture. The Word of God does not say that pleasing God without faith is merely difficult. It says that pleasing our Father without faith is *impossible*.

This verse tells us we "must believe that God exists." All Christians believe that God exists. We never would have asked Jesus to be our Savior if we did not believe this basic spiritual truth.

This passage of Scripture also says that we must believe that God will reward us "*if* we earnestly and diligently seek

Him out." Please note that *God's part* is to reward us. *Our part* is to seek Him earnestly and diligently.

We should not expect our Father to honor our faith in Him unless we consistently obey His instructions to seek Him *earnestly and diligently.* If we seek God earnestly, we will be very serious and determined about achieving this goal. We will persevere if we seek God diligently. Many complacent and apathetic Christians do *not* seek God earnestly and diligently. We cannot increase our faith in God in a casual manner.

Our Father does *not* always respond to our needs. Our Father cares very much about each of His beloved children. He is concerned about our needs, but we must understand that, if God responded entirely to our needs, no Christian anywhere would be sick. No Christian would have financial problems or any other kind of problem.

If we do not trust Him, our Father still loves us, but we are not pleasing to Him. Christian parents should love their children when they are disobedient, but not be pleased with the way they live. Our heavenly Father is no different. He loves us unconditionally, but we cannot please Him unless we have faith in Him.

Many Christians do not understand what Hebrews 11:6 says. They diligently try to please God by works – by doing what they think they should do. Our Father does not want us to spend tremendous amounts of time and energy doing what *we* think we should do. He wants us to learn what *He* wants us to do. Then He wants us to do exactly what He has instructed us to do.

Sometimes God allows us to be tested so that we can see just how strong our faith is. "…you may be distressed by trials and suffer temptations, so that [the genuineness] of your faith may be tested, [your faith] which is infinitely more precious than the perishable gold which is tested and purified by fire." (I Peter 1:6-7).

We may be "distressed by trials" and we may "suffer temptations," but we must see God's perspective. The trials and tribulations we go through on earth actually are *opportunities* for "the genuineness of our faith" in God to be tested. This passage of Scripture says that our faith is "precious" to God.

Our Father compares the preciousness of our faith in Him to gold. Sometimes gold is referred to as a precious metal. Our faith in God is "infinitely more precious" than any amount of gold. The word "infinite" means unlimited. Earthly riches, earthly achievements or anything else in this world cannot begin to compare with the importance of constantly increasing our intimacy with God and our trust in Him.

Many of the activities that some of us value very highly cannot compare to the value of developing deep, strong, unwavering and unshakable faith in God. If our faith is precious to God, it certainly should be precious to us. Our Father explains just how important our faith is. "…whatever does not originate and proceed from faith is sin [whatever is done without a conviction of its approval by God is sinful]" (Romans 14:23).

We should not expect God to help us if we knowingly sin against Him. This passage of Scripture tells us that *we sin against God if we do not have faith in Him.* The sins of worry, fear, doubt and unbelief are just as serious before God as the sins of murder, robbery and adultery.

When God repeats something in His Word, this repetition often is used for the purpose of emphasis. Our Father tells us at least *four times* in His Word that He wants us to *live by faith.*

We have added italics to the following passages of Scripture to clearly emphasize this point:

- "…the [rigidly] just and the [uncompromisingly] righteous man shall *live by his faith* and in his faithfulness" (Habakkuk 2:4).

- "…The man who through faith is just and upright shall live and shall *live by faith*" (Romans 1:17).

- "…The man in right standing with God [the just, the righteous] shall *live by and out of faith* and he who through and by faith is declared righteous and in right standing with God shall live" (Galatians 3:11).

- "…the just shall *live by faith* [My righteous servant shall live by his conviction respecting man's relationship to God and divine things, and holy fervor born of faith and conjoined with it]…" (Hebrews 10:38).

Can there be any doubt of the importance our Father places on His desire for us to live by faith? Our faith in God is tied to our *relationship* with Him. This relationship will become a burning fire that will stay ignited if we seek God throughout each day and night.

Each of these passages of Scripture says that the just shall live by faith. The word "just" means that we are justified before God. When we ask Jesus to be our Savior and trust completely in Him to pay the price for all of our sins, our position before God is the same as it would have been if we had never sinned. Every person who has asked Jesus to be his or her Savior is justified before God through the atoning blood of Jesus. We then have the opportunity to develop a vital living relationship with God.

All of God's children who are in this perfect standing with Him are instructed to live by faith. Living by faith means that every cell of our being is focused on Almighty God. Our Father wants us to be conscious of His indwelling presence throughout every day of our lives. He wants to be first in our lives. He wants every aspect of our lives to be centered on Him.

Our faith in God should be as instinctive as breathing or moving our hands, our arms or our legs. We should not have to think laboriously about faith in God. If we have paid the price of doing what our Father has instructed us to do to increase our faith in Him, this deeply rooted faith will be expressed spontaneously, normally and naturally.

Our Father does not want us to attempt to muster up faith in Him only when we face severe problems. He wants our faith to be constant. He wants us to trust Him to help us with everyday trials just as much as we trust Him to help us with the most severe problems we face.

Faith in God should be a way of life to us. All of our security should come from God Himself. Is your faith in God as important to you as it is to God? Are you absolutely determined to do exactly what your loving Father has instructed you to do to continually increase your faith in Him?

We pray that the scriptural facts you are reading in this book will convince you to expend the effort day in and day out to constantly increase your faith in God. We will face difficult times in the foreseeable future. If there ever has been a time to increase our faith in God, *now* is that time.

Chapter 9

A Solid Foundation for Faith in God

We live in a rapidly changing world that is becoming more unstable with each passing year. People whose lives are anchored on worldly security of any kind will be badly shaken by the events that will take place. In these uncertain times many people are looking for something solid and substantial to provide them with security. God is our solid rock. He has given us His Word as the *foundation* for our faith.

Unbelievers have no alternative except to trust in themselves and in external sources of security. Christians do have an alternative. Faith is not blind confidence or wishful thinking. Our faith in God should be solidly anchored on our close personal relationship with the living God and on His Word that is deeply rooted in our hearts.

I have learned the hard way that the faith I thought was very strong actually was completely inadequate. When I was thirty-five years old I faced bankruptcy and the impending failure of the business I had worked very hard to build. During the next eight years I carefully studied almost two hundred books about positive thinking, mind control, self-confidence and overcoming worry and fear.

I learned so much about these subjects that I began to speak on these topics in my local area. The positive reaction to these speeches gradually expanded so that I was asked to speak on these topics in several cities in the United States and Canada.

I especially remember a seminar I gave at Ohio State University that was entitled "The Power of the Subconscious Mind." This seminar received excellent audience response. I thought I had all the answers. However, not many months after I gave this seminar I found that my theories of positive thinking did not work.

Positive thinking is much better than negative thinking, but positive thoughts must have a *solid foundation*. I failed miserably when I needed this solid foundation. I found out the hard way that I had *no* foundation for my theories of positive thinking. I was filled with fear. I found myself on the edge of bankruptcy, business failure and a nervous breakdown.

At that time a man told me there was a way out of my problems. He told me that Jesus was the answer to my problems. This man told me that all Scripture is given by the inspiration of God (see II Timothy 3:16). He told me that I had read hundreds of books written by men and women, but I had never read the one Book that is inspired by God. He told me that the only solution to the problems I faced was to ask Jesus to be my Savior and then to saturate myself in the Word of God.

My friend explained my need for eternal salvation through Jesus. We prayed together that night as I asked Jesus to be my Savior on July 20, 1974. Jesus became the cornerstone of my life. The next day I went to a Christian book store and bought a Bible. The Bible, the Word of God, became the compass for my life that I needed so desperately. I studied and meditated on the Word of God constantly. With every month that passed I experienced the foundation of Jesus becoming more and more solid as God continually spoke to me through His Word as He revealed His Son to me.

Our business did not go bankrupt. This business still is prospering thirty years later. I am semi-retired from the business today. I can tell you from more than thirty years of intensive Bible study and meditation and from practical experience that Jesus is my *solid foundation*. The Bible is God-inspired daily instruction for my life.

To the best of my knowledge I have spent between twenty and thirty thousand hours studying and meditating on the Word of God. I do not believe I ever spent more than four or five hours reading any other book except for possibly a few college textbooks. *How can anyone spend thousands of hours reading one book?*

The Bible is not just "a book." The Bible is the Word of God. I study and meditate on the Word of God continually. I will not stop. I love the Word of God. I do my very best to anchor everything I think, believe, say and do on the solid foundation of the supernatural Word of God.

The undeniable facts in the first five chapters of this book indicate that a time of great shaking is about to come upon the whole world. The Word of God is unshakable just as its Author is unshakable. When we face difficult circumstances, we can pray that our Father will meet our needs based on the specific promises and instructions He has given us in His Word. "…they who seek (inquire of and require) the Lord [by right of their need and on the authority of His Word], none of them shall lack any beneficial thing" (Psalm 34:10).

This promise from God tells us that "none of us will lack any beneficial thing" *if* we pray to God that our needs will be met and our prayers are based "on the authority of His Word."

Our loving Father has made provision to meet every one of our needs (see Psalm 23:1, Matthew 6:26, Romans 8:31-32 and Philippians 4:19). He can and will meet all of these needs regardless of conditions in the world *if* our faith in Him is absolutely unwavering. This faith must be continually strengthened and deepened by His Word.

The Word of God does not come from this world. The Word of God comes to us from heaven. Our faith in God should be solidly anchored on this marvelous Book. "Forever, O Lord, Your word is settled in heaven [stands firm as the heavens]" (Psalm 119:89).

This passage of Scripture says that the Word of God is "settled" in heaven. The Hebrew word "natsan" that is translated as "settled" means "an established pillar that stands still and upright." The Word of God stands fast without change. The Word of God that is so solidly established in heaven is more than sufficient for *anything* any of us will face here on earth.

The Word of God is a spiritual bridge between heaven and earth. Can you name anything else in the world that comes from heaven that we can contact through our senses? We should be in absolute awe that we have been given the enormous privilege of being able to see with our eyes and hear with our ears the magnificent supernatural Word of God that comes to us from heaven.

We can place all of our weight on this magnificent bridge our Father has provided for us. We can be certain that it will hold us up. Faith in God requires us to step from the seen into the unseen. The unseen spiritual realm will become clearer to us than the visible world we temporarily live in if we faithfully obey our Father's instructions to constantly fill our minds and our hearts with His Word.

God is supernatural. Almighty God is much greater than anything in the natural realm. The holy Bible is filled with thousands of specific facts from the supernatural realm. We must not limit Almighty God by the limitations of the natural realm.

All Christians who have asked Jesus to be their Savior will live eternally in heaven. This world should not be natural to us. The spiritual realm should be natural to us. Each day we should learn and obey the laws of the spiritual realm that are explained to us in the Word of God. "…we consider and look not to the things that are seen but to the things that are unseen; for the things that are visible are temporal (brief and fleeting), but the things that are invisible are deathless and everlasting" (II Corinthians 4:18).

We should not place our primary focus on the things of this world – "the things that are seen." Our Father wants us to focus on the eternal spiritual realm – "the things that are unseen." We will learn the eternal truths of God's spiritual realm if we obey our Father's instructions to consistently study and meditate on His supernatural living Word. "…set your minds and keep them set on what is above (the higher things), not on the things that are on the earth" (Colossians 3:2).

We should keep our minds set on the "higher things" instead of the things that are on the earth. Walking in faith means turning away from the things of the world. We enter into an entirely different realm where everything depends on God.

The first four chapters of this book thoroughly document the evil effect that Satan has on the world today. Jesus referred to Satan as "…the ruler (evil genius, prince) of this world…" (John 12:31). Christians must not succumb to the influence that Satan has on all unbelievers. "We know [positively] that we are of God, and the whole world [around us] is under the power of the evil one" (I John 5:19).

The more we are caught up with the things of this world, the more we will come under the influence of Satan. You may think that you are a citizen of a city, county, state or country, but the Bible tells us that Christians actually are citizens of heaven. "…we are citizens of the state (commonwealth, homeland) which is in heaven, and from it also we earnestly and patiently await [the coming of] the Lord Jesus Christ (the Messiah) [as] Savior…" (Philippians 3:20).

We should constantly be aware that our real home is in heaven instead of where we temporarily abide on earth. Instead of dreading the coming of Jesus, we are instructed to "earnestly and patiently" wait for Him to come for us.

Why would we ever focus on the things of this world if we know that the Bible says we are "…aliens and strangers and exiles [in this world]…" (I Peter 2:11)? We should live each day of our lives knowing that we are "aliens" to the things of this world. Every aspect of our lives should focus on heaven. Because we are citizens of heaven, we must learn and obey the laws of heaven while we temporarily live here on earth.

We constantly have to choose between the world's ways and God's ways. We must understand that our Father absolutely does *not* want us to be preoccupied with the things of this world. "…Do you not know that being the world's friend is being God's enemy? So whoever chooses to be a friend of the world takes his stand as an enemy of God" (James 4:4).

No Christian wants to be "an enemy of God," but that is *exactly what we are* if we prefer the things of this world instead of continually learning and obeying God's instructions from heaven. Your heart will sing with joy if you make the quality decision to continually fill your eyes, your ears, your mind, your heart and your mouth with the supernatural power of the living Word of God. You will "know that you know that you know" that you *can* face the uncertainty of the future. You can face this uncertainty because the rock-solid foundation of the supernatural living Word of God is solidly anchored in your mind and in your heart. You will know God more intimately as you continue to learn His revealed character, plan and purpose.

In the next two chapters we will learn many interesting facts about the supernatural power of the Word of God. We should grow every day in our awareness of the glory and power of the Word of God. This growth serves to increase our intimacy with our Father God.

Chapter 10

Do Not Underestimate the Power of the Word of God

Worldly logic and reason say that words written on paper *cannot possibly be more powerful* than the extremely severe problems we will face during the end times. An unrenewed mind cannot comprehend the power of the holy Scriptures. We must turn away from the limitations of this worldly thinking. "…The Lord knows the thoughts and reasonings of the [humanly] wise and recognizes how futile they are" (I Corinthians 3:20).

Instead of looking at the holy Bible with the "futile" limitations of "the thoughts and reasons of the humanly wise," we should carefully study the Word of God to learn exactly what the Bible says about its supernatural power. Please approach the facts in the next two chapters with a completely open, humble and teachable mind.

Most Christians in the United States have one or more Bibles in their homes. These Bibles are spiritual powerhouses that are filled to overflowing with the supernatural power of Almighty God. We will make a tremendous mistake during these end times if we do not learn how to appropriate this enormous spiritual power that our Father has made available to us.

Our loving Father opens our spiritual consciousness when we ask Jesus to be our Savior. At that time He removes the spiritual "veil" that previously prevented us from being able to understand His ways. "…whenever a person turns [in repentance] to the Lord, the veil is stripped off and taken away" (II Corinthians 3:16).

I have told you about the almost two hundred books on positive thinking and similar subjects that I read for eight years before I became a Christian. Many of these books contained Scripture references. I had more than one hundred Scripture references categorized by subtopic *before* I asked Jesus to be my Savior. I could *not* grasp the supernatural power of the Word of God before I became a Christian *even though* I had all of this Scripture in my files.

Two significant changes took place in my life on the day I gave my life to Jesus. The Lord completely took away all desire to drink alcohol. I had been a fairly consistent drinker before that day, but I have not had any desire whatsoever to drink beer, liquor or any other alcoholic drink since that time. I have been drinking the living wine of the Holy Spirit since the day I was saved.

A second significant change took place in my life on the day I was saved – I found that I was able to understand the Bible. I was ravenously hungry for the spiritual food of the Word of God. I could not get enough of it. The more spiritual food I ate, the more I wanted. I have been stuffing myself with the Word of God for the past thirty years.

Give the holy Scriptures a chance to show you how much power they contain. We put ourselves at a tremendous disadvantage if the Word of God is not working continually in our lives. The Bible points us to Jesus and reveals God's unfolding plan for our lives.

The original Pilgrims who came to this country from England relied heavily on the Word of God. When English settlers first came to Jamestown, Virginia in 1607, most of them based every aspect of their lives on the Word of God. When the Pilgrims came to Plymouth, Massachusetts to face a harsh and bitter winter in 1620, most of them clung tightly to the holy Scriptures.

Many of the original leaders of the United States were Christians who treated the holy Bible with awe and respect. Thomas Jefferson said, "I always say that the studious perusal of this sacred volume will make better citizens, better fathers and better husbands." Andrew Jackson said, "That book, sir, is the rock on which our republic rests."

John Quincy Adams was the sixth president of the United States. His father, John Adams, served as vice president to George Washington and then succeeded George Washington as president. John Quincy Adams had a deep reverence for the Word of God. He once said, "So great is my veneration for the Bible that the earlier my children begin to read it, the more confident will be my hope that they will prove useful citizens to their country and respectable members of society. I say to you, Search the Scriptures! The Bible is the book of all others, to be read at all ages and at all conditions."

Christians are given the opportunity to go *past* the limitations of our human understanding to grasp the supernatural power of the Word of God. Abraham Lincoln said, "Take all of the Bible that you can by reason and the balance by faith and you will live and die a better person. It is the best book which God has given to humankind." President Lincoln also said, "I believe the Bible is the best gift God has given to man. All the good Saviour gave to the world was communicated through this Book."

Many misguided people today are trying to influence the United States government to take various courses of action that do not line up with the Word of God. We should listen to the advice of Alexander Hamilton, one of the original signers of the Constitution of the United States. Mr. Hamilton said, "The law dictated by God Himself is, of course, superior in obligation to any other. It is binding over all the globe, in all countries and at all times. No human laws should be contrary to this."

The Word of God should be the final authority. No human laws should supercede the instructions we have been given in the Word of God. In recent years the United States has turned away from many of the scriptural foundations that were established by the founders of our nation. We are headed for serious trouble if this widespread disregard for our country's scriptural foundation continues.

No book written by men and women can even remotely compare to the magnificent supernatural Word of God because the holy Bible is divine revelation from heaven. "Every Scripture is God-breathed (given by His inspiration) and profitable for instruction, for reproof and conviction of sin, for correction of error and discipline in obedience, [and] for training in righteousness (in holy living, in conformity to God's will in thought, purpose, and action), so that the man of God may be complete and proficient, well fitted and thoroughly equipped for every good work" (II Timothy 3:16-17).

This passage of Scripture tells us that *every Scripture is given to us by the inspiration of God.* The Bible should be very "profitable" to every Christian. We can and should learn from the Bible exactly how our Father wants us to live. Our Father has given us the Bible to instruct us, to show us when we sin, to show us how to change our ways and to guide us toward His will for our lives.

We should learn everything we can from the human authors of the Bible who wrote supernaturally anointed words that were given to them by divine inspiration. "The word that came to Jeremiah from the Lord: Thus says the Lord, the God of Israel: Write all the words that I have spoken to you in a book" (Jeremiah 30:1-2).

These words that were written by the prophet Jeremiah explain that the human authors of the sixty-six books of the Bible were inspired by Almighty God. We can see the divine inspiration of the holy Scriptures by the remarkable coherence of the Bible. How could approximately forty people write sixty-six books over a period of almost two thousand years and have everything they wrote fit together harmoniously unless the Bible truly is inspired by God? We should be in constant awe that our loving Father actually has given us His supernatural Bible with every word in it inspired by Him.

The human authors of the Bible had very different backgrounds. Some were common laborers. Others were tradesmen. Other men were highly educated. There is no possible way that these very different human beings living in different periods of time and in many different countries could have written the various books of the Bible unless everything they wrote was inspired by God.

Many learned scientists once believed that the earth was flat. They could have learned that the earth was round by reading in the Bible what the prophet Isaiah wrote under the inspiration of God when he spoke of "…God Who sits above the circle (the horizon) of the earth…" (Isaiah 40:22).

The Word of God told us the earth was a round "circle" almost fifteen hundred years before earthly scientists "discovered" that the earth was round. We will be in absolute awe of the holy Scriptures if we can even begin to grasp the magnitude of the Word of God.

When we study our Bibles each day we should treat the Word of God with the *same* reverence and awe we would extend to God if He physically came into the room while we were studying. We cannot separate God from His Word. God and His Word are one and the same. "In the beginning [before all time] was the Word (Christ), and the Word was with God, and the Word was God Himself" (John 1:1).

This passage of Scripture refers to God as the Word. It says that the Word of God is God Himself. Shortly after that we are told that Jesus is the living Word. "...the Word (Christ) became flesh (human, incarnate) and tabernacled (fixed His tent of flesh, lived awhile) among us..." (John 1:14).

The Book of Revelation contains many facts about the last days before Jesus returns. This wonderful book of the Bible refers to Jesus when it says "...the title by which He is called is The Word of God" (Revelation 19:13).

We *will* treat the holy Scriptures with the reverence and awe they deserve *if* we can grasp the undeniable fact that God and His Word are one and the same. God said, "...this is the man to whom I will look and have regard: he who is humble and of a broken or wounded spirit, and who trembles at My word and reveres My commands" (Isaiah 66:2).

Our Father wants us to faithfully obey His instructions to study and meditate on His Word each day. He looks for His children who are so broken, humble and teachable that they "tremble at His Word and revere His commands."

We should never approach the Word of God casually. We should approach the Word of God each day with reverence and awe. Our Father reserves revelation from the holy Scriptures for His children who "tremble" before the awesome magnificence of His supernatural Word. "Hear the word of the Lord, you who tremble at His word..." (Isaiah 66:5).

We should be very eager to learn from the holy Scriptures. We should be like the psalmist who said, "...my heart stands in awe of Your words [dreading violation of them far more than the force of prince or potentate]" (Psalm 119:161).

Is *your* heart in awe of the Word of God? Are you determined not to violate the instructions God has given you in His Word? Our Father rewards His children who approach His Word each day with tremendous awe and respect. "...he who [reverently] fears and respects the commandment [of God] is rewarded" (Proverbs 13:13).

God *will* reach down from heaven to protect us during the end times *if* our minds and our hearts are so filled with His Word that we have absolute, deeply rooted, unwavering and unshakable faith in Him. Our Father wants us to hunger and thirst to know Him more intimately as we learn everything we can from His supernatural living Word.

We should *not allow even one day* to go by without studying and meditating on the Word of God (see I Corinthians 4:16, Ephesians 4:23, Joshua 1:8 and Psalm 1:1-3). God's Word is filled with His power. We will fill our minds and our hearts with the power of God if we continually fill our minds and our hearts with the Word of God.

The Bible says that God has exalted His name and His Word above everything else. We then are told that God has exalted His Word *above* His name. "...You have exalted above all else Your name and Your word and You have magnified Your word above all Your name!" (Psalm 138:2).

If God in heaven places *this much importance* on His Word, shouldn't we give His Word the *same* priority? When we face seemingly impossible situations our Father wants us to understand that *nothing* is impossible because His Word is backed up by His mighty power. "For with God nothing is ever impossible and no word from God shall be without power or impossible of fulfillment" (Luke 1:37).

We will face many seemingly impossible situations during the last days before Jesus returns. We must place all of our hope and trust in God. This hope and trust should be solidly anchored on the supernatural promises from heaven that are contained in the Word of God. Unwavering faith in God and His Word can and will bring us safely through seemingly impossible situations.

Chapter 11

The Word of God is Filled with the Power of God

In these last days before Jesus returns we must understand that we live in a lost and dying world. Each day we should fill our minds and our hearts with the Word of God that is supernaturally filled with the life of God. Jesus said, "…The words (truths) that I have been speaking to you are spirit and life" (John 6:63).

The Word of God is spiritually alive. It is magnificent spiritual truth. "…the Word that God speaks is alive and full of power [making it active, operative, energizing and effective]; it is sharper than any two-edged sword, penetrating to the dividing line of the breath of life (soul) and [the immortal] spirit, and of joints and marrow [of the deepest parts of our nature], exposing and sifting and analyzing and judging the very thoughts and purposes of the heart" (Hebrews 4:12).

Please highlight or underline the words "alive and full of power." *Our Bibles are filled with the life and power of Almighty God.* The power of God will be activated deep down in our hearts *if* we faithfully obey our Father's instructions to study and meditate on His Word each day.

We can and should be "energized" by the supernatural power of the living Word of God. Our lives will be much more effective if we constantly saturate ourselves in God's Word. We will be able to see ourselves more and more as God sees us. "…we possess this precious treasure [the divine Light of the Gospel] in [frail, human] vessels of earth, that the grandeur and exceeding greatness of the power may be shown to be from God and not from ourselves" (II Corinthians 4:7).

Please highlight or underline the words "this precious treasure, the divine Light of the gospel." The Word of God is a magnificent treasure. The Word of God is "divine Light" that will help us when we are surrounded by the darkness of Satan. Christians are "frail human vessels" who are given the ability to tap into "the grandeur and exceeding greatness of the power" of Almighty God. We must take full advantage of this precious opportunity.

We must not confuse the Bible with books written by men and women. We should look at the Bible "…not as the word of [mere] men, but as it truly is, the Word of God, which is effectually at work in you who believe [exercising its superhuman power in those who adhere to and trust in and rely on it]" (I Thessalonians 2:13).

Every book except the Bible has been written by "mere men" (and women). The Bible "truly is the Word of God" that will be "effectually at work in you who believe." God wants us to get His Word deep down inside of our hearts. The Word of God will work effectively in our lives if we believe wholeheartedly in it. The amplification of this passage of Scripture tells us that the "superhuman power" of Almighty God will be released "in those who adhere to and trust in and rely on" the Word of God.

Please meditate carefully on II Corinthians 4:7 and I Thessalonians 2:13. The tremendous supernatural power of the Word of God is available to *you* if you will learn and obey the Word of God and place absolute trust and reliance on God's living Word. Many Christians do not even begin to comprehend the immensity of the supernatural power of the Word of God. They would avail themselves of this mighty power throughout every day and night of their lives *if* they knew that the Word of God is *much* more powerful than thermonuclear power or any other power on earth.

We should never be discouraged by any circumstance, no matter how difficult it may seem to be. The Word of God is superior to every circumstance. "Is not My word like fire [that consumes all that cannot endure the test]? says the Lord, and like a hammer that breaks in pieces the rock [of most stubborn resistance]?" (Jeremiah 23:29).

Our Father compares His Word to a fire that consumes everything in its path. He also compares His Word to a hammer that is able to break the hardest rock into pieces. We must understand that no problem we will ever face, no matter how severe this problem might seem to us, is more powerful than the supernatural power of Almighty God Who reveals Himself through the Bible.

Many Christians today are so preoccupied with accumulating wealth that they fail to fill their minds and hearts with the Word of God. We must not make this mistake. We should be like the psalmist who said, "The law from Your mouth is better to me than thousands of gold and silver pieces" (Psalm 119:72).

We must not put the pursuit of wealth or the pursuit of pleasure ahead of our consuming desire to continually fill our minds and our hearts with the supernatural living Word of God. How does the time that you devote to the pursuit of money compare with the time you spend studying and meditating on the Word of God? How do the hours you spend watching television compare to the time you spend in the Word of God? How do the number of hours you spend pursuing pleasure compare with the time you spend in the Word of God?

The Word of God is eternal. The eternal and unchanging spiritual truths of God's Word are *not* affected by anything that occurs in this temporal, lost and dying world. The promises in the Word of God can and will give us the permanence, certainty and stability we so badly need in these uncertain and continually changing times. "…everything [human] has its limits and end [no matter how extensive, noble, and excellent]; but Your commandment is exceedingly broad and extends without limits [into eternity]" (Psalm 119:96).

We must turn away from the limitations of human perception. Everything in the world is temporal. We make a tremendous mistake if we focus too much on people, places and things in the world instead of focusing constantly on the supernatural and eternal Word of God. "…All flesh is as frail as grass, and all that makes it attractive [its kindness, its goodwill, its mercy from God, its glory and comeliness, however good] is transitory, like the flower of the field. The grass withers, the flower fades, when the breath of the Lord blows upon it; surely [all] the people are like grass. The grass withers, the flower fades, but the word of our God will stand forever" (Isaiah 40:6-8).

Jesus said, "Sky and earth will pass away, but My words will not pass away" (Matthew 24:35). This world that we live in will pass away. The sky above us will pass away. The Word of God "will not pass away." We must not miss out on the priceless opportunity we have been given to continually fill our minds and our hearts with the supernatural power of "…the ever living and lasting Word of God" (I Peter 1:23).

The Bible is the most precious possession we have. If we suddenly had to flee our homes and we could only take one thing with us and we never could recover anything again, that one thing should be the holy Bible. We should not even think of taking anything else ahead of the Bible. We cannot afford to be without the Bible for even one day. We must comprehend the magnificence of the power of the Word of God during these difficult days before Jesus returns.

Our hearts will sing with joy if we continually fill our eyes, our ears, our minds, our hearts and our mouths with the mighty power of the Word of God. We will understand great spiritual truths that we cannot understand in any other way. The holy Scriptures will provide us with a magnificent source of strength and comfort during the end times.

We should be like the psalmist who had learned from practical experience that he could be "revived and stimulated" by the Word of God. The psalmist prayed to God saying, "…revive and stimulate me according to Your word…" (Psalm 119:25).

Soon after that the psalmist again asked God to strengthen him with His Word. He said, "My life dissolves and weeps itself away for heaviness; raise me up and strengthen me according to [the promises of] Your word" (Psalm 119:28).

When we face difficult problems we must understand that our Father *can* and *will* "raise us up and strengthen us according to the promises in His Word." The Word of God is *so powerful* that it is able to comfort, console and encourage us when we face adversity. The psalmist said, "This is my comfort and consolation in my affliction: that Your word has revived me and given me life" (Psalm 119:50).

The Word of God can and will provide everything we need during the end times. Are you continually being "revived" by the Word of God? God will lead us step by step if we remain in His presence and keep His Word open as our instruction manual.

If you continually study and meditate on the Word of God, you will be in awe of how much your Father has put between the covers of this one Book. No book written by any human author can even begin to approach the incredible depth, meaning and significance that is available to us in the holy Scriptures. This marvelous Book is filled with thousands of instructions and promises from heaven. Whenever we have to make a decision of any kind, we should ask ourselves, "…what does the Scripture say?…" (Galatians 4:30).

The Bible never grows old. The Word of God is always fresh and new. Even though the Bible was written many years ago, its supernatural contents can and will help us now. The Word of God is applicable to every aspect of *your* life today.

The supernatural Word of God applies to all ages and all people throughout the world. Just think of the tremendous changes that have taken place in the world since the words in the Bible were written. The Word of God always has been current and up to date through all of these changing times and circumstances. God anointed the contents of the Bible to provide instructions for all people at all times.

The Word of God can be used effectively by many different people all over the world. The same passage of Scripture that can be used to help a housewife with the problems she faces also can be used by the CEO of a large corporation who faces complex and difficult problems. This same passage of Scripture also can help a person living in poverty in a Third World country.

The Word of God can and will help each of us *according to our faith in God and our comprehension of God's magnificent provision.* The Bible does *not* contain any asterisks saying that its promises are null and void in case of certain events in the world. There are no asterisks in the Bible pertaining to the Dow Jones average, the state of the economy or the severe problems the world will face during the end times. The supernatural power of the holy Scriptures provide us with limitless horizons that can and will bring us safely through every problem we face according to our trust in God and our knowledge of and obedience to the Word of God.

The Bible is much more than a history book. It is filled with specific instructions from our Father in heaven telling us exactly how He wants us to live our lives on earth. The Bible enables us to turn away from Satan's darkness in this lost and dying world to be guided by the light of heaven.

We will develop a deep and abiding love for the holy Scriptures if we continually study and meditate on the Word of God and constantly learn more and more about its supernatural contents. We will be like the psalmist who said, "Your word is very pure (tried and well refined); therefore Your servant loves it" (Psalm 119:140).

Our Father wants us to be deeply in love with His Word. He wants us to love His Word so much that we will not be able to get enough of it. My life consists of constant immersion in the Word of God. The Word of God has saved my life. It can save your life too.

The Word of God is our Father's precious gift to us. We pray that these two chapters have motivated you to hold tightly onto the supernatural power of the Word of God to bring you safely through the difficult times that lie ahead. "Take firm hold of instruction, do not let go; guard her, for she is your life" (Proverbs 4:13).

We have learned that the Word of God is the manual for our faith in God through His Son Jesus. We have learned that the Word of God is *alive* and filled with the supernatural *power* of Almighty God. We now are ready to study the holy Scriptures to learn how to place *complete dependence* on God and to know the *absolute reliability* of His Word.

Chapter 12

We Can Trust Our Father Completely

In this chapter we will study numerous Scripture references that unequivocally *guarantee* us that our Father stands behind each and every one of His promises. Our loving Father is absolutely "faithful." He is completely "reliable." We *can* depend on Him. "God is faithful (reliable, trustworthy, and therefore ever true to His promise, and He can be depended on)…" (I Corinthians 1:9).

Every promise in the Bible is a written guarantee from God that is *just* as reliable as if God *signed His name* beneath each promise. Our Father cannot change what He has said He will do. Jesus said, "…the Scripture cannot be set aside or cancelled or broken or annulled…" (John 10:35).

We can be absolutely certain deep down in our hearts that every one of God's promises is completely dependable. "…Know in all your hearts and in all your souls that not one thing has failed of all the good things which the Lord your God promised concerning you. All have come to pass for you; not one thing of them has failed" (Joshua 23:14).

These words that Joshua spoke to the leaders of Israel apply to *you* today. This passage of Scripture tells us that we should "know" in our hearts and in our souls that God always does what He says He will do. God never fails. His Word never fails.

Meditate on this great spiritual truth until it begins to take root in your heart. You can be absolutely certain that God's promises cannot fail because God cannot fail. Our Father always does what He says He will do. God said, "…Yes, I have spoken, and I will bring it to pass; I have purposed it, and I will do it" (Isaiah 46:11).

God cannot let us down. God will not let us down. He asks only that we "believe in Him" and place all of our trust and reliance on Him. Our Father tells us again and again that *He always does exactly what He says He will do.* The apostle Paul assured us of God's faithfulness. Paul said, "…he who believes in Him [who adheres to, trusts in, and relies on Him] shall not be put to shame nor be disappointed in his expectations" (Romans 9:33).

Paul wanted to be certain the Romans understood the reliability of God. He repeated almost exactly the same words to them just a short time later. Paul said, "…No man who believes in Him [who adheres to, relies on, and trusts in Him] will [ever] be put to shame or be disappointed" (Romans 10:11).

Our Father has made provision for us to have a vital, alive and continual relationship with Jesus. Our job is to live in fellowship with Him and to trust Him completely. We need to learn exactly what He says He will do. He does not want us to doubt Him for even one minute.

All human beings have the capacity to lie, but our loving Father *cannot* lie. "God is not a man, that He should tell or act a lie, neither the son of man, that He should feel repentance or compunction [for what He has promised]. Has He said and shall He not do it? Or has He spoken and shall He not make it good?" (Numbers 23:19).

This chapter rings with the authenticity of the Word of God. Our loving Father has assured us again and again that we *can* depend on Him. God has obligated Himself by His promises. He must do everything He has said He would do. "...it is impossible for God ever to prove false or deceive us..." (Hebrews 6:18).

God is omniscient. He knows every minute detail about the lives of every person on earth. God is completely aware of how much each of us study, believe in, speak and act on His Word. He will honor our faith in Him. "...I am alert and active, watching over My word to perform it" (Jeremiah 1:12).

Our Father has this much repetition concerning the reliability of His Word because He wants us to be absolutely certain that we *can* trust Him. Some Christians place much more faith in other people and in sources of security here on earth than they do on God. Do you always know who the pilot is before you get on an airplane? Do you know the pilot's credentials? Are you absolutely certain that everything in the airplane has been carefully inspected?

There is no way we can be certain that the pilot of an airplane is completely dependable. There is no way we can be absolutely certain that the airplane has been properly inspected. We can believe that the airline only hires reputable pilots. We can believe that the airline has fulfilled every safety precaution. *How much more can we trust God?*

When you step into an elevator in a building and ride up several floors, are you absolutely certain that every part in that elevator is in perfect working order? Do you know that the manufacturer of that elevator is completely reliable and did not take any shortcuts?

Many Christians get on airplanes and elevators and ride in automobiles across bridges with blind trust in pilots, airplanes, elevators and bridges. *Why* would we ever hesitate to trust our loving Father more than we trust these earthly things or people we do not know?

The Bible is a legal document from heaven. The Bible is much greater and much more powerful than any legal document on earth. A legal document here on earth gives us certain rights. We should not give up these rights without receiving what we are entitled to receive. We should have this same attitude toward the Word of God. The security behind any contract on earth cannot even begin to approach the security we are given when we place all of our trust in the absolute reliability of Almighty God.

We are who God says we are. We can do what God says we can do. Our Father will do exactly what He says He will do. We have nothing to concern ourselves with *if* we can comprehend and believe wholeheartedly in the absolute reliability of the Word of God. We must always meet whatever conditions God requires for a specific promise to be fulfilled.

God has given each of us the freedom to choose what we will do and what we will not do. We each decide throughout every day of our lives whether or not we will obey our Father's instructions to study His Word each day, to meditate on His Word continually throughout the day and night, to believe His promises wholeheartedly, to constantly speak His Word with absolute faith and to step out with unwavering faith on the promises He has given us.

Many Christians fail to receive manifestation of God's promises because they do not do what their Father has instructed them to do. Now that we have learned all of these facts about the immense power of the Word of God and the absolute reliability of the Word of God, how can we not immerse ourselves in the supernatural living Word of God throughout every day of our lives?

The Israelites in the wilderness repeatedly showed that they did not trust God. In spite of the many miracles God performed during the years they were in the wilderness, their words and actions clearly showed their lack of faith in God. "…in spite of this word you did not believe (trust, rely on, and remain steadfast to) the Lord your God" (Deuteronomy 1:32).

Why would we expect God to honor His promises in our lives if we fail to obey His instructions to study His Word each day of our lives to learn what these promises are? Why would we expect our Father to do what He has promised to do if we have no faith, little faith or weak faith in Him because we have disobeyed His specific instructions to continually meditate on His Word throughout the day and night?

Have you asked Jesus to be your Savior? How did you learn about Jesus? How do you know that Jesus existed, that He came down from heaven, that He paid the price for your sins and that He rose from the dead? We know these facts about Jesus because the Bible reveals Him to us.

Jesus is our example in every area of our lives. Jesus relied on the holy Scriptures throughout His earthly ministry. If Jesus placed absolute reliance on the Word of God, we should follow His example. Every Christian can have complete confidence in the Word of God because of the enormous sacrifice Jesus made for us at Calvary. "…as many as are the promises of God, they all find their Yes [answer] in Him [Christ]…" (II Corinthians 1:20).

God has done His part. Jesus has done His part. *Will we do our part?* Will we do exactly what our Father has instructed us to do to progressively increase our faith in Him? Many of God's children are far too busy doing other things instead of doing what our Father has instructed us to do each day to steadily increase our faith in Him. We must have absolute faith in God regardless of the seeming severity of the circumstances we face.

Satan and his demons know that Christians whose hearts are filled with the Word of God are unshakable. These demonic forces will do everything they can to stop us from filling our hearts with the Word of God. Satan's demons will whisper in our ears when we face difficult circumstances. They will emphasize how difficult the problems are. They will do everything they can to undermine our faith in God.

We fight back against the evil influence of Satan and his demons by keeping our hearts so full of the Word of God that we absolutely refuse to give in to anything Satan and his demons say or do. "…the Word of God is [always] abiding in you (in your hearts), and you have been victorious over the wicked one" (I John 2:14).

We must show that we are absolutely certain that God's Word is true. When we face difficult circumstances we should open our mouths and say something like the following: "Dear Father, You said (repeat a specific promise from the Word of God). I know that You will do exactly what You said You will do. I have absolute faith in You. I will not give up. I will persevere in my faith in You. Thank You, Father, for this wonderful promise."

All Christians will say that God is trustworthy. However, what we say and do when everything is going well and what we say and do when we face severe problems often are quite different. Please take the time to go back over this chapter to meditate on the faithfulness of God. We can be absolutely certain that our loving Father stands completely behind every promise in His Word.

Chapter 13

Faith in God Begins
with a Renewed Mind

We will begin our study of *how* to increase our faith in God with the first requirement to increase our faith in God which is a continually renewed mind. *Webster's New World Dictionary* says that the word "renew" means "to make as if new again; make young, fresh … give spiritual strength to … to establish and revive … to replace by a fresh supply … to replace what is old, worn, exhausted." The Greek words "anakainoo" and "ananeoo" that are used in the New Testament as the word "renew" mean "to renovate."

Christians who continually renew their minds in the Word of God will find that their thinking is refreshed, renovated and revived. They will see life more and more from God's perspective. We cannot develop unshakable faith in Almighty God unless we begin by faithfully obeying our Father's instructions to continually renew our minds in His Word.

We explained in a previous chapter that Satan's demons draw a spiritual veil across the minds of unbelievers so they cannot understand the things of God. We have seen that this veil is removed when we ask Jesus to be our Savior. A tremendous spiritual change takes place within us when we ask Jesus to be our Savior. "…if any person is [ingrafted] in Christ (the Messiah) he is a new creation (a new creature altogether); the old [previous moral and spiritual condition] has passed away. Behold, the fresh and new has come!" (II Corinthians 5:17).

We become a "new creation" when we ask Jesus to be our Savior. Our previous value system "passes away." A "fresh and new" life is available to us as soon as we surrender our lives to Jesus.

Unbelievers cannot understand the Word of God. When we are saved, our Father gives each of us the ability to understand His Word. Jesus said, "… [Those who belong to God hear the words of God.] This is the reason that you do not listen [to those words, to Me]: because you do not belong to God and are not of God or in harmony with Him" (John 8:47).

We "belong to God" when we ask Jesus to be our Savior. At that time we become members of the family of God. We are "in harmony with God." From this time forward we are given the ability to renew our minds continually in the Word of God so that we will be able to see life more and more from God's perspective.

We must take full advantage of this marvelous blessing. We should be very excited about the opportunity we have been given to continually learn great spiritual truths from the supernatural living Word of God. We should be like the apostle Paul who said, "…I endorse and delight in the Law of God in my inmost self [with my new nature]" (Romans 7:22).

We are given a wonderful "new nature" deep down inside of ourselves when we surrender our lives to Jesus. Vast new spiritual horizons are open to us. We should "endorse and delight" in the Word of God. We should have a deep and constant desire to learn and obey all of the instructions our Father has given us in His magnificent Book of Instructions. "[Live] as children of obedience [to God]; do not conform yourselves to the evil desires [that governed you] in your former ignorance [when you did not know the requirements of the Gospel]" (I Peter 1:14).

Our Father wants us to turn completely away from the way we used to live before we became His children. He wants us to yearn to learn and obey His instructions. He wants us to "crave" His Word just as new babies crave their mother's milk. "Like newborn babies you should crave (thirst for, earnestly desire) the pure (unadulterated) spiritual milk, that by it you may be nurtured and grow unto [completed] salvation" (I Peter 2:2).

We should have a deep thirst for the supernatural "spiritual milk" that enables us to "be nurtured and grow unto completed salvation." We cannot possibly learn everything we need to learn by attending church once or twice a week. We need to renew our minds in God's Word on a *daily basis*. We will *not* be able to cope with the severe problems we will face in the end times if we have not faithfully renewed our minds in God's Word.

Our minds should be open. We should be humble and teachable. We should be eager to continually change our ways to conform our lives more and more to the ways of God. We should be like the psalmist who said, "Open my eyes, that I may behold wondrous things out of Your law. I am a stranger and a temporary resident on the earth; hide not Your commandments from me" (Psalm 119:18-19).

Our Father will "open our spiritual eyes" and reveal "wondrous things" to us if we obey His instructions to renew our minds each day in His Word. "Do not be conformed to this world (this age), [fashioned after and adapted to its external, superficial customs], but be transformed (changed) by the [entire] renewal of your mind [by its new ideals and its new attitude], so that you may prove [for yourselves] what is the good and acceptable and perfect will of God, even the thing which is good and acceptable and perfect [in His sight for you]" (Romans 12:2).

We can only turn *toward God* by turning *away from* the ways of the world. The amplification of this passage of Scripture speaks of the "external, superficial customs" of the world. Many people in the world are wrapped up in their appearance, their cars, their homes, their activities and many other things. God wants us to learn to live our lives in a much deeper and more meaningful way than an unrenewed mind can possibly comprehend.

Our Father tells us that we will be "transformed and changed by the entire renewal of our minds." The word that is translated as "transformed" in this passage of Scripture is the same Greek word "metamorphoo" that was used to describe the transfiguration of Jesus on a mountaintop (see Matthew 17:1-2). Jesus was transfigured when He went to the top of a mountain with two of His disciples. His appearance changed completely.

A metamorphosis can and will take place in our minds if we continually turn away from the superficial ways of the world to renew our minds each day in the Word of God. The amplification of this passage of Scripture says that we will have "new ideals and a new attitude" if we continually renew our minds in the Word of God.

We can learn great eternal truths from heaven from the holy Scriptures. We are given the opportunity to apply these godly principles to our everyday lives. Our lives will *not* be transformed if we ignore our Father's instructions to constantly renew our minds in His Word. We will live eternally in heaven, but we will not find and live in God's will during our lives on earth.

The apostle Paul explained that we will become more and more like God if we continually renew our minds in His Word. Paul said that we each will have an "…unveiled face, [because we] continued to behold [in the Word of God] as in a mirror the glory of the Lord, are constantly being transfigured into His very own image in ever increasing splendor and from one degree of glory to another; [for this comes] from the Lord [Who is] the Spirit" (II Corinthians 3:18).

We are able to "behold the glory of the Lord" when the veil that previously stopped us from understanding God's ways is removed. The glory of God is mirrored by His Word. The Word of God is a spiritual "mirror" where we can see ourselves more and more as we really are. We can see ourselves as God wants us to be. We can be "transfigured" into God's image.

The Greek word "metamorphoo" that is translated as "transfigured" in II Corinthians 3:18 is the same Greek word we saw in Romans 12:2 and in Matthew 17:1-2 regarding the transfiguration of Jesus and the transforming power of the Word of God. The Holy Spirit *will* guide us into a life of "ever increasing splendor" that will lead us "from one degree of glory to another" *if* we continually renew our minds in the Word of God.

We must take full advantage of the marvelous opportunity we have been given to renew our minds each day in the Word of God. Our spirits are changed instantly when we ask Jesus to be our Savior, but we still have the same mind. "Hear, my son, and be wise, and direct your mind in the way [of the Lord]" (Proverbs 23:19).

God does not think the way the world thinks. Our Father wants us to learn to think the way He thinks. He wants us to constantly abandon concepts that do not line up with His Word. He wants us to see Him, to see the world and to see ourselves from His perspective. Unbelievers and Christians who have not faithfully renewed their minds in the Word of God cannot possibly comprehend how faith in God works.

Christians are not limited to the natural realm of the world. We can and should live in the supernatural realm. We should constantly turn away from the limitations of worldly thinking. We must put the spiritual realm ahead of the natural realm. We must get into the spiritual realm and *stay there* throughout every day of our lives. Only then will we be able to grow and mature and develop our faith in God.

We cannot possibly trust God if we have carnal minds that are primarily aligned with the ways of the world. We must not make the mistake of living the way unbelievers live. "…you must no longer live as the heathen (the Gentiles) do in their perverseness [in the folly, vanity, and emptiness of their souls and the futility] of their minds" (Ephesians 4:17).

Worldly thinking is "futile." Unrenewed minds are centered around the "folly" of empty and selfish goals. Christians who do not consistently renew their minds in the Word of God often will be controlled by carnal worldly thinking. "…you are still [unspiritual, having the nature] of the flesh [under the control of ordinary impulses]…" (I Corinthians 3:3).

We will turn away from worldly goals when we renew our minds in the Word of God each day. As this process continues over a period of time, our thoughts will line up more and more with the mind of Jesus Who lives inside of every believer. "…we have the mind of Christ (the Messiah) and do hold the thoughts (feeling and purposes) of His heart" (I Corinthians 2:16).

Jesus makes His home in our hearts when we ask Him to be our Savior (see Galatians 2:20). Our "thoughts, feelings and purposes" will change dramatically if we obey our Father's instructions to continually renew our minds in His Word. Our thoughts will come more and more into alignment with the mind of Jesus.

The world often opposes and denies the ways of God. Some of us need to "unlearn" many of the precepts we have about life. This need is particularly prevalent in the United States. Our culture has become so worldly and so ungodly that even Christians who truly desire to live God's way must understand the absolute necessity of constantly renewing their minds in the Word of God to cleanse themselves from the influence of this lost and dying world we live in.

Chapter 14

We Must Reprogram Our Minds

Some Christians have little or no comprehension of how much their thoughts, habit patterns and value system have been influenced by the ways of the world. Many of us have been programmed by the world in a way that is much deeper and more subtle than we can understand. We have been molded by our parents, our teachers and our friends. We have been programmed by the events in our lives, by the news media, television, books and the internet. Many people also have been programmed by suggestive thoughts from Satan and his demons.

In the first four chapters of this book we read about the tremendous influence Satan is having on the ways of the world during these last days before Jesus returns. We must understand the absolute necessity of *reprogramming* our thinking.

The atmosphere around us is filled with God's angels and Satan's demons. These demons often attempt to put thoughts that are contrary to the Word of God into our minds. Some Christians do not understand that Satan and his demons actually are out there in the atmosphere around us attempting to influence our thinking. Other Christians realize that this activity is taking place, but they do not have enough spiritual maturity to discern the thoughts that Satan and his demons try to put into their minds.

As we continue to renew our minds in the Word of God, we will grow and mature to the place where we will be able to discern how Satan's demons are trying to influence us. We must cast out these thoughts immediately before they are able to establish a "foothold" in our lives. "Leave no [such] room or foothold for the devil [give no opportunity to him]" (Ephesians 4:27).

This passage of Scripture refers to allowing Satan and his demons to obtain a foothold in our minds in the area of anger. This principle also applies to every other technique Satan and his demons use to attempt to obtain a foothold in our minds. We cannot afford to allow Satan and his demons to become entrenched in our minds.

Many Christians also are bound by traditional thinking. They have been influenced by the world for so long that their thought patterns are significantly conditioned by the ways of the world to a degree that is much greater than they comprehend. Jesus explained what traditional thinking can do to us when He said, "…for the sake of your tradition (the rules handed down by your forefathers), you have set aside the Word of God [depriving it of force and authority and making it of no effect]" (Matthew 15:6).

These words that Jesus spoke to a group of Pharisees apply to each of us today. Many good and well-intentioned Christians are not aware of how the traditional thinking that has been handed down by other people can *block* the mighty power of the supernatural Word of God. The amplification of this passage of Scripture says that this traditional thinking can "set aside the Word of God depriving it of force and authority and making it of no effect."

We absolutely cannot afford to engage in any thinking that is able to make the mighty power of the Word of God "*of no effect.*" We must not allow the influence of Satan and his demons, the influence of the ways of this world and traditional thinking to weaken our faith in God. We must understand the tremendous importance of changing our thoughts by renewing our minds in God's Word. We should constantly bring our thoughts into alignment with God's thoughts, God's ways, God's instructions and God's promises.

Some of us must understand that our minds have been influenced for *many years* by the ways of the world, by Satan and his demons and by traditional thinking. Our minds are similar to computers. We do not need to do anything to program our minds with the ways of the world, the influence of Satan's demons and traditional thinking. This carnal programming takes place *automatically* in our minds.

Our memories are like gigantic filing cabinets. We each have recorded numerous thoughts and experiences for many years. We must make a constant decision to continually "reprogram" our minds to God's ways.

Ideally, children should be brought up in a Christian home. They should live with Jesus as their constant Savior and Lord. They should learn, obey and trust in God's Word. God planned our lives to be lived this way, but only a very small percentage of the people in the world have consistently programmed their minds with the Word of God from childhood.

Some of us have a tremendous reprogramming job to do. I was forty-three years old when I asked Jesus to be my Savior. For more than thirty years I have worked diligently to reprogram my thinking from the thoughts and worldly values that were established in my mind during the first forty-three years of my life.

We can reprogram our minds with God's Word. We can constantly substitute new thoughts, beliefs and concepts for the thoughts, beliefs and concepts that have dominated some of us for many years. Many Christians operate partially in the ways of the world and partially in the ways of God. The Word of God should be *the standard for our lives.*

The amount of time we can invest to reprogram our minds is *much greater* than many of us think. Most Christians spend approximately forty to fifty hours of their week earning a living. They spend approximately fifty hours each week sleeping. A week consisting of seven twenty-four hour days has a total of one hundred and sixty-eight hours. If we spend one hundred of these hours working and sleeping, we have almost seventy hours remaining to eat our meals, to take care of ourselves physically and to perform other tasks. Anyone who takes a hard look at his or her life will see that we each have many discretionary hours to spend in whatever way we choose.

We must get serious about God and His Word in these last days before Jesus returns. We may not have much time left. Have you failed to renew your mind in the Word of God each day and to meditate constantly on the holy Scriptures? If so, we strongly suggest that you make a decision to significantly increase the amount of time you are investing into studying and meditating on the Word of God.

We all know how hard it is to break bad habits. *Good habits are just as difficult to break as bad habits.* Once we establish a habit pattern of renewing our minds in God's Word each day, this good habit can be very beneficial to us. If we can even begin to understand the magnitude of the changes that will be coming on us, we must understand that *now* is the time to accelerate the renewing of our minds in God's Word.

We cannot increase our faith in God without cleaning out doubtful, worried, anxious and fearful thoughts that have become established in our minds. We must replace these thoughts with the supernatural power of the living Word of God. Negative thoughts in our minds are like the contents of wastebaskets that need to be dumped regularly.

We need to clean out all thinking that has been affected by Satan and his demons and the influence of the world. We should sweep these thoughts out of our minds just as we use a broom to clean out a room. We need to continually replace these thoughts with fresh, uplifting, positive and encouraging concepts from the Word of God.

We actually weed out thoughts that do not line up with the Word of God when we renew our minds in the Word of God each day. We know what happens to gardens if they are not weeded. The weeds in a garden ultimately can become so powerful that they greatly affect the harvest of whatever seeds have been planted in the garden. Many people who are worried and anxious must learn how to clean out the weeds of negative thoughts that fill their minds. They must learn to replace these thoughts with wonderful cleansing promises from the Word of God (see our book *Exchange Your Worries for God's Perfect Peace*).

The Word of God is much more powerful than any thoughts in our minds. Our Father tells us exactly what we should do with these thoughts. "Strip yourselves of your former nature [put off and discard your old unrenewed self] which characterized your previous manner of life and becomes corrupt through lusts and desires that spring from delusion; and be constantly renewed in the spirit of your mind [having a fresh mental and spiritual attitude], and put on the new nature (the regenerate self) created in God's image, [Godlike] in true righteousness and holiness" (Ephesians 4:22-24).

We cannot afford to allow any "corrupt lusts and desires" to become established in our minds as a result of "delusion." This passage of Scripture tells us that we should "strip" ourselves of the way we used to think with our unrenewed minds. We will have a "fresh mental and spiritual attitude" if we *constantly* renew our minds in the Word of God. Please highlight or underline the word "constantly" in this passage of Scripture. We must understand the vital necessity of renewing our minds *every* day of our lives.

As this process continues over a period of weeks, months and years, we will learn more and more how our Father wants us to live. We will become more like God because of this continual renewal of our minds. "...you have stripped off the old (unregenerate) self with its evil practices, and have clothed yourselves with the new [spiritual self], which is [ever in the process of being] renewed and remolded into [fuller and more perfect knowledge upon] knowledge after the image (the likeness) of Him Who created it" (Colossians 3:9-10).

Once again we see that the word "stripped" is used in regard to the way we used to think. We are instructed to "clothe ourselves" with our "new spiritual selves" that should constantly be "renewed and remolded" into the image of God.

Do you agree with the facts in the first five chapters of this book about the last days before Jesus returns? Anyone who completely agrees with these facts will be very careful of how they spend their discretionary time. Do you engage in many activities that have absolutely no eternal significance? We must constantly renew our minds in the Word of God.

As this process takes place over a period of time, fearful thoughts will not be able to establish a foothold in our minds. "...we do not become discouraged (utterly spiritless, exhausted, and wearied out through fear). Though our outer man is [progressively] decaying and wasting away, yet our inner self is being [progressively] renewed day after day" (II Corinthians 4:16).

This passage of Scripture tells us that fear can cause us to become "spiritless, weary, exhausted and discouraged." Anyone who has experienced significant fear knows that fear can drain us physically, mentally and emotionally. *How* can we offset the fear that will paralyze the minds of many people during the last days before Jesus returns? This passage of Scripture tells us that we can accomplish this goal by renewing "our inner selves progressively day after day." The words "day after day" once again emphasize that our Father wants us to renew our minds *continually*.

This passage of Scripture says that our bodies "progressively decay and waste away" as we grow older. We *can* offset some of the issues that are caused by the aging process if we "progressively" renew our minds with the supernatural power of the living Word of God. The Bible instructs us to "...brace up your minds..." (I Peter 1:13).

A brace is something that strengthens something else and makes it firm by supporting its weight. Our Father wants us to strengthen our minds by renewing our minds in His Word every day of our lives. We must "brace up" our minds continually in these last days before Jesus returns.

God created us in such a way that our minds cannot think of two things at the same time. Whenever we are tempted to think worried, doubtful and fearful thoughts or any other thoughts that are in opposition to the Word of God, we should substitute thoughts from the living Word of God. We *can* push negative thoughts *out* of our minds by constantly studying and meditating on the Word of God.

We all know that we should fill up the gas tank in an automobile when it is low. None of us would think of driving past a gas station when the fuel gauge in a car shows that the gas tank is empty. Unfortunately, many Christians attempt to go through life without continually filling up their tanks with the supernatural power of God's high test living Word.

Chapter 15

How Do We Renew Our Minds?

Studying the Bible is a comprehensive subject that only can be dealt with completely in a book. We recommend our book, *How to Study the Bible*, and our two cassette tapes that also are titled *How to Study the Bible*. This book and these tapes expand on the brief information that is contained in this one chapter.

Our Father wants us to give the renewal of our minds a very high priority in our lives. The time that we spend in the Word of God each day should be joyful, fulfilling and exciting. Some Christians think that Bible study is boring and unfulfilling. I have found that *just the opposite is true*. I have been renewing my mind in the Word of God for more than thirty years. I can honestly say that nothing in my life is as exciting and fulfilling as receiving constant revelation from God through His supernatural living Word.

The last two chapters explained the victorious life our Father has provided for us *if* we will obey His instructions to continually renew our minds in His Word. We should have such a strong desire to increase our faith in God during these last days before Jesus returns that we will give our daily Bible study first priority.

We must have the discipline to stick to a definite daily program to renew our minds in the Word of God. The words "disciple" and "discipline" are similar. If we want to be disciples of Jesus, we should have the *discipline* to renew our minds in the Word of God each day.

We need to *study* our Bibles instead of just *reading* them. "Study and be eager and do your utmost to present yourself to God approved (tested by trial), a workman who has no cause to be ashamed, correctly analyzing and accurately dividing [rightly handling and skillfully teaching] the Word of Truth" (II Timothy 2:15).

Please highlight or underline the word "study" in this passage of Scripture. We should "be eager and do our utmost" to pass God's tests of our character by the way we respond to trials and tribulation. We can only deal successfully with adversity by continually studying the Word of God and doing exactly what we are instructed to do.

We should pay careful attention to every detail in the holy Scriptures. We should apply ourselves diligently as we continually renew our minds. We will receive more and more information from God as we study His Word each day.

We cannot study the Bible the same way we would read a book. Studying and reading are very different. My former business partner, Christian brother and close friend, Ed Hiers, once gave me an excellent explanation to compare studying the Bible with reading the Bible. I have never forgotten these words of wisdom.

Ed spoke of an imaginary book titled *How to Survive When You Are Lost in the Woods*. He said that people could *read* this book in the comfort of their homes. However, if these same people were lost in the middle of a large forest and had this book with them, they would do much more than just read this book. They would *study* it. They would *devour* it. They would pay close attention to every word because their lives could depend on doing what this book instructed them to do.

The Greek word "spoudazo" that is translated "study" in II Timothy 2:15 means "to make an effort, to be diligent, to labor." Our lives in the end times could depend on the effort we put into studying our Bibles. We cannot adequately prepare for the difficult times ahead by just reading our Bibles. We need to *study* our Bibles effectively each day to prepare ourselves for the future.

I have learned that the *morning* hours are far and away the best time for me to renew my mind in God's Word. Our Father wants to visit us each morning. Will you be there waiting for Him? "What is man that You should magnify him and think him important? And that You should set Your mind upon Him? And that You should visit him every morning…" (Job 7:17-18).

Our Father places a high priority on quality time with His children. If our loving Father wants to "visit us every morning," we should be there waiting to hear what He has to say. "…He wakens Me morning by morning, He wakens My ear to hear as a disciple [as one who is taught]. The Lord God has opened My ear, and I have not been rebellious or turned backward" (Isaiah 50:4-5).

This passage of Scripture is a prophetic word from the prophet Isaiah referring to Jesus during His earthly ministry. This same principle applies to us today. Our Father wants to *teach us* in the morning. He wants us to have a deep and sincere desire to seek Him "diligently" during the early morning hours. "…those who seek me early and diligently shall find me" (Proverbs 8:17).

Our Father *will* honor our commitment if we set aside time each morning to draw closer to Him. I believe that we should begin each day with quiet time with God. We can pray to Him, worship Him, fellowship with Him, listen to Him and study and meditate on His precious Word.

We should give our Father the *best* part of each day. I believe the best part of the day to give to our Father is the early morning hours when we have been refreshed by sleep. I have found that I receive much more revelation from the Word of God in the morning than I do if I try to study the Word of God at the end of a busy day.

I believe that our Father blesses us when we honor Him with the firstfruits of each day. The Bible tells us that God blessed the farmers who gave Him the firstfruits of their harvest. This same principle applies to the time we spend with the Lord each day.

Our Father wants us to draw close to Him when we are fresh and vibrant. We should establish contact with heaven each morning so that we will have a solid foundation to build our lives on for the upcoming day.

I have found that the early morning hours are extremely productive. Telephones are not yet ringing. Daily activities have not started. Many people are sound asleep. The atmosphere is quiet. What better time could there be to receive daily revelation from God as we renew our minds in His supernatural Word?

There are many ways to study the Bible. I have studied the Bible on a *topical* basis for more than thirty years. The following is a brief alphabetical list of some of the topics I believe we could study in the Word of God to strengthen ourselves during the last days before Jesus returns:

- **Adversity**: How to successfully cope with problems we face
- **Angels**: How they minister to us and to others
- **Burdens**: How to give problems to the Lord and leave them with Him
- **Change**: How to cope with the sweeping changes that lie ahead
- **Close to God**: How to continually draw closer to God
- **Confession**: The vital importance of the words we speak
- **Doubt and Unbelief**: How to resist negative thoughts
- **Emotions**: How to successfully yield our emotions to God
- **Faith**: How to increase our faith in God
- **Fear and Worry**: How to overcome fear and worry
- **Fear of the Lord**: Reverence and awe for God
- **Grace of God**: God's blessings that we do not deserve
- **Hearing**: Our faith increases by continually hearing the Word of God
- **Hearts**: Our hearts are the key to our lives
- **Holy Spirit**: A close relationship with our Comforter and Helper
- **Humility**: God gives grace to the humble
- **Impossibilities**: Nothing is impossible to God
- **Joy**: We must not give up the joy of the Lord
- **Love**: God's love for us, our love for God and our love for one another

- **Meditation on God's Word**: The key to understanding the holy Scriptures
- **Name of Jesus Christ**: The Name that is above all names
- **One Day at a Time**: Refuse to be imprisoned by the past or the future
- **Obedience**: God blesses His obedient children
- **Patience and Perseverance**: We must not give up
- **Peace of God**: Receive God's great peace that surpasses human understanding
- **Praise and Worship**: Glorify God continually
- **Prayer**: The privilege of making our requests to God
- **Presence of God**: Enter into and remain in God's presence
- **Pride**: God resists the proud
- **Rest**: Trust God completely and enter into His rest
- **Satan**: Satan and his demons are defeated foes
- **Strength**: God promises to exchange His strength for our weakness
- **Thanksgiving**: We should be exceedingly grateful at all times
- **Victory of Jesus Christ**: How to walk in His victory
- **Will of God**: Seek, find and carry out God's will for our lives
- **Word of God**: God's wonderful instructions and promises

This list is not meant to be comprehensive. It is only a brief example of the different topics I have studied that could be applicable to the end times. My complete list of topics and subtopics consists of several hundred different areas that I continually study in the Word of God.

Even if you do not use the topical method of studying the Bible, you still can make notes by topic whenever you come across a passage of Scripture that deals with a specific topic. I found many of the Scripture references in this book when I was studying the Bible for another purpose. Whenever I find any Scripture that applies to a particular topic, I make a note of the topic, the chapter and the verse or verses. I then file this information in an alphabetical topical filing system.

We each must find the system of Bible study that is effective for us. Each day we should pray asking God to reveal wonderful spiritual truths to us as we faithfully study and renew our minds in His Word. If you will carefully review the list of our books, Scripture Meditation Cards and cassette tapes at the end of this book, you will find that we have provided Bible study aids on a wide variety of topics. Each of our publications and cassette tapes is solidly anchored on the Word of God. We have spent thousands of hours compiling this material to help you to study the Bible effectively.

Our book and Scripture tapes titled *How to Study the Bible* will give you comprehensive suggestions on how to use a Bible concordance, a Bible dictionary, a chain reference Bible and other Bible study aids. Bible study does *not* have to be complex. The most effective way for me to study the Bible is to pick a topic I need to learn about and then to prayerfully study everything I can find on that particular subject. The following comments on our book *How to Study the Bible* might interest you:

- "My wife and I are utilizing the Bible study method that you explained in *How to Study the Bible*. We are really growing spiritually as a result. Our old methods of study were not nearly as fruitful. Thank you for writing about your method." (Idaho)

- "I read almost all of your books and they are outstanding. The one that blessed me the most was *How to Study the Bible*. The study part was excellent, but the meditation chapters were very, very beneficial. I am indebted to you for sharing these. I purchased thirty copies to give to friends. Every earnest student of God's Word needs a copy." (Tennessee)

- "I have finally found what I've been looking for. *How to Study the Bible* provides the most logical and sensible way for a new Christian to study and meditate on the Word of God. Thank you for caring." (Virginia)

- "Your book *How to Study the Bible* has helped me very much. I am an organized person and I like to write down and file information. This method is exactly what I've been praying for. Thank you for writing this book." (Mississippi)

- "Your book *How to Study the Bible* has really helped me. I don't read the Bible any more. I study it and I thank God for the big improvement this book has made in my life." (Texas)

- "Thank you for pioneering in God's Word. Your book *How to Study the Bible* has somehow caused my rebelliousness, confusion and resistance to God's grace to dissipate. I am now able to quit arguing and confidently accept that 'all Scripture is given by the inspiration of God' and build upon that. I am growing in my relationship with God. Thank you." (Alabama).

Judy uses a much different system than I do. I study the Bible topically. Judy studies the Bible as God's revealed plan. She marks categories that interest her as she reads. As your Bible study progresses, we believe that the Lord will show you the specific techniques He wants you to use.

There are many selections of Bibles. You can find one that presents the Bible in chronological order. You can find one that takes you through the Bible in one year. Judy recommends reading one chapter in the New Testament and two chapters in the Old Testament each day. This plan will take you through the Bible in one year. You can write a brief summary of each chapter for review and to help you set the progression of the Bible in your mind.

This chapter has given you a brief overview of studying the Bible. You can greatly expand this chapter by utilizing our book and cassette tapes titled *How to Study the Bible*. We definitely recommend that you add the cassette tapes to the book. These tapes were recorded several years after the book was written. They contain a considerable amount of additional information. You also can facilitate your Bible study by availing yourself of the wide variety of scriptural material we have prepared for you in our other books, our Scripture Meditation Cards and our other cassette tapes.

Chapter 16

There Are No Hopeless Situations with God

In the last three chapters we learned numerous facts about renewing our minds in the Word of God. In this chapter we will discuss what the Bible says about *hope* and the relationship between hope and renewing our minds in the Word of God.

The scriptural definition of "hope" is quite different from the way we use the word today. Many people use the word "hope" today in a similar context to the word "wish." When they are asked if they believe God will honor their faith they say, "I hope so."

The Greek words "alpizo" and "elpis" that are translated as "hope" in the New Testament mean "anticipation, expectation and confidence." New Testament hope is *much stronger* than the wishy-washy use we make of the word "hope" today. The hope of unbelievers is based on worldly sources of security. The hope of Christians is based on confident expectation of help from God.

The Hebrew words that are translated as "hope" in the Old Testament also are much stronger than our word "hope" today. The Hebrew word "tizuch" in the following passage of

Scripture means "expectancy." The psalmist David said, "…You are my hope; O Lord God, You are my trust from my youth and the source of my confidence" (Psalm 71:5).

The Old Testament points to Jesus. The New Testament confirms that *Jesus is our hope.* Jesus went to Calvary, gave His life, took upon Himself the sins of the entire world, descended into hell and rose again from the dead so that everyone who receives Him as Savior can have hope. "…By His boundless mercy we have been born again to an ever-living hope through the resurrection of Jesus Christ from the dead" (I Peter 1:3).

Our hope should be constant. This passage of Scripture refers to "ever-living hope." If our hope is not in Jesus, we have no hope. If our hope is in Jesus, we will have glorious hope regardless of the circumstances we face. We must not give up hope when we face severe adversity. "Rejoice and exult in hope; be steadfast and patient in suffering and tribulation; be constant in prayer" (Romans 12:12).

God's ways are much higher and very different from the ways of the world. Our hearts should sing with joy when we face adversity. The word "exult" means to "leap for joy." We should be "patient and steadfast in suffering and tribulation" because we have not given up hope. We should pray continually with "constant" hope because we have absolute faith that God will answer these prayers.

Christians can and should have hope for the future regardless of worldly conditions. We do not deserve this hope. We have not earned this hope. Our loving Father has given us supernatural hope by His grace. "…God our Father, Who loved us and gave us everlasting consolation and encouragement and well-founded hope through [His] grace (unmerited favor)" (II Thessalonians 2:16).

Our loving Father will give us "everlasting consolation and encouragement" and "well-founded hope" during the difficult days that lie ahead of us. Our hope has a solid foundation. We must not give up hope.

Unbelievers have good reason to feel hopeless. They will be very apprehensive when they look at the seemingly hopeless situations in the world during the end times. "…you had no hope (no promise); you were in the world without God" (Ephesians 2:12).

This passage of Scripture applies to the eternal destiny of unbelievers. This same principle of eternal hopelessness also applies to the remainder of the lives of unbelievers here on earth. The hope of unbelievers is based on favorable circumstances. They often feel hopeless when circumstances become much worse. Our prayer is that they reach out to Jesus Who is the Hope of Glory.

Many people in the world today feel hopeless. They are emotionally drained by the problems they face. All they can see ahead of them is a dreary life filled with more of the same. Hopelessness permeates their minds because they do not see any possible solution to the problems they face.

Christians should turn away from attempting to find their security from worldly sources. Our hope does not come from the world. True hope comes from God. We must realize that there *is* hope in the spiritual realm when there does not seem to be any hope whatsoever in the natural realm. This chapter is filled with *facts* about hope.

Many people who feel hopeless have yielded themselves to the influence of the devil. Hopelessness is a fertile feeding ground for Satan's demons. They will hammer away at us continually in an attempt to influence us to give up hope. They exert even more pressure when they hear words of hopeless-ness coming out of our mouths.

Christians deny the Word of God if they believe that any situation is hopeless. There is *no* place in the Word of God where we are told that anything is hopeless. God never looks at anything as hopeless. His power and might are beyond the limitations of our human comprehension. If we think some-thing is hopeless, we are identifying more with the seemingly hopeless circumstances we face than we are with the tremen-dous power of Almighty God.

God knew that we would need hope in these last days be-fore Jesus returns. Thousands of years ago He anointed ap-proximately forty human authors to write sixty-six Books of the Bible. "…whatever was thus written in former days was written for our instruction, that by [our steadfast and patient] endurance and the encouragement [drawn] from the Scriptures we might hold fast to and cherish hope" (Romans 15:4).

This passage of Scripture tells us that God has given us His anointed holy Bible "for our instruction." Our Father wants us to learn continually from His supernatural Word so that we will have "steadfast and patient endurance" whenever we are tempted to give up hope. Our Father wants us to receive "en-couragement drawn from the Scriptures" so that we can "hold fast to and cherish hope" if we feel like giving up.

This passage of Scripture explains the relationship be-tween hope and receiving *continual encouragement* from the Word of God. We must renew our minds in the Word of God each day so that we will not give up hope. We are in-structed to "hold fast" to hope. Our loving Father has given us "…mighty indwelling strength and strong encouragement to grasp and hold fast the hope appointed for us and set before [us]" (Hebrews 6:18).

Our hope is Jesus. Our Father has provided all of the strength within us that we will need to face whatever the future holds (see II Corinthians 12:9-10 and Philippians 4:13). Once again we are told that our Father has given us "strong encouragement" so that we can "hold fast" to hope. "…we have this [hope] as a sure and steadfast anchor of the soul [it cannot slip and it cannot break down under whoever steps out upon it – a hope] that reaches farther and enters into [the very certainty of the Presence] within the veil" (Hebrews 6:19).

This passage of Scripture tells us that hope is "a sure and steadfast anchor of the soul." Our souls consist of our minds, our emotions and our will. All of our thoughts, all of our emotions and all of our decisions will be solidly anchored if we refuse to give up hope. The amplification of this passage of Scripture says that this hope "cannot slip and it cannot break down under whoever steps out upon it" because of "the very certainty of the Presence" of our Lord Jesus.

Scriptural hope is a supernatural anchor. An anchor is something that holds a boat in place. Hope can and will *hold our souls in place* when we are in the midst of the storms of life. We must not give up hope no matter what we face. We can keep our hopes up by renewing our minds in the Word of God each day.

People who are hopeless *do not protect their minds.* They allow dire circumstances and the thoughts that Satan's demons attempt to put into their minds to dominate their thinking. Hope cannot prevail if our minds are filled with negative thoughts based on the circumstances we face and the continual influence of Satan's demons.

We must protect our minds when we face difficult problems. Our minds will be filled with the Word of God if we faithfully obey our Father's instructions to renew our minds in

His Word each day. Seemingly hopeless circumstances *cannot prevail* in a mind that is constantly being filled with the supernatural power of the living Word of God.

We must learn how to renew our minds in the Word of God so that we can get God's promises and instructions up from the printed pages of the Bible into our minds. We then must learn how to get the Word of God from our minds down into our hearts. We *think* with our *minds*. We *believe* with our *hearts*. "…with the heart a person believes (adheres to, trusts in, and relies on Christ)…" (Romans 10:10).

Both hope and faith are essential to trusting God. We will fail if we attempt to trust God *only* with the *hope* that is in our *minds*. We also will fail if we attempt to trust God *only* with the *faith* that is in our *hearts*. Hope and faith work together. We must understand the function of hope and the function of faith. Hope in our minds *sets the goal* so that faith in our hearts will have something definite to bring into manifestation.

If we desire to drive an automobile to a certain destination, we must point the automobile toward that destination. This automobile could have more power than any other automobile in the world, but all of this power will not help us if the car is headed in the wrong direction. Hope points us in the right direction. Unwavering, persevering and unshakable faith in God releases the power of God to bring our hopes into manifestation.

We will learn many wonderful promises from God if we study the Word of God each day. The cumulative result of studying these promises develops hope in our minds. Specific passages of Scripture that we study can be used to help us set the goal for our faith.

Many Christians do not understand the difference between hope and faith. We must know the difference between hope and faith so that we can use hope for what hope is intended for instead of attempting to use hope for what only faith can accomplish. Hope and faith fit together perfectly. We must use our hope as God intended hope to be used. We must use our faith as God intended faith to be used.

We should renew our minds in the Word of God each day so that our hope will not waver when we face difficult circumstances. "...let us seize and hold fast and retain without wavering the hope we cherish and confess and our acknowledgement of it, for He Who promised is reliable (sure) and faithful to His word" (Hebrews 10:23).

This passage of Scripture instructs us to "seize and hold fast and retain without wavering" what we are hoping for. These instructions are similar to the instructions we previously saw in Romans 15:4 where we were instructed to "hold fast to and cherish hope." When we "cherish" something, we value it and take good care of it.

We also are instructed to "confess and acknowledge" our hope. If we faithfully renew our minds in the Word of God each day, we will be able to open our mouths and speak about our hopes. We will be able to confess our hopes because they will be anchored on the holy Scriptures. Our Father "is reliable, sure and faithful to His Word."

We usually cannot see what we are hoping for. Hope serves no function if we already can see the result. Our Father wants us to calmly and patiently hope with absolute certainty that the Holy Spirit will strengthen us and help us to receive whatever we are hoping for. "...hope [the object of] which is seen is not hope. For how can one hope for what he already sees? But if we hope for what is still unseen by us, we wait for it with patience and composure. So too the [Holy] Spirit comes to our aid and bears us up in our weakness..." (Romans 8:24-26).

In the last four chapters we have learned how to develop *hope* in our *minds* by renewing our *minds* each day as we study the Word of God. We cannot receive manifestation of God's promises only by hoping in our minds. Many Christians make this mistake. We now are ready to learn how to increase our faith in God by learning how to get the Word of God from our minds down into our *hearts*.

The power of the Holy Spirit will be released in our hearts when our hearts continually are being filled with the Word of God. The apostle Paul said, "May the God of your hope so fill you with all joy and peace in believing [through the experience of your faith] that by the power of the Holy Spirit you may abound and be overflowing (bubbling over) with hope" (Romans 15:13).

This passage of Scripture gives us a spiritual bridge between hope and faith. Paul referred to God as "the God of our hope." He then told us that true faith "by the power of the Holy Spirit" will cause us to "abound and be overflowing (bubbling over) with hope."

In the next three chapters we will study what the Word of God says about the importance of what we believe in our *hearts*. In subsequent chapters we will learn exactly what the Bible instructs us to *do* to develop faith in our hearts.

Chapter 17

Our Hearts Are the Home for God's Word

We cannot survive the difficult times that lie ahead of us unless our *hearts* are filled to overflowing with the supernatural power of the living Word of God. Some Christians read the Bible. Some Christians study the Bible. Some Christians memorize Scripture. We *are* doing what our Father wants us to do when we read His Word, study His Word and memorize Scripture, but *we must not stop there.*

We have seen that continually filling our minds with the Word of God enables us to have hope. Our faith in God cannot be added to this hope until we learn how to get the Word of God from our minds down into our hearts.

When the Bible speaks of our hearts it does not refer to the organ in our chests that pumps blood. When the Bible speaks of our hearts it refers to the very center of our being. It refers to what we really are deep down inside of ourselves.

I have learned through thousands of hours of experience that the Word of God drops from our minds down into our hearts when we continually *meditate* on the holy Scriptures. Our Father instructs us to meditate on His Word throughout the day and night. If you are not familiar with Joshua 1:8 and Psalm 1:1-3, you might want to stop for a moment to look at these passages of Scripture. There is no question that we are instructed to meditate on the Word of God *throughout the day and night*. Are *you* faithfully obeying these instructions?

We will study Joshua 1:8 and Psalm 1:1-3 in detail in subsequent chapters when we study meditation on the Word of God. For now we merely want to point out our Father's specific instructions to meditate continually on His Word throughout the day and night. We cannot develop the deep, unwavering and unshakable faith in Almighty God that we absolutely will *have to have* during the end times if we ignore our Father's specific instructions to meditate continually on His Word.

The real us that the Bible refers to when it refers to our hearts is not the person casual acquaintances see. We each have an outer person and an inner person. The outer person is the personality that everyone who has occasional contact with us can see. The inner person is the person who only is seen by God and by the people who are closest to us. The Bible refers to this person as "…the hidden person of the heart…" (I Peter 3:4).

Some people do not even begin to understand what they really are like deep down inside of themselves. The Word of God is a spiritual mirror. The Holy Spirit will give us an ongoing reflection of what we really are like if we continually meditate on the holy Scriptures.

Our faith in God must grow within the "hidden person of the heart." The Word of God must get past the intellectual comprehension of our minds to drop down into our hearts before we can have deep and unwavering faith in God. The Word of God becomes a lifeline and a love letter from God as our intimacy with God increases.

As our hearts are continually filled with the Word of God, the inner person and the outer person come more and more into harmony. We cannot have too much of God's Word living in our hearts. Hearts that are filled to overflowing with the Word of God are able to survive incredible pressure.

We find out what we really are like deep down inside of ourselves when we face a crisis. Severe crises often come upon us suddenly. We do not have a lot of time to think and plan how we will react. Our immediate reaction will be based on whatever we *really believe* deep down inside of our hearts.

Everyone on earth will face many crises in the last days before Jesus returns. Now is the time to prepare ourselves for the crises that surely will come. Now is the time to fill our minds and our hearts with the supernatural power of the living Word of God so that our actions in a crisis situation automatically will be directed by the Holy Spirit and our unwavering faith in God deep down inside of ourselves.

Some Christians have great intellectual knowledge of the Word of God. These scholars study the Word of God constantly. We will *not* be able to cope with the severe problems we will face in the end times with intellectual faith. We must have real intimacy with our Father that requires more than just intellectual knowledge of His Word.

We are not in any way demeaning scholarly Christians, but we must understand that we will not be able to survive the difficult times that lie ahead by paying mental assent to the Word of God. Faith in God is spiritual knowledge that has been *accepted by our hearts*.

God's ways are very different from the ways of the world. God has created us in such a way that our hearts can accept spiritual truths that do not seem to be reasonable to our minds.

A heart that is filled with the Word of God is able to trust God completely in situations that seem to be absolutely impossible to the intellectual comprehension of our minds.

We should fill our eyes and our ears continually with the supernatural power of the living Word of God until it drops from our minds down into our hearts. Once we have established this process, we should maintain it. As this process continues over a period of months and years, we will find that the Word of God in our hearts overrides traditional worldly thinking. Our hearts will be programmed with the Word of God. Our lives will be directed by the abundance of God's Word living in our hearts. Our lives will be yielded to the Holy Spirit.

We are in trouble if our lives are dominated by our minds. Our Father wants us to be absolutely certain deep down inside of ourselves that everything will work out just fine, even though we may not be able to explain our faith in God intellectually. We should desire to understand "the hidden person of the heart." We know God with this inner person. We trust God with this inner person. "…as he thinks in his heart, so is he…" (Proverbs 23:7).

Please highlight or underline the word "heart" in this passage of Scripture. This passage of Scripture does *not* say "…as he thinks in his *mind*, so is he…" We will face problems in the future that will overwhelm our minds unless we have consistently renewed our minds in the Word of God *and* filled our hearts each day with the supernatural power of the living Word of God. Unbelievers and casual Christians will be overwhelmed by the problems in the world. They do not understand how to get the Word of God off the printed pages of the Bible, into their minds and, from there, down into their hearts.

God does not look at our lives the way that many human beings look at their lives. Many people are externally oriented.

Their lives revolve primarily around people, places, things and events. God looks at what we are like deep down inside of ourselves. "…the Lord sees not as man sees; for man looks on the outward appearance, but the Lord looks on the heart" (I Samuel 16:7).

Some of us are too concerned with what we are like on the outside. We are not saying that we should not present a neat and tidy appearance. However, the Word of God teaches us that we should place *much more* emphasis on the "hidden person of the heart" and the Holy Spirit Who lives in our hearts than we do on our external appearance and on external circumstances in the world

Our Father wants us to fill the wonderful new hearts He gives us when we are saved with the supernatural power of His living Word. He wants our hearts to be so full of His Word that His ways and our ways will become increasingly similar. "My son, give me your heart and let your eyes observe and delight in my ways" (Proverbs 23:26).

Our Father does *not* want us to focus primarily on the accumulation of wealth and an excess of worldly possessions. He wants us to place our focus instead on filling our hearts with His Word. We should pray as the psalmist prayed when he said, "Incline my heart to Your testimonies and not to covetousness (robbery, sensuality, unworthy riches)" (Psalm 119:36).

The holy Bible is not effective when it is sitting on a desk or in a bookcase. The Word of God only can be effective in our lives when it comes up off the printed pages of the Bible into our minds and then drops down into our hearts. God created us in such a way that our minds and our hearts are meant to be *the home for His Word.* "Let the word [spoken by]

Christ (the Messiah) have its home [in your hearts and minds] and dwell in you in [all its] richness…" (Colossians 3:16).

The Word of God is very good in our minds. However, the supernatural power of the Word of God truly comes alive on the inside of us when it dwells in our hearts. We cannot call time out when we face a sudden crisis. We can't say "Wait a minute. I'm going to run home and get my Bible and study it to see what it says about how to deal with this situation." We can only react by whatever we *truly believe* in our *hearts*.

We have learned that the Word of God is alive and filled with the superhuman power of Almighty God. Our Father wants His living Word to fill our hearts so that we will be able to respond to the crises we face with hearts that are filled with His Word.

The Bible teaches us that the Word of God is the Truth. Jesus said, "…Your Word is Truth" (John 17:17). Jesus is the Truth. He said, "…I am the Way and the Truth and the Life…" (John 14:6). Shortly after this statement Jesus referred to the Holy Spirit as "the Spirit of Truth…" (John 14:17).

Filling our hearts with supernatural Truth from the Word of God is essential throughout our lives on earth. The time and effort we spend filling our hearts with the supernatural Truth of God's Word *also* will bless us throughout eternity. The Bible speaks of "…the Truth which lives and stays on in our hearts and will be with us forever" (II John 2).

This chapter is filled with basic facts from the holy Scriptures pertaining to the importance of God's Word living in our hearts. We hope that these facts have influenced you to have a deep and strong desire to fill *your heart* to overflowing with the Word of God.

Chapter 18

More Facts about God's Word in Our Hearts

The Word of God is a magnificent spiritual treasure chest. The Bible is filled with many precious gems from heaven. Nothing on earth can compare to it. We should have a deep, sincere and constant desire to put as much of this wonderful treasure inside of us as we possibly can so that we will be able to draw on it whenever we need it.

We will treat the Bible with the absolute reverence and awe it deserves when we begin to comprehend the magnificent supernatural power of the living Word of God. Each and every day of our lives we should carry out a deep commitment to fill our minds and our hearts with the precious treasure of God's Word that is so great that nothing in the world can even begin to compare to it. Jesus explained that every person's heart contains whatever he or she perceives to be his or her treasure. He said, "…where your treasure is, there will your heart be also" (Matthew 6:21).

We make a big mistake if we allow anything in the world to be more of a treasure to us than the Word of God. Nothing else will be sufficient to help us in the difficult times that lie ahead of us. When we reach deep down inside of ourselves for the strength we will need during the end times, we should be able to draw upon an abundance of the Word of God living in our hearts.

The Bible refers to our hearts as spiritual tablets that can be compared to a pad of paper. Our Father has instructed us to continually "write" the holy Scriptures "upon the tablet of our hearts." "…write them upon the tablet of your heart…" (Proverbs 3:3).

We actually write God's Word on the tablet of our hearts when we meditate continually on the holy Scriptures. We must understand the vital importance of storing up large amounts of the Word of God inside of us so that we *will* have everything we need when we need it. "…keep my words; lay up within you my commandments [for use when needed] and treasure them. Keep my commandments and live, and keep my law and teaching as the apple (the pupil) of your eye. Bind them on your fingers; write them on the tablet of your heart" (Proverbs 7:1-3).

The amplification of this passage of Scripture tells us that the Word of God inside of us should be there "for use when needed." We definitely will need the supernatural power of the living Word of God in the difficult days that lie ahead. Is the Word of God *so important to you* that it truly is "the apple of your eye?" Have you continually written the Word of God "on the tablet of your heart" by obeying our Father's instructions to continually meditate on His Word throughout the day and night?

Many people have the desire to store up treasure for the future. We have learned that the Word of God is much greater and much more powerful than the money of this world. People who focus continually on storing up money make a tremendous mistake. These people trust the money of this world as their primary source of security. "Wise men store up knowledge [in mind and heart]..." (Proverbs 10:14).

If we truly are wise in the ways of God, we will not store anything from this world in our minds and in our hearts. Instead, we will understand the vital importance of continually storing up more and more of the Word of God. We should be like the psalmist who said, "...You desire truth in the inner being; make me therefore to know wisdom in my inmost heart" (Psalm 51:6).

Other people can teach the Word of God to our minds, but I do not believe that anyone else can put God's Word into our hearts. I do not believe we should allow *anything* to come ahead of our deep and fervent commitment to constantly fill our minds and our hearts with the supernatural power of the living Word of God. We may not have a great deal of time before Jesus returns. We do not have time to waste doing anything that is not ordained of God. "...attend to my words; consent and submit to my sayings. Let them not depart from your sight; keep them in the center of your heart" (Proverbs 4:20-21).

When God tells us to "attend to" His Word, He is telling us to pay close attention to His Word. How do we accomplish this goal? We give our daily meditation on the Word of God such a high priority that the Word of God will "not depart from our sight." We only can accomplish this goal by faithful obedience to the instructions our Father has given us in Joshua 1:8 and Psalm 1:1-3 to meditate on His Word throughout the day and night. If we obey our Father's specific instructions in this area, we will keep the Word of God "in the center of our hearts."

This passage of Scripture goes on to give us more specific instructions about the vital importance of God's Word living in our hearts. "…they are life to those who find them, healing and health to all their flesh. Keep and guard your heart with all vigilance and above all that you guard, for out of it flow the springs of life" (Proverbs 4:22-23).

We have learned that the Word of God is supernaturally alive. If we obey our Father's instructions to meditate continually on His Word, we will store up more and more of the spiritual life of His Word in our hearts. This passage of Scripture explains the important relationship that exists between enjoying good health, receiving healing from sickness and hearts that are filled to overflowing with the Word of God.

Do you want to improve your health? Do you need physical healing? If so, meditate often on Proverbs 4:20-23 so that you can experience the relationship between Scripture meditation, divine healing and divine health.

We are instructed to "keep and guard our hearts with all vigilance and above all that we guard." Do *you* have the *same* priority that God speaks of here in regard to the spiritual condition of your heart? Is the spiritual condition of your heart vitally important to you?

We must understand that "springs of life" can and should flow out of our hearts. We must understand the correlation between receiving wisdom, power and guidance from the Holy Spirit Who lives in our hearts and the amount of the Word of God that continually is being fed into our hearts. We will guard our hearts continually *if* we can comprehend how important our hearts are to God.

Please go back and carefully meditate on Proverbs 4:20-23. Think about the importance that Almighty God places on the contents of your heart. If you have not already made this decision, please make the decision now to constantly fill *your mind* and *your heart* with the supernatural power of the living Word of God. Make the decision to prepare yourself now for the difficult times that surely will come upon us. "...garrison and mount guard over your hearts and minds in Christ Jesus" (Philippians 4:7).

God has given us the ability to direct our thoughts and our emotions. We must not allow difficult circumstances to dominate our thoughts and our emotions. Instead, we should carefully "garrison and mount guard over" what we allow to come into our hearts and into our minds. The word "garrison" in this passage of Scripture is a military term that compares guarding our hearts and our minds with a fort where the people in the fort are protected by the walls of the fort, soldiers and weapons.

Seemingly severe problems will *not* be able to get into our minds and our hearts *if* we obey our Father's instructions to constantly fill our minds and our hearts with His Word. The supernatural power of the Word of God is *so great* that negative thoughts about the problems we face *cannot* possibly dislodge God's Word. The only way we will continually dwell on the difficult circumstances we face is if we ignore our Father's instructions to renew our minds in His Word every day of our lives and to meditate on His Word constantly throughout the day and night.

When we face a crisis situation, our primary asset is the spiritual condition of our hearts. We have learned that our hearts are the real us. If God has our hearts, He will have our minds and our bodies. All superficial veneer is stripped away when we face a severe crisis. Whatever we truly believe will be manifested when we are under severe pressure.

We will *not* be able to persevere in faith when we face severe adversity if we have not prepared ourselves *in advance* by continually filling our hearts with the Word of God. In Chapter Ten and Chapter Eleven we learned many facts about the supernatural power of the living Word of God. We learned that the Word of God is spiritually alive and full of the power of God (see Hebrews 4:12). Our hearts are *filled with God's power* to the degree that our hearts are filled with God's Word.

Our Father wants us to absorb His Word. He wants each of us to learn how to get His promises and instructions up off the printed pages of the Bible to come alive in our minds and in our hearts. The more of God's Word we have living in our hearts, the more of God we will experience. Our Father's tremendous strength, power, wisdom and ability are available to us to the degree that we faithfully obey His instructions to continually fill our minds and our hearts with His Word.

The Word of God is like spiritual currency. Our hearts can be compared to a spiritual bank. We should deposit spiritual currency into our hearts on a daily basis. We should make these deposits constantly over a period of time so that we always will have enough of the Word of God on deposit in our hearts to cover whatever withdrawals of faith we have to make when we face difficult circumstances.

We cannot wait until difficult problems come upon us to begin increasing our faith in God. We must develop our faith in God *in advance* so that we will be equipped for every situation. If we do not make these deposits by faithfully meditating on God's Word throughout the day and night, we will reach down inside of ourselves to make a withdrawal only to find that nothing is there.

We will be able to persevere in the face of severe adversity if we continue to faithfully study and meditate on the Word of

God. Nothing will be able to knock us off our feet. "The law of his God is in his heart; none of his steps shall slide" (Psalm 37:31).

The beauty of having our hearts filled to overflowing with the Word of God is that we take this reservoir of supernatural power with us wherever we go. We never will be caught short because the power of God's living Word will be with us twenty-four hours a day throughout every day of our lives.

Chapter 19

We Can Encourage and Strengthen Our Hearts

During these last days before Jesus returns, we will face many difficult circumstances that could cause us to be discouraged. Our Father has instructed us to "encourage our hearts." We can "strengthen" our hearts with the supernatural power of His Word. "Comfort and encourage your hearts and strengthen them [make them steadfast and keep them unswerving]..." (II Thessalonians 2:17).

The word "discourage" means "to deprive of courage." Discouragement comes from Satan, not from God. There is no place in the Word of God where we are instructed to be discouraged. My friend Charlie Jones says, "Discouragement is a luxury we cannot afford." Most of us would not think of squandering our money the way that some people squander their emotions when they allow themselves to be discouraged. We must not indulge in this luxury. The price is far too great.

When we encourage ourselves, we constantly put supernatural spiritual courage from the Word of God into our hearts. Our faith in God will be strengthened if we constantly encourage our hearts with the Word of God. We can and should receive constant "comfort" from meditating on the Word of God. Our hearts will be "steadfast and unswerving." The problems we face will *not* be able to overcome us

We will be courageous if we trust God to do in us and through us what we know we cannot do ourselves. We will not allow the circumstances of life to pull us down when our faith is in God and not in ourselves. "…be strong in the Lord [be empowered through your union with Him]; draw your strength from Him [that strength which His boundless might provides]" (Ephesians 6:10).

How do we become "strong in the Lord?" The amplification of this passage of Scripture says that we will "be empowered through our union with Him." If we faithfully set aside precious time to be with the Lord each day, we will develop a close personal relationship with Him. We will be able to "draw our strength from Him." His "boundless might" will provide us with all of the strength we need.

Discouragement comes from focusing on the seeming severity of the problems we face. Encouragement comes from focusing continually on God Who lives in our hearts. Encouragement comes from constantly filling our minds and our hearts with the supernatural power of the living Word of God.

The word "encourage" consists of two parts – "en" and "courage." The prefix "en" means "in." We need to put courage *into* our hearts continually so that we will not allow discouragement to take courage *out* of our hearts. We will make constant deposits of courage deep down inside of ourselves if we faithfully obey our Father's instructions to meditate on His Word throughout the day and night. We will have such a bank of courage to draw on that the circumstances in our lives will not be able to overcome us. We will *not* give in to discouragement if we have paid this price that our Father has instructed us to pay.

We will pour a steady stream of heavenly encouragement into our hearts if we obey our Father's instructions to meditate continually on His Word. We will trust God completely to do everything He has promised to do. When we face difficult circumstances, we will not be discouraged *if* our lives are centered around our close personal relationship with Jesus. We will not be discouraged *if* the Word of God fills our hearts to overflowing. Jesus said, "If you live in Me [abide vitally united to Me] and My words remain in you and continue to live in your hearts, ask whatever you will, and it shall be done for you" (John 15:7).

When we "abide" in Jesus, we stay close to Him continually. Abiding in Jesus should be a way of life. Abiding in Jesus is something we should do twenty-four hours a day, seven days a week and twelve months a year throughout every year of our lives. We should not allow anything or anyone to come ahead of Him. Our personal relationship with Jesus is more important than anything else in our lives.

This passage of Scripture tells us that we should "abide vitally united to Jesus." If we want our prayers to be answered, every aspect of our lives should revolve around Jesus. We must understand the *vital importance* of a close personal relationship with Him.

The second condition to this wonderful promise of having all of our prayers answered is for the Word of God to "remain in us and continue to live in our hearts." *Every one* of our prayers *will* be answered *if* we have a constant, close relationship with Jesus and if we continually fill our hearts with the supernatural living Word of God.

As we grow and mature as Christians, we will have a constantly increasing awareness that Jesus really does live in our hearts. "…Do you not yourselves realize and know [thoroughly by an ever-increasing experience] that Jesus Christ is in you?…" (II Corinthians 13:5).

The same Jesus Who rose from the dead and won the greatest victory this world has ever known lives inside of *you* if you have asked Him to be your Savior. *Refuse* to focus on any problems, no matter how difficult they may seem to be. Focus *instead* on the victorious Jesus Who lives in your heart.

John 15:7 and II Corinthians 13:5 are important promises from heaven that will sustain us in these last days before Jesus returns. We will make a tremendous mistake if we center our lives around anything except the indwelling presence of Jesus and minds and hearts that overflow with the supernatural power of the living Word of God.

Jesus has done His part. Will we do our part? Our part is to live in close communion with Him by setting aside precious quality time each day to draw closer to Him and to gladly surrender control of our lives to Him (see Galatians 2:20). Our part is to continually fill our hearts with the Word of God. If we do our part, we can be absolutely assured that Jesus will do exactly what John 15:7 says He will do.

Some Christians pay mental assent to the fact that Jesus lives in their hearts, but their words and actions throughout every day of their lives do not indicate that they really believe this great spiritual truth. *Why* would we ever be afraid of anyone or anything if we *really* believe that the all-conquering, victorious Jesus Christ lives in our hearts? "May Christ through your faith [actually] dwell (settle down, abide, make His permanent home) in your hearts!…" (Ephesians 3:17).

We should have absolute faith that Jesus really does "make His permanent home in our hearts." We must not underestimate the power of Jesus living in our hearts. We must not underestimate the power of God's Word living in our hearts. If we are humble and teachable, we will turn to the Word of God each day with a deep and sincere desire to learn whatever the Holy Spirit reveals to us. "…in a humble (gentle, modest) spirit receive and welcome the Word which implanted and rooted [in your hearts] contains the power to save your souls" (James 1:21).

Unfortunately, many Christians fail to continually humble themselves with awe and reverence before the mighty supernatural power of the living Word of God. Constant meditation on the Word of God causes it to be "implanted and rooted in our hearts." The Word of God is a spiritual seed (see Luke 8:11). We will plant supernatural spiritual seeds in the spiritual soil of our hearts if we faithfully obey our Father's instructions to meditate continually on His Word. The Word of God will put down deep roots in our hearts.

This passage of Scripture tells us that the Word of God "contains the power to save our souls." Our souls consist of our minds, our emotions and our will. Whatever we think, whatever we feel and whatever we decide should be solidly anchored on hearts that are filled with the Word of God.

How can we control our thoughts in the face of a crisis situation? How can we control our emotions? How can we control the decisions we make when we are under severe pressure? The answer to each of these questions is determined by the amount of God's Word we have planted in our hearts *before* we face difficult problems.

Unfortunately, some Christians have developed hard hearts. Satan wants our hearts to harden. Our Father wants our hearts to be soft and pliable. How can we tell if our hearts have hardened? We can tell whether we have hard hearts by taking an objective look at the amount of quality time we consistently spend with the Lord.

Do you set aside an ample amount of precious quiet time each day for prayer, worship and fellowship with the Lord? Do you obey your Father's instructions to renew your mind in His Word each and every day? Do you obey your Father's instructions to meditate on His Word throughout the day and night? Do you faithfully attend church (see Hebrews 10:25)?

Our Father wants us to revere Him. He wants us to hold Him in constant awe. He does not want us to allow our hearts to become hard. We are headed for serious problems if our hearts are hard. "Blessed (happy, fortunate, and to be envied) is the man who reverently and worshipfully fears [the Lord] at all times [regardless of circumstances], but he who hardens his heart will fall into calamity" (Proverbs 28:14).

Our Father will bless us if we keep Him in first place at all times "regardless of circumstances." This passage of Scripture does *not* contain an asterisk saying that this magnificent promise of God's blessing will be null and void during the end times. Our Father *will* bless each of His children who "reverently and worshipfully fear Him." We will "harden our hearts and fall into calamity" if we fail to obey these instructions from God.

Some of us had a wonderful relationship with the Lord immediately after we were saved. However, as time goes by, some Christians gradually turn away from the confidence they had in the Lord when they were saved. Their hearts become hard. "…we have become fellows with Christ (the Messiah) and share in all He has for us, if only we hold our first newborn confidence and original assured expectation [in virtue of which we are believers] firm and unshaken to the end. Then while it is [still] called Today, if you would hear His voice and when you hear it, do not harden your hearts…" (Hebrews 3:14-15).

Do you want to be a "fellow with Christ" because of your close relationship with Jesus? Do you want to "share in *all* He has for you?" You can and will receive these magnificent blessings *if* you "hold your first and newborn confidence firm and unshaken to the end."

Our hearts will harden if we disobey our Father's instructions to renew our minds daily in His Word and to meditate continually on the holy Scriptures. We will not be able to hear His voice. Sin will creep into our lives. We will not have the humble and teachable attitude our Father desires. We open ourselves to the evil influence of Satan if we do not seek the Lord with all our hearts. "…he did evil because he did not set his heart to seek (inquire of, yearn for) the Lord with all his desire" (II Chronicles 12:14).

Many Christians seem to be religious, but they actually have given Satan a foothold in their lives because they do not seek God wholeheartedly. They fail to continually fill their hearts with the supernatural power of God's Word. Our Father wants us to be like the psalmist who said, "With my whole heart have I sought You, inquiring for and of You and yearning for You; O let me not wander or step aside [either in ignorance or will-fully] from Your commandments. Your word have I laid up in my heart, that I might not sin against You. Blessed are You, O Lord; teach me Your statutes" (Psalm 119:10-13).

Do you seek the Lord with your "whole heart?" Do you "yearn" for a close personal relationship with Him? We must not allow ourselves to "wander" spiritually through "ignorance" of what the Word of God instructs us to do to constantly draw closer to our precious Lord.

We will not "sin against" the Lord if we truly yearn for a close personal relationship with Him and if we have a deep and sincere desire to continually fill our minds and our hearts with His Word. Our minds and our hearts should be so filled with the Word of God that we will continually surrender ourselves to live our lives the way our Father instructs us to live.

During these last days before Jesus returns, we will not be able to get by with the habits that some of us have established over the years. Only Christians who have filled their hearts with God's Word will be able to obey the instructions of Jesus Who said, "…Do not let your hearts be troubled, neither let them be afraid. [Stop allowing yourselves to be agitated and disturbed; and do not permit yourselves to be fearful and intimidated and cowardly and unsettled]" (John 14:27).

Please highlight or underline the words "let," "allowing" and "permit" in this passage of Scripture. We each make a continual *choice* whether or not we will allow the circumstances we face to get into our hearts. We each decide whether we will be "fearful, intimidated, cowardly and unsettled."

We cannot stop the influence of fearful thoughts through sheer willpower. However, we can successfully resist adversity and the fearful thoughts that Satan's demons will try to put into our minds and our hearts. We will be able to resist adversity *if* we have faithfully obeyed our Father's instructions to constantly fill our minds and our hearts with His Word (see James 4:7).

Some Christians allow negative thoughts to enter into their hearts that our Father does not want in our hearts. We have seen that our Father has instructed us to guard our hearts diligently (see Proverbs 4:23). Satan wants us to allow the problems we face, anxiety about these problems and the pursuit of selfish goals to get into our hearts to block the mighty power of the Word of God. Jesus said, "…the cares and anxieties of the world and distractions of the age, and the pleasure and delight and false glamour and deceitfulness of riches, and the craving and passionate desire for other things creep in and choke and suffocate the Word, and it becomes fruitless" (Mark 4:19).

Some Christians actually have "choked and suffocated the Word of God" in their lives to the point where it has "become fruitless." *How* do we make this terrible mistake? We allow worry and anxiety, the distractions of the world, selfish desires, the pursuit of money and yearning for the things of the world to live in our hearts. We must not make the mistake of allowing "other things to creep in and choke and suffocate the Word." We absolutely must be single-minded and focused during the last days before Jesus returns.

People whose hearts are filled with worry, fear and worldly desires will not be able to cope with the difficult problems of the end times. Only Christians who constantly fill their hearts with the Word of God will be able to deal with them successfully. "…the [uncompromisingly] righteous (the upright, in right standing with God) shall be in everlasting remembrance. He shall not be afraid of evil tidings; his heart is firmly fixed, trusting (leaning on and being confident) in the Lord. His heart is established and steady…" (Psalm 112:6-8).

This passage of Scripture says that we should be "uncompromisingly righteous" at all times. We are made righteous before God when we ask Jesus to be our Savior. We should choose to live for God, not for ourselves. God knows the people who have made this decision. The "uncompromisingly righteous" people who are mentioned in the Bible are people who make this decision. This decision then becomes discipline and finally it becomes a reflex. Deeply committed Christians who obey these instructions will "be in everlasting remembrance" of God. Every aspect of their lives will revolve around God.

These Christians "will not be afraid of evil tidings." They will not allow difficult circumstances to overwhelm them. They will not be swayed by the circumstances they face or the thoughts that Satan's demons try to put into their minds. Their hearts will be "firmly fixed, trusting, leaning on and being confident in the Lord."

Christians who have constantly filled their hearts with the Word of God will be "established and steady." Christians who have filled their hearts with the supernatural power of God's living Word will *not* give in to the problems they face no matter how difficult these problems may seem to be. They will *know* that the supernatural power of God in their hearts is much greater than any circumstances, no matter how difficult these circumstances might seem to be. "The precepts of the Lord are right, rejoicing the heart..." (Psalm 19:8).

Our hearts will rejoice and sing with joy if they are filled to overflowing with the supernatural power of the living Word of God. Christians who have faithfully obeyed God's instructions to meditate continually on God's Word will never have a heavy heart. A heavy heart comes from allowing worry, fear and anxiety to get inside of us. Our Father does not want us to have heavy hearts. He wants us to have glad hearts. "Anxiety in a man's heart weighs it down, but an encouraging word makes it glad" (Proverbs 12:25).

We will have glad hearts in the face of difficult circumstances *if* we have constantly *encouraged* ourselves by faithfully meditating throughout the day and night on the Word of God. Anxiety cannot get into hearts that continually are being filled with supernatural encouragement from the holy Scriptures. Too many Christians have heavy hearts as a result of the circumstances they face. Their hearts would *sing with joy* if they had obeyed God's instructions to constantly fill their hearts with encouragement from His Word.

The deep inner peace, joy and confidence that come from hearts that are filled with God's Word are difficult to describe with the limitations of our human vocabulary. Christians who have chosen to live in the joy of the Lord will not be "weighed down" by circumstances. "All the days of the desponding and afflicted are made evil [by anxious thoughts and forebodings], but he who has a glad heart has a continual feast [regardless of circumstances]" (Proverbs 15:15).

The amplification of this passage of Scripture tells us that all of our days will be made evil if we allow "anxious thoughts and forebodings" to enter into our hearts. Many people will give in to thoughts of worry, fear and concern during the difficult times that lie ahead. The only way we can overcome this tendency to allow these fearful thoughts to enter into our minds and our hearts is to faithfully obey our Father's instructions to continually fill our minds and our hearts with the supernatural power of His living Word.

Christians who worry give Satan and his demons a foothold in their lives. Christians whose hearts are filled with the Word of God will have "a glad heart." The amplification in this passage of Scripture says that our hearts will sing with joy "regardless of circumstances." We must not allow the circumstances in our lives to pull us down.

A heart that is filled with the Word of God is a healthy heart. The Word of God is our Father's spiritual "medicine" for us. We will enjoy good mental, emotional, physical and spiritual health if our minds and our hearts are filled with the Word of God. "A happy heart is good medicine and a cheerful mind works healing, but a broken spirit dries up the bones" (Proverbs 17:22).

The Word of God repeatedly tells us that we *can* have a "glad heart," a "happy heart" and a "merry heart." *Why* would any Christian ever fail to constantly fill his or her mind and heart with the living Word of God that supplies the supernatural spiritual fuel for a joyous heart?

Are you physically sick? Do you need to be healed? The Word of God says that you will receive the spiritual medicine you need to receive manifestation of healing *if* you have "a happy heart and a cheerful mind."

We will hold tightly onto God's promises and instructions when our hearts are filled with God's Word. Our lives will be anchored on and guided by the Word of God. Every aspect of our lives will revolve around the Word of God that lives in our hearts. "…Let your heart hold fast my words; keep my commandments and live" (Proverbs 4:4).

Our faith in God *will* be measured whenever we face extremely difficult problems. We will find what we really believe in our hearts. We will clearly see whether we have prepared ourselves in advance for any crisis situation we might encounter. We will find out if the Word of God is so ingrained in our hearts that we will persevere in faith, no matter how severe the problems we face might seem to be.

There is *no* limit to the power of God's Word that lives in our hearts except any limit *we* set. How many years have passed since you asked Jesus to be your Savior? Have you faithfully obeyed God's instructions to continually fill your mind and your heart with His Word? Can you give an approximate estimate as to how many passages of Scripture are alive in your heart? Is your heart filled with ten passages of Scripture? …

fifty? … one hundred or more? … more than one thousand?
… several thousand?

Make the decision to constantly fill your mind and your heart with the supernatural power of the living Word of God. The remainder of this book will give you hundreds of specific instructions from the holy Scriptures that will tell you exactly what *you* should *do* so that *your* mind and *your* heart will overflow with the supernatural power of God's living Word.

Chapter 20

God's Instructions Pertaining to Scripture Meditation

Our loving Father has given us His holy Bible that is filled with thousands of instructions and promises from heaven. We need to study and meditate on the Bible throughout each day and night of our lives to know God, to learn and obey His instructions and to learn and believe wholeheartedly in His promises.

Unfortunately, many of God's children do not spend enough time in His Word to know Him. They know very few specific instructions and promises from God. Many Christians do not understand the difference between reading the Bible, studying the Bible, memorizing Scripture and meditating on the Word of God.

We have discussed the difference between reading the Bible and studying the Bible. We have seen that we renew our minds by studying the Word of God. We have learned that studying the Bible enables us to get God's instructions and promises up off the printed pages of the Bible into our minds. We have learned that studying the Bible is essential because this daily Bible study gives us hope for the future.

We must learn how to receive "head knowledge" from the Word of God before we can receive "heart knowledge." We *must not stop* with studying the Word of God. Some Christians think they have strong faith in God when this faith actually is only mental assent to the promises of God. We cannot understand what God promises to do for us until we study His Word. We cannot believe with absolute certainty that God will do exactly what He says He will do unless we meditate continually on His Word.

We have referred many times to Scripture meditation. We now are ready to study in detail exactly what the Bible teaches about meditating on the Word of God. We must not confuse Scripture meditation with memorizing Scripture. Memorizing Scripture is very important. However, memorizing Scripture gets the Word of God into our minds. Meditating on the holy Scriptures causes the Word of God to drop from our minds down into our hearts.

Some Christians do not even read the Bible. Some Christians read the Bible, but they do not study the Bible. Some Christians read the Bible and study the Bible but they never have taken the next step of continually meditating on the Word of God to get God's Word from their minds down into their hearts. They do not experience the Holy Spirit revealing great spiritual truth to them.

Please study these chapters on Scripture meditation very carefully. *These chapters are the heart of this book.* We can see how important Scripture meditation is to God by reading the first chapter of the Book of Joshua. When Moses was one hundred and twenty years old, the Lord told him that Joshua should be appointed as his successor as the leader of the Israelites (see Deuteronomy 31:14).

Joshua was a young man who had served as a captain in Israel's army and as an assistant to Moses. Even though Joshua had served with distinction in these roles, he probably was somewhat apprehensive about the awesome responsibility he would be given as the leader of Israel.

God spoke directly to Joshua to encourage him. He said, "...be strong and very courageous, that you may do according to all the law which Moses My servant commanded you. Turn not from it to the right hand or to the left, that you may prosper wherever you go. This Book of the Law shall not depart out of your mouth, but you shall meditate on it day and night, that you may observe and do according to all that is written in it. For then you shall make your way prosperous, and then you shall deal wisely and have good success" (Joshua 1:7-8).

When Joshua was the leader of the Israelites, he faithfully obeyed God's instructions to meditate on His Word throughout the day and night. This constant meditation kept Joshua in touch with God and enabled him to successfully do what God called him to do. This same principle applies to each of us today. God did not give these instructions to Joshua only for his personal benefit. He wants each of us to continually be encouraged as we fill our hearts with His Word.

I believe this passage of Scripture is one of the most important passages of Scripture in the entire Bible for those of us who live in the last days before Jesus returns. We *must* learn how to "be strong and very courageous" during the difficult days that lie ahead of us.

In Joshua 1:8 God told Joshua three things that he should do as leader of the Israelites. Our Father wants each of us to follow these specific instructions. He wants our mouths to *speak* His Word continually. He wants us to *meditate* on His Word constantly throughout the day and night. He wants us to *do* what He has instructed us to do.

We *will* receive manifestation of *three* definite promises from God *if* we continually obey these three instructions. Our Father promises that we will be *prosperous*, that we will be *wise* and that we will be *successful*.

Do *you* want to be prosperous, wise and successful from God's perspective? Almost every Christian will answer this question affirmatively. Ask yourself if *you* have been *speaking* the Word of God continually, *meditating* on the Word of God throughout the day and night and constantly learning and *doing* exactly what the Word of God instructs you to do.

I have given many seminars on the subject of Scripture meditation. Each time I asked how many people in the audience wanted to be prosperous, wise and successful, every person raised his or her hand. Each time I asked how many people could honestly say that they were speaking the Word of God continually, meditating on the Word of God constantly throughout the day and night and learning and obeying all of God's instructions, only a few hands were raised.

After many years of giving these seminars and after writing several books that contained information on Scripture meditation, I can share the results with you. *Less than five percent* of the Christians we have surveyed can honestly say that their mouths are opening to speak God's Word continually, that they actually are meditating on the Word of God throughout the day and night and that they constantly are learning and doing what God has instructed them to do.

When Joshua 1:8 tells us that we will be prosperous if we obey these instructions from God, we must understand that the word "prosperous" is much greater than the financial success the word "prosperity" refers to in the world today. The Hebrew word "tsalach" that is translated as "prosperous" in this passage of Scripture refers to having the financial wherewithal we need, but it also means to "push forward, break out and go over." In these last days before Jesus returns we absolutely *must* be able to "push forward, break out and go over."

Did you know that Joshua 1:8 is the *only* place in the entire *Amplified Bible* and the *King James Bible* where the word "success" is used? Do *you* want to be successful from God's perspective? Doesn't it make sense that any Christian who wants to be successful from God's perspective should know and obey God's specific instructions for success?

The Hebrew word "sakal" that is translated as "success" in Joshua 1:8 indicates that success from God's perspective includes "intelligence, expertise, prudence and wisdom." We cannot survive in the difficult times that lie ahead of us unless we faithfully obey the three specific instructions our Father has given to His children who sincerely desire to receive the prosperity, wisdom and success He promised to Joshua.

Very few Christians even know what Joshua 1:8 tells us to do in order to be prosperous, wise and successful from God's perspective. Our Father has done His part. He told how us to live in victory. We must do our part. We cannot expect to receive the results that are promised to us in the last part of Joshua 1:8 *unless* we learn and faithfully obey the three specific instructions our Father has given us in the first part of this passage of Scripture.

Our Father told us in one other place in the Bible about the tremendous blessings we will receive if we consistently meditate on His Word throughout the day and night. "Blessed (happy, fortunate, prosperous, and enviable) is the man who walks and lives not in the counsel of the ungodly [following their advice, their plans and purposes], nor stands [submissive and inactive] in the path where sinners walk, nor sits down [to relax and rest] where the scornful [and the mockers] gather. But his delight and desire are in the law of the Lord, and on His law (the precepts, the instructions, the teachings of God) he habitually meditates (ponders and studies) by day and by night" (Psalm 1:1-2).

This passage of Scripture tells us that we cannot expect to live as God planned if we seek advice from "ungodly" people who do not know and understand God's ways. We then are told that we will receive God's blessings if we "delight" in the holy Scriptures and if we have a deep, constant and sincere "desire" to live our lives the way our Father wants us to live. We will receive wonderful blessings from God if we "habitually meditate, ponder and study" the Word of God throughout the day and night.

God will not necessarily bless us abundantly as soon as we begin to study and meditate on His Word on a daily basis. However, we can promise you based on our experience and the promises in God's Word that your loving Father *will* bless you abundantly *if* you continue to obey His instructions to fill your eyes, your ears, your mind, your heart and your mouth with His Word throughout every day and night. We must not be swayed from our resolve to meditate continually on the supernatural living Word of God.

Our Father has told us what we can expect if we habitually meditate on His Word. "And he shall be like a tree firmly planted [and tended] by the streams of water, ready to bring forth its fruit in its season; its leaf also shall not fade or wither; and everything he does shall prosper [and come to maturity]" (Psalm 1:3).

Please highlight or underline the word "prosper" in Psalm 1:3. The Hebrew word "tsalach" that we discussed in Joshua 1:8 is the same word that is used here. There is *no* question that Scripture meditation is absolutely essential for every one of God's children who want to experience the prosperity and success our Father has made available to us.

We are instructed to "habitually" meditate on the Word of God. When we do something habitually, we do it regularly. Our Father does not want us to meditate on His Word some of the time or most of the time. He wants us to meditate on His supernatural living Word *continually* throughout *every day* and night of our lives.

If we obey these instructions, we are told that we will be "like a tree that is planted next to a stream of water." We will be able to "bring forth fruit in season." Please visualize several rows of trees in an orchard next to a stream of water. Imagine that a long season of drought caused the leaves on these trees to "fade and wither." Please visualize that every row of trees in this orchard is brown, faded and withered *except the one row of trees that is next to the stream of water.*

Psalm 1:3 tells us that the leaves on these trees will *not* fade or wither. These trees *will* "bring forth fruit" in the proper season. *Why* will this one row of trees be green and lush and continue to produce fruit in the midst of a drought? The answer is that the trees next to a stream of water are able to reach their roots down into the stream to bring up water from the stream even though *no* rain is coming down from the sky.

This passage of Scripture is directly applicable to these last days before Jesus returns. We absolutely *must* meditate continually on the supernatural living Word of God if we want to prosper and be successful from God's perspective during the difficult times that lie ahead of us. Everything we do *will* "prosper and come to maturity" *if* we obey these instructions from God

God's promises are timeless. The requirements and promises in Joshua 1:8 and Psalm 1:1-3 are just as applicable in these last days before Jesus returns as they were when these passages of Scripture were written.

How can any thinking Christian *ignore* the specific and exact instructions our loving Father has given us in Joshua 1:8 and Psalm 1:1-3? There is *no* question that we cannot expect to prosper and be successful in the difficult times that lie ahead unless we faithfully *meditate* throughout the day and night on the Word of God, *speak* the Word of God continually and *do* exactly what the Word of God instructs us to do.

We are not saying that we should use the Bible selfishly for our own benefit. God knows if our hearts are truly His. If our hearts truly are committed to God, we will faithfully obey these instructions from our Father in heaven. Our Father will bless us for our obedience.

Chapter 21

How Do We Meditate
on the Word of God?

We have seen the relationship between deep, strong, unwavering and unshakable faith in God and meditating on the Word of God throughout the day and night. We now are ready to learn *how* to meditate on the Word of God.

I believe the first thing we should do when we meditate on the Word of God is to be very specific about the Scripture we choose to meditate on. If we have financial problems, we will not solve these problems by meditating on healing Scripture (see our Scripture Meditation Cards and cassette tape titled *Financial Instructions from God*). If we have concerns pertaining to our health, we are not as likely to be healed if we meditate on God's promises pertaining to finances instead of meditating on God's healing promises (see our Scripture Meditation Cards and cassette tape titled *Receive Healing from the Lord*).

If we have a particular need in a specific area, we should find *as much* Scripture on that specific subject as we possibly can. We should meditate continually on these passages of Scripture. We will be using a spiritual rifle instead of a shotgun when we do this. All of our Scripture meditation will be focused on the specific area where we need help.

These passages of Scripture will become more and more real to us as we meditate on them continually and speak them again and again. We will increasingly understand this specific area from God's perspective. Our faith for God's provision in this area will increase continually.

The amplification of the word "meditate" in Psalm 1:2 says that we should "ponder and study by day and by night." We have already explained what it means to study the Word of God. Now we need to consider what it means to "ponder." *Webster's New World Dictionary* tells us that the word "ponder" means "to weigh mentally, think deeply about and consider carefully." When we meditate on the Word of God, we should examine this portion of Scripture very deeply, very carefully and very thoroughly.

We must understand the significant difference between meditating on the holy Scriptures and the meditation that is taught by many Eastern religions. Most of the meditation that is taught by Eastern religion teaches that our minds should be empty when we meditate. This meditation is *exactly the opposite* of Scripture meditation.

Our minds should not be empty when we meditate. Our minds should be *filled* with the Word of God. When we meditate on the holy Scriptures, we should turn completely away from whatever circumstances we face in the world to continually fill our eyes, our ears, our minds, our hearts and our mouths with specific promises from the living Word of God.

What exactly do we do when we meditate on the Word of God? Many years ago God showed me that worrying and Scripture meditation are similar. Worry utilizes the *same* principles as meditating on the Word of God even though worry and Scripture meditation are very different.

We all know people who are chronic worriers. If they cannot find something to worry about, they will make something to worry about. Chronic worriers constantly think about the problems they face or the problems they might face in the future. These problems consume them. They turn these problems over and over in their minds. They look at them from every conceivable angle. They magnify these problems continually. They talk constantly about these problems.

Chronic worriers think about these problems throughout the day and night. The problems they are concerned about never leave their minds. The more they dwell on these problems, the worse the problems seem to be. They visualize exactly what will happen to them when these problems are manifested in their lives. They often visualize what they are worrying about so strongly that they bring exactly what they are worrying about into manifestation in their lives.

We see an example of this principle in the life of Job. Job was a wealthy man who continued to be completely devoted to God even after he lost everything he owned. However, Job was a human being just like us. He was not perfect.

On one occasion Job spoke words that illustrate exactly what happens to chronic worriers. He said, "...the thing which I greatly fear comes upon me, and that of which I am afraid befalls me. I was not or am not at ease, nor had I or have I rest, nor was I or am I quiet, yet trouble came and still comes upon me" (Job 3:25-26).

This passage of Scripture explains the relationship between what we continually think about and its manifestation. People who are constantly worried inevitably will find that whatever they worry about ultimately happens.

We cannot afford to make this mistake. There will be a great deal to worry about in the years ahead for people who are inclined toward worrying. These people will focus continually on the many problems the world will face during the end times.

Our Father wants us to do what chronic worriers do, but He wants us to turn completely in the opposite direction. He wants us to apply these principles positively, not negatively. Instead of meditating continually on anticipated *problems*, we must meditate continually on God's Word.

Three chapters of this book have been devoted to the supernatural power of the living Word of God and the rock-solid foundation our Father has given us to develop unwavering faith in Him. The next chapter explained in detail that Almighty God stands completely behind every promise in His Word.

Bad news will be prevalent in the future. The secular news media will pour out bad news twenty-four hours a day. We must *not* make the mistake of meditating on this constant flow of bad news.

We should *not* ignore what is taking place in the world. We can acknowledge the problems, but we must not *dwell* on them. There is no place in the Bible where we are instructed to dwell on bad news. Instead, we are instructed to meditate continually on the good news that fills the Word of God.

The mountains in our lives are *not* mountains to God. We must not be staggered by seemingly impossible circumstances. We should look at these challenges more and more from God's perspective and less and less from the perspective of this lost and dying world.

We should take full advantage of every available minute to saturate ourselves in God's Word. During trying times, our mouths should boldly proclaim the Word of God. The greater the pressure we face, the greater our determination should be to trust God because we know He will see us through to the other side.

We must learn everything we can about the supernatural power of the Word of God, the foundation for faith that it gives us and the reliability of every promise in the Bible. We should focus continually on God's supernatural promises that are absolutely reliable and completely trustworthy regardless of the circumstances the world faces. We must obey our Father's instructions to meditate continually on His supernatural living Word.

When we meditate on a promise from God, we visualize this specific promise being fulfilled. We should constantly think about each promise we are meditating on. We should open our mouths to continually speak each promise.

As we obey our Father's instructions to constantly meditate on His Word, we are meditating on what God has promised to do for His beloved children who trust Him completely. Human beings are the only creatures God has created who have the power to imagine. When we meditate continually on the Word of God, we do *not* misuse the tremendous power of imagination the way that chronic worriers do.

Our Father wants each of us to use the ability to imagine that He has given us to visualize by faith the manifestation of specific promises from His Word. Satan wants us to use our

God-given ability to imagine to visualize that the things we are worrying about will come into manifestation.

Sometimes life seems to be almost unbearable. Sometimes we face frustrating circumstances. *These are the times* when we must boldly speak the Word of God. We will be encouraged if *our ears* continually hear *our mouths* boldly speaking magnificent promises from heaven. The circumstances in our lives that could tempt us to be discouraged no longer will have power over us. Encouragement from God will rise up on the inside of us if we focus only on the supernatural living Word of God.

When we meditate on the Word of God, we focus on a specific passage of Scripture and turn it over and over in our minds. We should look at this passage of Scripture from every conceivable angle. We should personalize this Scripture. We should look at it as a personal message from our Father in heaven to us.

The holy Bible *is* a specific individual message from God to every person on earth. The Bible will come alive to us when we personalize it. Deep down inside of our hearts we will "know that we know that we know" that God Himself is speaking to each of us individually through the supernatural power of His eternal living Word.

The Word of God is our spiritual food. We *eat* this spiritual food when we *study* the Word of God. We *chew* and *digest* a specific morsel of spiritual food whenever we *meditate* on a passage of Scripture.

Chewing the spiritual food of God's Word is similar to chewing the food we put into our mouths. We should chew our food thoroughly and slowly if we want to digest this food properly. In this impatient fast food age we live in, many people want to gulp down their food quickly. Our Father wants us to chew on the spiritual food of His Word slowly and thoroughly as we meditate on the holy Scriptures.

We should not rush when we meditate on Scripture. When I show you exactly how I believe we should meditate on the Word of God, you will be able to see how we can chew each morsel of spiritual food from our Father in heaven again and again. This chewing enables us to assimilate the supernatural spiritual food our Father has provided for us.

Sometimes I meditate on a passage of Scripture for ten or twenty minutes and then stop. On other occasions I have meditated on a passage of Scripture for an entire day or even for several days. We rush ahead of God whenever we hurry. We will miss learning what our Father wants us to learn if we do not meditate slowly and thoroughly on His Word. "…to be overhasty is to sin and miss the mark" (Proverbs 19:2). Rushing ahead of God always causes problems. "…everyone who is impatient and hasty hastens only to want" (Proverbs 21:5).

Our Father wants us to *fully absorb* the immense spiritual power that is contained in His Word. As we continually meditate on a specific promise from God, this promise takes root deep down inside of ourselves. As we continue to meditate thoroughly on this promise, it will grow and develop in our hearts. As this process continues over a period of time, we will have absolute confidence that God *will* do in our lives exactly what He says He will do.

When I first became a Christian, the man who led me to the Lord told me that I would never escape the problems I faced unless I saturated myself in the Word of God. At that time I knew nothing about Joshua 1:8 and Psalm 1:1-3. All that I knew was that this man told me to saturate myself in the Word of God. I was determined to do exactly what he told me to do.

I can vividly remember meditating on Philippians 4:13 day after day after day. I meditated on the King James Version of the Bible at that time. I now use the *Amplified Bible* exclusively because of the additional shades of meaning that are given to the original Hebrew and Greek. We can clearly see the value of this amplification when we look at Philippians 4:13 from the *Amplified Bible.* "I have strength for all things in Christ Who empowers me [I am ready for anything and equal to anything through Him Who infuses inner strength into me; I am self-sufficient in Christ's sufficiency]" (Philippians 4:13).

If I was meditating on this particular passage of Scripture today, I would open my mouth to say something like the following, "Dear Father, this promise from You tells me that I have strength for *all things*. I know that my human strength is insufficient, but I do have strength for all things *because* the strength of Jesus is available to me.

"I believe the amplification of this passage of Scripture is a personal promise to me from You, dear Father. It tells me that I am ready for anything and equal to anything. It says that inner strength is available to me because Jesus lives in my heart. I am *absolutely certain* that I have all the strength I will ever need no matter what circumstance I face because of the mighty power of Jesus Who lives in my heart."

I then would go on and speak out loud more and more personalized facts pertaining to this passage of Scripture. In my early days as a Christian I sometimes meditated at least one hundred times on Philippians 4:13 in one day. I used to write a number on a piece of paper every time I opened my mouth and meditated on Philippians 4:13. I kept writing these numbers until I had numbered from one to one hundred.

I learned during the difficult times I faced then *how much I can be lifted up* by meditating again and again on one encouraging passage of Scripture. I often used to meditate on Philippians 4:13 for hours at a time. I became absolutely convinced that God would bring me through the difficult problems I faced. God did bring me safely through each of these seemingly overwhelming problems. Thank You, dear Father.

In the next five chapters we will examine in detail many additional facts about meditating on the Word of God and the results that will occur if we obey our Father's specific instructions in this area. I urge you to carefully study these chapters on Scripture meditation. I believe that our lives in the difficult years ahead could depend on the effectiveness of our Scripture meditation.

Chapter 22

Additional Facts Pertaining to Scripture Meditation

The Hebrew word "hagah" that is translated as "meditate" in both Joshua 1:8 and Psalm 1:2 means "to murmur, mutter, speak, talk, utter." We should *speak* the Word of God out loud when we meditate. *Our ears* should continually hear *our mouths* boldly speaking, personalizing and expanding on the supernatural promises that are contained in the Word of God.

We must understand that we *release spiritual power with our mouths*. We release this spiritual power when we speak the Word of God continually as we meditate on it. The cumulative effect of speaking these words from heaven again and again steadily increases our faith in God.

We have learned that we can establish hope by *studying* the Word of God. When we meditate on God's Word, our Father wants us to speak continually about what we hope for. We undergird what we are hoping for when we continually speak specific promises from the Word of God. We give substance to what we are hoping for as we continually speak these promises from God.

Our faith will not increase by rote repetition of Scripture verses. Our faith will increase because we are developing a closer relationship with God. God wants each of us to align our entire being with His Word.

We must understand the vital importance of *hearing* the Word of God throughout every day of our lives. Our ears were created to hear the Word of God. Our ears should hear our mouths opening continually to boldly speak the Word of God. Our lives should be a constant prayer to God as we faithfully pray His Word back to Him.

As this process continues over a period of time, we will receive increasing revelation from the Holy Spirit about what we are meditating on. The Holy Spirit honors our continual meditation. He will reveal wonderful spiritual truths that will not be revealed to Christians who disobey God's instructions to meditate continually on His Word.

As we continually meditate on the Word of God, we change "logos" which is the written Word of God into "rhema" which is the spoken Word of God that is quickened and made alive and active. Logos is a spiritual seed. Rhema constantly plants these spiritual seeds to produce a harvest.

Scientists have proven that people can speak as many as one hundred thousand words in twenty-four hours. How many of the words that come out of your mouth are *increasing* your faith in God? How many of the words that you speak are *decreasing* your faith in God? The percentage of faith-filled words that we speak will increase dramatically if we faithfully obey our Father's instructions to meditate on His Word throughout the day and night. We must understand the absolute importance of saying and praying what God says again … and again … and again.

Let me give you another example of how I meditate by showing you how I would meditate on the following passage of Scripture. "…Him Who, by (in consequence of) the [action of His] power that is at work within us, is able to [carry out His purpose and] do superabundantly, far over and above all that we [dare] ask or think [infinitely beyond our highest prayers, desires, thoughts, hopes, or dreams]…" (Ephesians 3:20).

If I was meditating on this passage of Scripture, I would say something like, "The mighty power of God that is working inside of me is fully able to do in me and through me exactly what my Father wants done. God knows no limits. My Father is able to do much more in me and through me than I think He can do.

"Dear Father, I will not limit You in any way by the limitations of my human understanding of Your desire to carry out Your purpose for my life. Instead, I will focus continually on this magnificent promise that assures me that You can and will do in me and through me much, much more than anything I can ask for, hope or dream."

These words are just the beginning of what I would say. I would personalize this passage of Scripture more and more each time I meditated on it. Again and again I would repeat this passage of Scripture, personalizing it, expanding it and steadily increasing my faith in God as this process continued.

I often feel as though I am floating on a sea of Scripture. I continually fill my eyes, my ears, my mind, my heart and my mouth with the Word of God. I have been doing this quite consistently during the past thirty years. Every day of my life revolves around the supernatural power of the living Word of God.

When God created us He provided two external entrances into our minds – our eyes and our ears. God gave us our eyes and our ears for many things, but I believe the primary reason He gave us eyes and ears was to receive His Word throughout each day and night of our lives.

God's Word enters into our *minds* through our *eyes* when we obey God's instructions to study His Word by renewing our minds daily as we study the Bible. We have seen previously that Proverbs 4:21 says we should not allow the Word of God to depart from our sight. We obey these instructions when we meditate on the Word of God throughout the day and night.

God's Word is able to enter into our *hearts* through the openings our Father has provided in our *ears*. As we continually speak the Word of God, this Scripture will drop from our minds down into our hearts.

Unfortunately, many Christians spend their entire lives without having more than a trickle of God's Word coming into their minds and hearts through their eyes and ears. Instead of a trickle, our Father wants us to receive a *torrent* of His Word that will flood our consciousness every day of our lives.

We are receiving *supernatural power from heaven* when our eyes and our ears continually are being filled with the living Word of God. We devoted Chapters Nine and Ten of this book to a detailed study of the supernatural power of the living Word of God. In these last days before Jesus returns we absolutely must develop and maintain a continual flow of this supernatural power from heaven through our eyes and our ears into our minds and our hearts.

There is *only one thing* in this entire world that comes from heaven that we can contact with our senses. The Word of God comes to us from heaven. We can *see* God's Word with our eyes. We can *hear* the Word of God with our ears. We should take full advantage of the privilege we have been given to constantly fill our eyes and our ears with the supernatural power of God. Jesus said, "The eye is the lamp of the body. So if your eye is sound, your entire body will be full of light. But if your eye is unsound, your whole body will be full of darkness..." (Matthew 6:22-23).

We each determine whether we will use our eyes to be filled with the light of God or the darkness of Satan. Many secular newspapers, magazines and books are filled with spiritual darkness. Television and the internet are filled with spiritual darkness. We each determine what will get inside of us by what we consistently allow to come in through our eyes.

Our ears are the other external openings God has provided for us to receive His Word. Our ears are *the key* to our faith in God. Our faith in God increases by *hearing* the Word of God. "...faith comes by hearing [what is told], and what is heard comes by the preaching [of the message that came from the lips] of Christ (the Messiah Himself)" (Romans 10:17).

This passage of Scripture tells us that faith *comes* to us when we *hear* the Word of God. A definite relationship exists between our faith in God and the amount of God's Word we hear. Some Christians only hear the Word of God once or twice a week when they attend church. Our faith in God can increase when we hear an anointed servant of God boldly speaking the Word of God. However, we cannot bring the preacher home with us to speak to us during the week.

My faith in God increases steadily when I listen each day to cassette tapes from anointed preachers and teachers. I have found that my faith in God increases the most when *my ears hear my mouth* boldly speaking the Word of God day after day, week after week, month after month and year after year.

We hear external sounds with our external ears. We hear our own voices with our internal ears. Have you ever heard a tape recording of your voice when you had not heard it before? People who hear their own voice for the first time often are surprised at how much different their voice sounds than they thought it sounded.

The reason for this difference is that we are hearing our own voice for the first time with our external ears. Until we heard our own voice as it was recorded, we always have heard our voice with our inner ear. Our inner ear is very sensitive to the words it hears spoken by our mouths. Our faith in God increases steadily when our inner ears hear our mouths continually speaking words of faith. Fear will increase in our lives if our inner ears hear our mouths continually speaking words of fear.

Sometimes Christians fail to meditate thoroughly on passages of Scripture they know well. We must understand that Romans 10:17 does *not* say that faith comes from "having heard" the Word of God in the past. We are told that faith comes from "hearing" the Word of God.

If we want to keep our faith in God strong, our ears need to hear the Word of God flowing into them day after day, week after week, month after month and year after year, no matter how many times we have meditated on a particular passage of Scripture in the past. Our faith in God cannot remain strong unless a continual flow of the Word of God pours into our ears on a daily basis.

Faith comes from hearing the Word of God over and over and over again. Faith in God is cumulative. Our faith in God should increase because we should obey our Father's instructions to hear His Word by meditating continually on the holy Scriptures.

We should protect these precious gateways to our minds and our hearts. We should be *very selective* about what we allow to come into our minds and our hearts through our eyes and our ears. We can be assured that our eyes and our ears will constantly receive what our Father wants us to pour into them if we faithfully obey His instructions to meditate on His Word.

We will think like God thinks if we meditate continually on His Word. We will believe what God wants us to believe. We will act the way God wants us to act. Christians who spend too much time watching television will think the way the world thinks. They will believe what the world believes. They will act the way the world acts.

We will constantly grow and mature if we obey our Father's instructions to meditate continually on His Word. I believe that meditating on the Word of God is like climbing a mountain. When we first begin to climb, we cannot see very much except things that are close to the ground. As we climb higher and higher, we are able to see many things we could not see before. When we finally get to the top of the mountain, we can see distant things we could not see from the ground.

The depth of the Word of God is so great that its true depth cannot be appreciated without faithfully obeying our Father's instructions to meditate continually on His Word. Continual meditation on the Word of God opens vast new spiritual horizons that we could not perceive in any other way.

The more we meditate on God's promises, the more we will comprehend how powerful these mighty promises are. The reality of the promises of God and the magnitude and power of God's supernatural Word will rise up on the inside of us as we meditate constantly on God's Word over a period of weeks, months and years.

We will live in God's presence. We will be able to clearly see ourselves receiving manifestation of His supernatural promises. As this process continues, we will understand the enormous benefits of dwelling continually in the midst of God's promises.

This book is filled with specific instructions from the holy Scriptures telling us exactly what we should do to increase our faith in Almighty God. Can you imagine what it must have been like for Moses to stand at the edge of the Red Sea and raise a rod toward the water with so much faith in God that the water completely dried up? A wide path was created through the water for more than two million people and all of their animals to pass over on dry land (see Exodus 14:1-31). This same degree of faith is available to each of us today *if* we will obey our Father's instructions to diligently pay the price each and every day of our lives to meditate on His Word.

Just knowing in our minds what a passage of Scripture says is not sufficient. I often have meditated on passages of Scripture that I knew by heart and still learned great new spiritual truths as a result of this continual meditation. We must not make the mistake of thinking that the Word of God is in any way similar to words written by human beings. God's Word is always new. The Holy Spirit will give us fresh revelation if we continue to meditate on a passage of Scripture we have meditated on many times before.

Chapter 23

We Should Love the Word of God

Some people who are reading this book may look somewhat skeptically at our comments pertaining to Scripture meditation. These people have this skeptical attitude toward Scripture meditation because they have done little or no Scripture meditation. They also will have this attitude because they probably do not know other Christians who have meditated on the Word of God to the degree that we recommend.

Most readers of this book *do* know Christians (or know of Christians) who have consistently meditated on the Word of God. Please stop for a moment and think about Christian leaders who have had a great influence on you. Perhaps the pastor in your church has influenced you greatly. Perhaps these leaders are national and international evangelists, preachers and pastors who consistently set aside time to draw close to God through His Word.

We all should have role models who are Christian leaders. Perhaps we have seen them on Christian television, read their books or listened to their teaching cassette tapes, DVDs or CDs. Hopefully the pastor of your church is a tremendous role model to you. Perhaps this pastor is so anointed by God that you go home from church each week with increased faith in God.

I can tell you one thing that *every one* of these anointed Christian leaders does for certain – he or she meditates on the Word of God continually. All true Christian leaders are filled with the Word of God. They always are able to reach deep down inside of themselves for several passages of Scripture to illustrate their point. The Word of God pours out of their mouths.

We can see Jesus in these servants of God. Only Christians who pay the price of time with God and meditating continually on His Word radiate Jesus. His power flows through them to others.

I am on the mailing list of approximately twenty-five major ministries because I continually order cassette teaching tapes and books from them. I listen to these cassette tapes almost every time I drive my car and at many other times as well. I cannot fill my ears too much with the supernatural power of the living Word of God.

I have listened to hundreds of cassette tapes and read hundreds of books that come from nationally and internationally known ministry leaders. I have never known *any* of these Christian leaders who have not filled their minds, their hearts and their mouths to overflowing with the supernatural living Word of God.

These men and women are consumed by God. Every aspect of their lives revolves around God. Their faith in God is strong, vibrant and unwavering. They are wonderful role models for us. Carefully observe the leaders in your church, leaders on Christian radio or television and any other Christian leaders you know. I can guarantee you that these men and women *have paid the price* of immersing themselves in the Word of God over a period of many years.

All of these Christian leaders have the same Bible you have. Each of these anointed men and women began with the *same* amount of faith you received from God. God gave each of us enough faith to ask Jesus to be our Savior. What we do with this original measure of faith that God has given to us is up to each of us individually.

When we hear these Christian leaders speaking the Word of God, we should learn from them. We should do what they do. "Remember your leaders and superiors in authority [for it was they] who brought to you the Word of God. Observe attentively and consider their manner of living (the outcome of their well-spent lives) and imitate their faith (their conviction that God exists and is the Creator and Ruler of all things, the Provider and Bestower of eternal salvation through Christ, and their leaning of the entire human personality on God in absolute trust and confidence in His power, wisdom, and goodness)" (Hebrews 13:7).

Sometimes we observe leaders with strong faith and say, "I wish I had that much faith in God." If we want to increase our faith in God, we should observe these Christian leaders carefully. We should "imitate their faith" by following their example of continually meditating on the Word of God.

During the months and years ahead, all Christians *must* do what these Christian leaders have done and continue to do. All of God's children should immerse themselves in the Word of God. We will pay a severe price during the difficult days that lie ahead of us if we disobey our Father's instructions to meditate continually on His Word.

Meditation on the Word of God will not change our lives overnight. Scripture meditation is a *lifestyle,* not a quick fix. I can guarantee that you *will* experience significant changes in your life if you will faithfully obey your Father's instructions to meditate continually on His Word.

We must pay the price of constantly studying and meditating on the Word of God so that we will be able to enter into and remain in God's rest. We must not allow doubt and unbelief to pull us down. "…he who has once entered [God's] rest also has ceased from [the weariness and pain] of human labors, just as God rested from those labors peculiarly His own. Let us therefore be zealous and exert ourselves and strive diligently to enter that rest [of God, to know and experience it for ourselves], that no one may fall or perish by the same kind of unbelief and disobedience [into which those in the wilderness fell]" (Hebrews 4:10-11).

When we face severe adversity, we often cannot solve these difficult problems through "the weariness and pain of human labor." We will face challenges that are too much for us to handle. We need to rest in God. We can enter into God's rest only if we are "zealous and exert ourselves and strive diligently to enter the rest of God."

We must pay a definite price to experience God's rest. I believe this price is meditating continually on His supernatural Word. We must not allow doubt and unbelief to affect us the way it affected the Israelites in the wilderness many years ago.

God gave each of us freedom of choice when He created us. We all would be mere robots if God did not give us freedom of choice. We each make many choices throughout every day of our lives. These choices often determine the blessings we will receive from God or the problems we will experience.

Unfortunately, the cumulative result of the choices that many of us have made have brought severe problems into our lives.

Because of the choices they have made, many of God's children are living *far below* the quality of life our loving Father has provided for us. He wants us to live joyous lives in absolute obedience to His specific instructions in His comprehensive and complete Book of Instructions. Our Father wants us to learn His promises and to develop our faith in Him to the point where our lives will be a living testimony to His faithfulness.

Many Christians are not persistent in developing their faith in God during good times. They do not renew their minds in the Word of God each day because things are going well. That is a mistake. We should develop our faith in God before we have problems. We need to keep on continually developing our faith in God right up until the time we go to be with God in heaven.

Will we do our part to continually increase our faith in God? Will we be so preoccupied with the personal goals that are important to us and the pursuit of pleasure that we will not set aside the necessary time to continually draw closer to our loving Father each day?

God knows the future. He knows exactly what will happen in the end times. We believe that we live in the last days before Jesus returns. We pray that many readers of this book *will* make the choice to obey God's specific instructions to significantly increase their faith in Him now.

Unbelievers who do not know Jesus as their Savior and Christians who have not meditated continually on the Word of God will not be able to cope with the difficult problems they will face during the end times. Our Father will not increase our faith for us. He has given us everything we need to increase our faith in Him. This book is filled with hundreds of specific scriptural instructions telling us exactly how to increase our faith in God.

You may have to almost force yourself to study the Bible each day when you first begin to renew your mind in God's Word. If you have not been renewing your mind in the Word of God on a daily basis, you can be certain that Satan's demons will do everything they can to attempt to stop you soon after you begin to study and meditate on the Word of God.

If we truly love God, we will not be able to get enough of His Word. We will have a constant hunger for this marvelous spiritual food our loving Father has provided for us. Our daily Bible study and meditation is a *tremendous privilege*.

We should persevere when we first begin this Bible study and meditation until we come to the point where we eagerly look forward to this daily time with God. We should take full advantage of the opportunity we have been given to receive magnificent revelation from God in heaven as we faithfully study and meditate on His supernatural Word.

As you begin to comprehend the power and might of God's living Word, you will not be able to get enough of it. You will delight in meditating on the Word of God. Continual meditation on the Word of God is not the chore some people think it is. If you persevere, you will find that meditating on the Word of God will be one of the *greatest blessings* in your life.

The Bible is God talking to us. We should approach the Word of God each day with a humble and teachable attitude. We should approach the Word of God with absolute awe and respect. We should have a deep and sincere desire to learn from the holy Scriptures.

The very Bible that unbelievers and some Christians look at as boring is just the opposite. The time that I spend in the Bible each day is the most exciting time in my life. The Bible is filled with magnificent supernatural truths from heaven. *How* can we possibly become bored if we are hearing from heaven throughout every day and night of our lives?

My time in the Word of God is the highlight of my day. This time is the foundation and the anchor for every other aspect of my life. I love the Word of God. I revere the Word of God because I revere God and God and His Word are the same. I place the Word of God on the highest possible pedestal. I am in absolute awe, knowing that the Word of God is the *only* thing that comes from heaven that I can see with my eyes and hear with my ears.

The depth of the Word of God is beyond the limits of human comprehension. The more we get into the Word of God and the more the Word of God gets into us, the more we will hunger and thirst for additional revelation from heaven.

Our Father wants us to love His Word. If you do not have a deep love for the Word of God as you begin to renew your mind each day and as you begin to meditate on the holy Scriptures, I can promise you that your love for God's Word will increase with every passing month.

You soon will find that studying and meditating on the Word of God is not an obligation or a duty. You will find that your daily time in God's Word is exciting and fulfilling. You will look forward to this time with great anticipation.

The psalmist gave us an example of the tremendous love we should have for the Word of God when he said, "Oh, how love I Your law! It is my meditation all the day. You, through Your commandments, make me wiser than my enemies, for

[Your words] are ever before me. I have better understanding and deeper insight than all my teachers, because Your testimonies are my meditation" (Psalm 119:97-100).

The psalmist spoke of the tremendous wisdom and understanding he received because the Word of God never departed from his sight (see Proverbs 4:20-23). This same wisdom and understanding is available to *you* if you will continually study and meditate on the Word of God. Another passage of Scripture indicates that the psalmist also meditated on God during the night. He said, "…I remember You upon my bed and meditate on You in the night watches" (Psalm 63:6).

Our Father wants every area of our lives to be in harmony with His supernatural Word. He wants us to have a deep and sincere desire to please Him with our Bible study and meditation and the words we speak. He wants us to be like the psalmist who said, "Let the words of my mouth and the meditation of my heart be acceptable in Your sight, O Lord, my [firm, impenetrable] Rock and my Redeemer" (Psalm 19:14).

Chapter 24

Commit Yourself to Scripture Meditation

Many Christians get more of the Word of God when they attend church each Sunday than they receive the other six days of the week. They have disregarded God's instructions to renew their minds in His Word each day. They do not obey their Father's instructions to meditate on His Word throughout the day and night. These Christians fail to comprehend the tremendous blessing they will receive if they faithfully obey God's instructions regarding Bible study and meditation.

I do not hold myself up as any shining example. I was almost paralyzed by fear when I first became a Christian. I soon found that the Word of God was the lifeline that enabled me to keep functioning.

I kept careful records of the time I spent studying and meditating on the Word of God during my early months as a Christian. In my first month as a Christian I spent 89 hours in the Word of God. I spent 72 hours the next month, 80 hours the month after that and 89 hours the month after that. I spent 93 hours in the Word of God the next month. As I look back on the records I kept thirty years ago, I can see that I spent seven hours one Saturday increasing my faith in God. I must have faced extremely difficult problems on that particular day.

I no longer keep these records. They are not necessary. Studying and meditating on the Word of God is the foundation of every day and night of my life. I have been faithfully studying and meditating on God's Word for so many years that I have formed a deeply ingrained habit.

We should have so much respect for the Word of God that we will be like the psalmist who said, "I will meditate on Your precepts and have respect to Your ways [the paths of life marked out by Your law]. I will delight myself in Your statutes; I will not forget Your word" (Psalm 119:15-16).

The psalmist was delighted to meditate on the Word of God. He did not want to forget God's precious instructions and promises. The psalmist was so enthusiastic about his daily Scripture meditation that he lifted up his hands to God's commandments that he loved. He said, "My hands also will I lift up [in fervent supplication] to Your commandments, which I love, and I will meditate on Your statutes" (Psalm 119:48).

The psalmist loved the Word of God. The amplification of this passage of Scripture says that he lifted up his hands "in fervent supplication." Supplication means a request or a prayer to God. When we do something fervently, we do it intensely and passionately.

I have made a tremendous commitment to the Word of God during the past thirty years. We have just seen the commitment of the psalmist to the Word of God. In the last chapter I referred to the commitment that many Christian leaders have made to intense daily Bible study and meditation. Have *you* made this commitment in your life?

The Holy Spirit is always ready to reveal magnificent spiritual truths to us that will bring us safely through the difficult days before Jesus appears to take the Church out of the world.

There is nothing we can do that will be more beneficial to prepare for adversity than to continually fill our minds and our hearts with the supernatural power of the living Word of God.

Lamplight Ministries is dedicated to helping as many Christians as possible to make a definite commitment to effectively study and meditate on the Word of God on a daily basis. We chose the word "Lamplight" as the name for our ministry because of the following description of the Word of God. "Your word is a lamp to my feet and a light to my path" (Psalm 119:105).

Our loving Father has given us His Word as a "lamp" to shine light on the paths He wants us to follow. Our Father has given us His Word as a "light" to guide us safely through the darkness that Satan and his demons try to engulf us in. "…show yourselves to be blameless and guileless, innocent and uncontaminated, children of God without blemish (faultless, unrebukable) in the midst of a crooked and wicked generation [spiritually perverted and perverse], among whom you are seen as bright lights (stars or beacons shining out clearly) in the [dark] world, holding out [to it] and offering [to all men] the Word of Life…" (Philippians 2:15-16).

Our Father wants us to fill our eyes and our ears continually with His Word so that we will live the way He wants us to live "in the midst of a crooked and wicked generation." I believe this passage of Scripture specifically refers to the people who live in the world today (see II Timothy 3:2-4). Our Father wants His Word to light up our lives so that we will be "as bright lights, stars or beacons shining out clearly in this dark world." Our lives should be constant examples of obedience to the instructions we have been given in the Word of God.

We spent thousands of hours during five intense years of hard work to develop a comprehensive set of Scripture Meditation Cards and accompanying cassette tapes. These Scripture cards and tapes will help Christians to obey God's instructions to meditate on His Word throughout the day and night. We believe the following list of ten sets of Scripture Meditation Cards can save you many hours of hard work trying to find and correlate the Scripture references that already have been included in each of the topics covered in these Scripture cards:

1. *Continually Increasing Faith in God*
2. *Freedom from Worry and Fear*
3. *Our Father's Wonderful Love*
4. *Receive God's Blessing in Adversity*
5. *Financial Instructions from God*
6. *Enjoy God's Wonderful Peace*
7. *A Closer Relationship with the Lord*
8. *God is Always with You*
9. *Receive Healing from the Lord*
10. *Find God's Will for Your Life*

Each set of Scripture Meditation Cards consists of fifty-two 2 1/2 inch by 3 1/2 inch cards. Each set of fifty-two cards is enclosed in a plastic folder that will easily fit into a pocket or purse. These Scripture cards will provide you with a proven and effective method to faithfully obey our Father's instructions to meditate on His Word throughout the day and night.

You cannot carry your Bible with you throughout every day and every night. You *can* put these Scripture cards in a pocket, in a purse, on the dashboard of your car, on your desk or a workbench where you work, on a shelf in your home, on a mirror in your bathroom, on the door of your refrigerator, on the walls of your home and in many other places.

Each set of fifty-two Scripture Meditation Cards contains between seventy and eighty Scripture references because several Scripture cards have more than one Scripture reference.

Each card has specific instructions and comments pertaining to the Scripture(s) on that card.

We could not even begin to include enough information on each Scripture card to assist you in meditating effectively on each passage of Scripture. I have recorded an eighty-five minute cassette tape to go with each of the ten sets of Scripture cards. We have seen that the Bible says faith comes from *hearing* the Word of God (see Romans 10:17). Please consider purchasing the Scripture cards *and* the detailed cassette tape that goes with each set of Scripture cards. Many people have told us that they listen to these tapes over and over again.

Our ten sets of Scripture Meditation Cards contain a total of between 700 and 800 passages of Scripture. We invite you to partake of this feast of God's Word that we have prepared for you. These Scripture cards and cassette tapes will enable you to fill *your* mind and *your* heart continually throughout the day and night with the supernatural power of the living Word of God. These Scripture cards will provide you with enough information from the holy Scriptures to last you for a long time.

We believe that our Father wants us to meditate on His Word during our quiet time alone with Him as we begin each day. We can meditate on His Word while we are preparing our-selves for the upcoming day. We can meditate on His Word while we are driving to and from work. There are many opportunities to keep God's Word in front of us each day.

Some people do not believe they can meditate on the Word of God while they are working. You can take one Scripture Meditation Card and put it on your desk or wherever else is convenient where you work. You will find many occasions throughout the day when you can stop for a moment to think about a passage of Scripture and meditate on it. You can meditate on the Word of God during your lunch hour.

Our Father also has instructed us to meditate on His Word during the evening hours. These Scripture cards and cassette tapes will help you to accomplish this goal. We should understand the importance of meditating on the Word of God just before we go to sleep. Our minds and our hearts should be filled with precious principles from God's Word so that we can subconsciously turn the Word of God over and over in our minds and our hearts while we sleep.

Our Father wants us to establish a habit pattern of effectively meditating on His Word. Christians who faithfully obey God's instructions pertaining to Scripture meditation will find that their faith in God will grow steadily. Christians who fail to obey God's instructions regarding Scripture meditation will find that their faith will be woefully insufficient when they suddenly face a crisis situation.

We must not give in to the problems we will face during the last days before Jesus returns. These Scripture cards and cassette tapes will allow you to continually fill your eyes and your ears with the supernatural power of God's living Word instead of dwelling on the widespread problems the world will face during the end times.

We should not ignore the problems we face. We need to acknowledge the problem we face whenever we face a crisis situation, but we must not *dwell* on any problem. We should *turn completely away* from focusing on these problems as we choose instead to meditate continually on the Word of God as we boldly speak our Father's promises.

Negative thoughts will *not* be able to establish a foothold in our minds and our hearts if we faithfully obey God's instructions to meditate continually on His Word. Our minds and our hearts will be so full of God's Word that the circumstances in our lives and the thoughts that Satan's demons try to put into our minds will be ignored.

We are encouraged by the many favorable comments we have received on our Scripture Meditation Cards. We have included just a few of these comments so you can see for yourself the help *you* can receive from these Scripture cards:

- "Out of everything I ever seen or read, your Scripture cards are the most simple but inspirational tools of God. As I'm visiting friends here in Florida, each morning we walk on the beach and take a set of Scripture cards with us and read them. We read them throughout the day and before we go to bed at night. I rang my sister in Australia and shared with her how inspirational the cards are. I am so excited about finding something so simply and easily shared with everyone I meet." (Australia)

- "I received the Lord just two months before I came to Bible school. My life is 180 degrees from what it was. I was bound by fear. I began to go over the *Freedom from Worry and Fear* Scripture Meditation Cards in the daytime and I listened to the tape at night. The verses jumped off the cards and into me! They became part of me. It was awesome. It was really a blessing!" (Florida)

- "My back was hurting so badly that I couldn't get comfortable. I was miserable whether I sat or stood or lay down. I didn't know what to do. Suddenly I thought of the Scripture cards on healing that my husband had purchased. I decided to meditate on the Scripture in these cards. I was only on the second card when, all of a sudden, I felt heat go from my neck down through my body. The Lord had healed me. I never knew it could happen so fast. The pain has not come back." (Idaho)

- "I was recently involved in an automobile accident that was so severe that my car spun 360 degrees. While this was happening, I was amazed at how calm I was because I had been meditating on one of your Scripture cards with the Scripture reference, 'Fear not, I am with you always.' I wasn't afraid. I knew the Lord was with me." (Haiti)

- "I picked up ten sets of Scripture cards. I gave one to each of our six children, two to friends and kept two for my husband and myself. I have nothing but praise for them. Our world is in such a turmoil. You can feel the Holy Spirit rise up. I felt that this morning as I was reading these cards. I love these cards! You can feel the anointing!" (Arizona)

- "My husband is incarcerated in prison. I can't tell you how much your Scripture cards and cassette tapes have helped me. I meditate on them continually. I gave the cards and tapes on healing to a friend of mine. She was very pleased. She said it was like I had given her a million dollar gift." (Florida)

- "I just read your Scripture cards on healing and listened to the tape. I feel like I have eaten a T-bone steak. This is wonderful spiritual food. Many people will be helped by your cards and your tapes." (Oklahoma)

- "Your Scripture reference cards titled *A Closer Relationship with the Lord, Our Father's Wonderful Love* and *Receive Healing from the Lord* are fantastic. Please send me ten copies of each." (Oregon)

- "Thank you very much for the many dynamic blessings that come from your meditation cards. They are very unique, very rich, full of life and very real." (Zambia, South Africa)

We believe that our Scripture Meditation Cards and our cassette tapes will be a tremendous blessing to you. We believe these Scripture cards and tapes will provide you with hundreds of hours of profitable preparation for the difficult times that lie ahead of all of us.

Chapter 25

Activate God's Promises through Scripture Meditation

I would like to ask you some questions that only you and God can answer. I am not asking these questions to accuse you in any way. I ask these questions so that you can give an honest answer before God about how well *you* have been preparing for the difficult times that lie ahead of all of us. Please be completely honest as you answer these questions.

Do you believe you have spent an ample amount of time renewing your mind each day in the Word of God as God instructs you to do in II Corinthians 4:16 and Ephesians 4:22-23? Have you faithfully meditated on the Word of God throughout each day and night as God instructs you to do in Joshua 1:8 and Psalm 1:1-3?

We each are given the same twenty-four hours a day. We each decide how we will spend these precious hours. How does your investment of time studying and meditating on the Word of God compare with the amount of time you spend watching television, engaging in your favorite hobby or pursuing pleasure in any other way?

Continual study and meditation on the Word of God are characteristic of Christians who *really do* put God in *first* place in their lives. Everything else *will* work out in God's way and in God's perfect timing if we really do put God in first place in our lives and keep Him there. Jesus said, "…seek (aim at and strive after) first of all His kingdom and His righteousness (His way of doing and being right), and then all these things taken together will be given you besides" (Matthew 6:33).

When Jesus referred to "all these things," He was referring to the necessities of life such as food, clothing and shelter. Jesus said that all of these necessities *will* be provided for us *if* we truly do seek God and keep Him first in our lives. Once again, we want to emphasize that this magnificent promise does *not* have any asterisk saying that it will be null and void during the end times.

We keep God first when we faithfully set aside time each day to be quiet before Him and to listen to Him. We keep God first when we pray continually. We keep God first when we praise Him continually. We keep God first when we continually learn and obey the instructions in His Word. We keep God first when we continually learn more of His promises and believe wholeheartedly that He will do exactly what He says He will do.

Your answers to the questions at the beginning of this chapter will clearly indicate whether you are prepared for the difficult times that are coming. You may decide to significantly increase the amount of time you spend studying and meditating on the Word of God. We have found that people from Third World countries who read our books are *much* more open to our emphasis on consistent Bible study and meditation than most Christians in the United States are. Most of these people in Third World countries face poverty and extremely difficult conditions. They are very interested in anything from God that will help them to improve their situation.

In the United States only a small percentage of Christians faithfully renew their minds in the Word of God and meditate continually on the holy Scriptures. Even Christians who are well-intentioned have to fight the pull of the world. They are drawn away by many activities and attractions in the world and by the tendency to depend on external sources of security. They have very few, if any, Christian friends who faithfully renew their minds each day and meditate continually on the holy Scriptures.

We believe that conditions in the United States and other relatively prosperous countries will change dramatically in the near future. We believe that the attitude of many Christians in these countries then will become more like the attitude of Christians in Third World countries. They will be much more open to receiving the instructions and promises in the Word of God.

In the natural realm, time limits how fast we grow. No one can become a mature adult at the age of five. We must go through childhood and adolescence. We must learn during our years as young adults. We must go through the unique experiences of middle age. We must go through the twilight years of our lives before we die and our lives on earth come to a close. We can and should grow and mature during each of these stages of life.

The same situation does *not* always apply in the spiritual realm. *We each can decide how rapidly our faith in God will increase.* In the natural realm, our growth is limited by our chronological age. In the spiritual realm, our faith in God can grow as rapidly as we truly desire.

Life is very different from God's perspective. Our Father has given each of us the precious opportunity to enter into the spiritual realm and *remain* there. As we faithfully study and meditate on God's Word, we will learn that many things that seem impossible in the natural realm are not difficult or impossible for God. We must develop our faith in God so that we will trust Him to do in us, through us and for us what we cannot possibly do by ourselves.

A widespread spirit of fear will increase steadily during the last days before Jesus returns. We will have to take specific actions to turn *away* from this fear to trust God completely during these difficult times. We must do exactly what our Father has instructed us to do if we want to have deep, strong, unwavering and unshakable faith in Him.

The Word of God is our spiritual food. In the natural realm, many of us attempt to limit the food we eat. Our Father wants us to stuff ourselves with the spiritual food of His Word. No one can study and meditate on the Word of God too much.

Two people can ask Jesus to be their Savior on the same day. Two years later one of these Christians can have much stronger faith in God than the other person. Did God give more faith to one of them than He gave to the other? God does not do this. Our loving Father always is fair and impartial (see Acts 10:34).

The difference is in the amount of time and effort that one Christian put into increasing his or her faith in God. The Christian with only a little faith in God probably is like many Christians in the United States today. This person goes to church once or twice a week, spends a few minutes each day in prayer and pretty much lives the remainder of his or her life the way that a moral person lives.

Our lives will be absolutely transformed if we will spend as much time fervently meditating on the Word of God as we do watching television and pursuing pleasure in other ways. Many Christians live and die knowing little or nothing about the supernatural power of the Word of God that is available to them. They know little or nothing about the magnificent revelation they would receive from the Holy Spirit if they would continually study and meditate on the Word of God.

Many of us do exactly what our doctor, attorney or accountant tell us to do. *Why* do so many Christians ignore the specific instructions our Father has given to us about studying and meditating on His Word? *Why* would we honor the instructions of any person who was created by God more than we honor the specific instructions we have been given by God Himself?

Our faith in God will increase significantly if we faithfully obey His instructions for increasing our faith in Him. We cannot afford to be careless in this area. After Jesus died on the cross at Calvary, many of His followers were not aware that He had risen from the dead just as He said He would. Jesus referred to these people as "…foolish ones [sluggish in mind, dull of perception] and slow of heart to believe…" (Luke 24:25).

This description could apply to many Christians today. Some of God's children are "foolish" people who miss out completely on what our loving Father wants us to learn. The amplification of this passage of Scripture says that we are foolish if we are "sluggish in mind and dull of perception." Some of God's children are "slow of heart to believe."

The magnificent spiritual Truth in the Word of God is only as effective in our lives as our receptivity to that Truth. Many Christians have not even begun to break through in the area of Bible study and meditation. They do not have a hunger and thirst for the Word of God. They mistakenly think that Bible study and meditation is a dull chore.

Nothing could stop us from continually studying and meditating on the holy Scriptures if we had any comprehension of how important it is to increase our faith in God. Christians who now are unwilling to study and meditate on the Word of God will hunger and thirst to fill their eyes and their ears with the living Word of God when they receive this revelation.

The supernatural power of the Word of God will build up on the inside of us as we faithfully study and meditate on God's Word. Our faith in God will steadily increase. We will be absolutely certain that the power of God on the inside of us is much greater and much more powerful than any problem we will face.

The Word of God is a spiritual seed. Jesus said, "…The seed is the Word of God" (Luke 8:11). Jesus went on to explain that we should plant this seed in the spiritual soil of our hearts. He said, "…as for that [seed] in the good soil, these are [the people] who, hearing the Word, hold it fast in a just (noble, virtuous) and worthy heart, and steadily bring forth fruit with patience" (Luke 8:15).

Jesus referred to our hearts as "good soil." There is no question that we should continually plant the seed of God's Word into the good soil of our hearts. We will "steadily bring forth fruit with patience" if we faithfully obey these instructions.

Different seeds have different germination periods. Some seeds take longer to produce a harvest than others. We will experience a wonderful harvest in God's perfect timing if we faithfully obey our Father's instructions to continually plant the seeds of His Word in our hearts.

No farmer would think of attempting to reap a harvest without having planted any seeds. Many Christians make this mistake every day in the spiritual realm. They think that God will give them a particular result even though they have not planted any seeds from His Word in their hearts.

Jesus compared the kingdom of heaven to a man planting a mustard seed. He said, "…The kingdom of heaven is like a grain of mustard seed, which a man took and sowed in his field. Of all the seeds it is the smallest, but when it has grown it is the largest of the garden herbs and becomes a tree, so that the birds of the air come and find shelter in its branches" (Matthew 13:31-32).

The mustard seed is a tiny seed, but it becomes a large tree when it is full grown. A mustard seed tree is so large that many birds "can find shelter in its branches." Our faith in God will become strong enough to move mountains if we continually plant seeds of faith from God's Word in our hearts. Jesus said, "…For truly I say to you, if you have faith [that is living] like a grain of mustard seed, you can say to this mountain, Move from here to yonder place, and it will move; and nothing will be impossible to you" (Matthew 17:20).

Is your faith in God growing continually the way that a mustard seed turns into a tree? If so, your faith in God will grow to the extent where you will be able to speak to the "mountains" in your life. You will be able to tell them to move and *they will move* (see Mark 11:22-24). *Nothing is impossible* to Christians who have deep, strong, unwavering and unshakable faith in Almighty God.

We each decide how much effort we will expend to increase our faith in God. *There are no short cuts*. We live in an instant gratification generation where fast food restaurants have drive-through windows so that customers will not even have to leave their automobiles. Microwave ovens, instant cameras, one hour dry cleaning, cell phones and jet airplanes are other examples of the desire our generation has for quick results.

This type of instant thinking and increasing our faith in God are very different. Our Father did not instruct us to renew our minds in His Word for a few days or a few months. Our Father wants us to renew our minds in His Word every day of our lives. Our Father wants us to meditate faithfully on the holy Scriptures throughout every day and every night. We must continually plant spiritual seeds from God's Word in our hearts if we want to receive the harvest of manifestation of God's promises.

Very difficult times lie ahead of us. We either will pay the price of continually studying and meditating on the Word of God before these difficult times come upon us or we will pay a significant price in the future for our lack of faith in God. We cannot escape paying a price at one time or another.

This principle applies to several areas of our lives. Many people think they are getting away with something by not paying the price in a particular area because they do not see any immediate consequences. We must develop enough spiritual maturity to see our lives from God's long term perspective instead of living our lives the way we think we should live (see Proverbs 14:12).

In the next chapter we will carefully study a detailed plan for immersing ourselves in the Word of God. You will see the importance of *saturating yourself* in the Word of God day after day, week after week, month after month and year after year.

Chapter 26

Continual Immersion in the Living Word of God

The scriptural principles we will discuss in this chapter will sound extreme to some readers. They will change their minds when the bottom falls out and everything seems to be going wrong. I can tell you from more than thirty years of personal experience, from the experience of many people I have taught in more than nine hundred Bible study classes and from written comments we have received from our readers that constant immersion in the Word of God is extremely beneficial.

The only way we can live in victory during the severe adversity that will sweep across the world is to be *filled with* God's Word. The mighty Truth of the Word of God will sustain us. Jesus said, "…If you abide in My word [hold fast to My teachings and live in accordance with them], you are truly My disciples. And you will know the Truth, and the Truth will set you free" (John 8:31-32).

The Greek word "meno" that is translated "abide" in this passage of Scripture means "to stay in a given place, to remain, stand, tarry." Jesus wants us to get into the Word of God and *stay there*. The amplification of this passage of Scripture says that we abide in the Word of God when we "hold fast to its teachings and live in accordance with them." We should program ourselves continually with the Word of God so that our thoughts, words and actions will be in accordance with God's teachings. Christians who obey these instructions are "disciples" of Jesus.

The Word of God is the Truth (see John 17:17). This magnificent Truth *will* "set us free" *if* we continually fill our hearts with the supernatural power of the living Word of God. We will be able to turn away from all of the bad news of the world to *abide* in the Word of God as we immerse ourselves in it constantly.

As the world plunges headlong toward destruction, Christians must go in the opposite direction. We have learned that the Word of God is alive and filled with supernatural power. Our Father wants us to saturate ourselves in His Word so that nothing that occurs in the world will move us from trusting Him.

Christians who do not immerse themselves in the holy Scriptures cannot understand the immensity of the supernatural power of the living Word of God. They cannot comprehend staking their lives on God and the total and absolute reliability of His Instruction Manual, the Bible. Many complacent and apathetic Christians have no sense of urgency about continually filling their hearts with the Word of God.

We each will require megadoses of the Word of God in the difficult times that are coming. This extensive Bible study and meditation is *vastly different* from the lifestyle of the average American who reads only one or two books a year and spends an average of *more than one hundred hours a month* watching worldly television. Our Father wants us to turn away from the ways of the world to constantly draw closer to Him. One of the best ways to draw closer to God is to spend a lot of time studying and meditating on His supernatural living Word.

Do you *really believe* that every word in the Bible is inspired by God as II Timothy 3:16 says it is? If you really believe this great spiritual truth, *why* wouldn't you utilize every possible hour to fill your heart with the Word of God? We cannot make a better investment of our time.

Let's imagine that someone has been a Christian for ten years. Let's assume that this person was taught the importance of meditating daily on the Word of God from the day he or she turned to Jesus for eternal salvation. Let's assume that this person meditated on *only two* passages of Scripture each week. I think you will agree that two passages of Scripture in a week is a minimal amount of Scripture meditation.

This Christian would have *more than one thousand* promises and/or instructions from Almighty God living in his or her heart at the end of ten years from meditating on only two passages of Scripture each week. The power of God's Word that can come alive in our hearts through constant Scripture meditation is overwhelming.

We will hunger and thirst for more of God's Word as we consistently partake of the Word of God and experience what takes place deep inside of ourselves. We will gladly trade pursuing temporary pleasures for continually meditating on God's Word.

We each should have such a hunger and thirst to get the Word of God into us that we would not consider missing even one day of meditating on the holy Scriptures. We should be like a gigantic sponge soaking up the supernatural power of the living Word of God.

I can tell you from many years of experience that I have not always felt like studying and meditating on the Word of God. This habit is so deeply ingrained in me that I do it anyway.. On many occasions I have refreshed myself by taking a nap, a brief walk or washing my face with cold water so that I could continue Scripture meditation.

We need to get into God's Word and *stay there* day after day, week after week, month after month and year after year. This repetition is very important to our spiritual growth. Scripture meditation will become an integral part of our daily lives when we solidly establish the habit of continual meditation on the Word of God.

We must become addicted to the Word of God if we want to have deep, strong, unwavering and unshakable faith in God. Most addictions are negative. I do not believe we can have a more positive addiction than to be addicted to the Word of God. We have learned that the Bible instructs us to guard our hearts vigilantly (see Proverbs 4:23). One of the best ways to guard our hearts is to constantly fill our hearts with the supernatural power of the living Word of God.

Most of us would not think of going one day without a bath or shower. Our Father wants us to take a "spiritual bath" in His Word each day. "How shall a young man cleanse his way? By taking heed and keeping watch [on himself] according to Your word [conforming his life to it]" (Psalm 119:9).

This passage of Scripture tells us exactly how to "cleanse our way." We cleanse ourselves from the ways of the world by "keeping watch" on ourselves based on the instructions in the Word of God. We cleanse ourselves by conforming every aspect of our lives to God's instructions.

We have learned previously that God's Word is spiritual food. We now can see that the multifaceted Word of God also is a spiritual detergent. We will cleanse ourselves from the spiritual stagnancy of this lost and dying world if we continually meditate on God's Word as our Father has instructed us to do.

We cannot afford to allow the dirt of the world to contaminate us. Our Father wants us to cleanse ourselves continually in His Word so that we will live consecrated lives. "...since these [great] promises are ours, beloved, let us cleanse ourselves from everything that contaminates and defiles body and spirit, and bring [our] consecration to completeness in the [reverential] fear of God" (II Corinthians 7:1).

This passage of Scripture tells us to "cleanse ourselves" from contamination by continually appropriating the "great promises" of God that have been given to us. The spiritual power of the Word of God living in our hearts can "bring our consecration to completeness" as we fear God with reverent awe.

We *must* continually cleanse ourselves from the impurities of the world so that we can carry out each assignment God has for us. "...whoever cleanses himself [from what is ignoble and unclean, who separates himself from contact with contaminating and corrupting influences] will [them himself] be a vessel set apart and useful for honorable and noble purposes, consecrated and profitable to the Master, fit and ready for any good work" (II Timothy 2:21).

Do you "separate yourself" as much as possible from the evil ways of the world? Have you set yourself apart so that Jesus can use you in any way He wants during these last days? Are you cleansing your spirit as faithfully as you cleanse your body? Are you soaking in the Word of God every day and night of your life? We refresh ourselves spiritually when we meditate continually on the Word of God. We keep God's Word fresh in our hearts.

Christians who continually saturate themselves in the Word of God will become very enthusiastic. The word "enthusiasm" comes from the Greek words "en" and "theos." The prefix "en" means "in." The word "theos" means "God." Enthusiasm literally means "in God."

We always are moving either forward or backward in the spiritual realm. *We never stand still.* We may seem to stand still at times, but this is an illusion. The backward movement is so subtle and imperceptible that we are not aware of it. We must keep the Word of God at the forefront of our consciousness at all times. "…we ought to pay much closer attention than ever to the truths that we have heard, lest in any way we drift past [them] and slip away" (Hebrews 2:1).

We cannot afford to allow the Word of God to "slip away" from us. We need to move forward constantly in the spiritual realm. We must obey our Father's instructions to meditate on His Word continually so that our faith in God will grow steadily. As we constantly immerse ourselves in the Word of God, we will find that we are "…springing from faith and leading to faith [disclosed through the way of faith that arouses to more faith]" (Romans 1:17).

The amplification in this passage of Scripture tells us that faith in God leads to more faith which in turn leads to more faith. We must have spiritual momentum to continually increase our faith in God. God's promises will become very uplifting and encouraging to us as we saturate ourselves in the Word of God over a period of months and years.

Our Father can and will bring us through every situation we will face during the end times. Our certainty that God will bring us safely through difficult circumstances *will increase steadily* as we faithfully meditate on His supernatural living Word.

The power of God will rise up inside us more and more as this process continues. We will not have bad days in our lives. How can we have a bad day if we are continually filling our hearts with the supernatural power of the living Word of God? How can negative thoughts and emotions dominate our lives if saturate ourselves in His Word?

How can we be worried, discouraged or depressed if we absolutely refuse to focus on the circumstances that could tempt us to be worried, discouraged or depressed? How can we allow negative thoughts and emotions to obtain a foothold in our hearts if our hearts are filled to overflowing with the supernatural power of the Word of God?

Some people make the problems in their lives seem like big, big problems and God to seem like a little, little God. They focus far more on their problems than they do on God's supernatural power. We should do just the opposite. We will achieve this goal if we immerse ourselves in the Word of God on a daily basis.

We will see life more and more from God's perspective as we saturate ourselves in His living Word. We will focus continually on our loving Father instead of focusing on the seeming immensity of the difficult circumstances we face. Nothing can pull God down. Nothing will be able to pull us down *if* we faithfully fill our hearts with the Word of God.

Our Father will honor our dedication and commitment. He will reveal great spiritual truths to us as we immerse ourselves in His Word. Our faith in God will become deeply rooted. Our faith in God will grow steadily. The Word of God is our

Father's precious gift to us. We must not fail to take full advantage of this precious gift from heaven.

Now that we have finished ten chapters that overflow with scriptural facts pertaining to the spiritual condition of our hearts and meditating continually on the holy Scriptures, we are ready to move on to the final chapter on this subject. In the next chapter we will learn how continual Scripture meditation will enable us to receive revelation from the Holy Spirit.

Chapter 27

Receive Revelation from the Holy Spirit

Some Christians know little or nothing about the Holy Spirit. We become children of God when we ask Jesus to be our Savior. We make the decision to turn from all that is evil, to confess our sins and we are forgiven by God because the blood of Jesus was sacrificed for us. At that time our loving Father sends the Holy Spirit to live in our hearts. "…because you [really] are [His] sons, God has sent the [Holy] Spirit of His Son into our hearts, crying, Abba (Father)! Father!" (Galatians 4:6).

The Holy Spirit will open our spiritual understanding *if* we continually turn away from preoccupation with the things of the world to obey our Father's instructions to study and meditate daily on His Word. He will illuminate wonderful spiritual truths to us as we fill our hearts more and more with God's Word. I have learned that boldly speaking what I am meditating on helps me to receive revelation from the Holy Spirit.

Our Father wants us to fill our minds and our hearts with magnificent Truth from His supernatural Word. We have seen previously that Jesus said, "…Your Word is Truth" (John 17:17). Jesus referred to Himself as "…the Way and the Truth and the Life…" (John 14:6). He referred to the Holy Spirit as "…the

Spirit of Truth Who comes (proceeds) from the Father…" (John 15:26).

We can see the definite connection that exists between the Truth, God's Word, Jesus Christ and the Holy Spirit. We align ourselves more and more with the Spirit of Truth as we fill our minds and our hearts with the Truth of God's Word. Jesus said, "…Everyone who is of the Truth [who is a friend of the Truth, who belongs to the Truth] hears and listens to My voice" (John 18:37).

This passage of Scripture explains the relationship between minds and hearts that are full of the Word of God and hearing God's voice. Our spiritual comprehension will increase as we meditate more and more on God's Word. If you have received Jesus as your Savior, the same Holy Spirit Who anointed the written words of the Bible lives in *your* heart. The Holy Spirit speaks to every one of God's children continually. He is like a twenty-four hour radio station.

We can hear the voice of the Holy Spirit, but we must learn how to tune in to His spiritual frequency. We tune in to the frequency of the Holy Spirit through what I like to call "spiritual radio station WORD." Many voices are speaking in the atmosphere around all cities at all times. We can only hear these voices when we tune in to the proper AM or FM frequency on a radio.

If we want to hear the Holy Spirit speaking to us, we can "tune in" to His voice by constantly meditating on the Word of God. The Holy Spirit speaks to us through our human spirit that was completely transformed when we were saved. The Holy Spirit will assure us that God is our Father and that we are His beloved children. "The Spirit Himself [thus] testifies together with our own spirit, [assuring us] that we are children of God" (Romans 8:16).

Some Christians do not believe that God talks to them. God talks to *all* of His children. Many Christians do not know how to hear His voice. We will learn to hear our Father's voice when we spend a lot of quiet time alone with Him. People we know well do not need to identify themselves when they call on the telephone. We instantly recognize their voice. This same principle applies to the voice of God.

Our natural ears hear what other people say. Our spiritual ears hear what God says. The Bible contains general promises and instructions for all of God's children. The Holy Spirit will cause these messages to be *individualized* as we continually study and meditate on the Word of God. We will see exactly how the Scripture we are meditating on applies to our own lives.

We have learned that Bible study is hard work. The Holy Spirit will honor our diligence as we pay the price of continually studying and meditating on the Word of God. In these last days before Jesus returns, we must learn how to receive continual guidance and revelation from the Holy Spirit.

The Holy Spirit knows exactly how much time we spend in the Word of God. He knows how much of God's Word lives in our hearts. The Holy Spirit will honor our efforts if we faithfully obey our Father's specific instructions to meditate continually on His Word.

We hear from God by faith. The Scripture in this chapter tells us that the Holy Spirit does speak to us. We must *believe* this Scripture and act accordingly. When we meditate on the Word of God, we should meditate with an attitude of expectancy. We should expect the Holy Spirit to constantly reveal fresh new spiritual truth to us.

The Holy Spirit will give us wonderful revelation if we approach our daily Scripture meditation in a humble and teachable manner with simple childlike trust. Christians who are not humble and teachable have hard hearts. Hard hearts block us from hearing the voice of the Holy Spirit. "…Today, if you will hear His voice, do not harden your hearts…" (Hebrews 3:7-8).

I have found over the years that I must write down each revelation from the Holy Spirit as soon as I receive it. If I do not write this message down quickly, it will slip away very rapidly and I won't remember it. I always carry a small memo pad and a ballpoint pen in my pocket. I continually write down notes as the Holy Spirit speaks to me.

I often receive revelation from the Holy Spirit during the day. I also have found that He speaks to me when I am asleep. I write down many notes from this revelation when I wake up during the night or immediately after awakening in the morning. "[One may hear God's voice] in a dream, in a vision of the night, when deep sleep falls on men while slumbering upon the bed…" (Job 33:15).

The Holy Spirit also brings up from our hearts applicable Scripture we have meditated on in the past. Have you ever found yourself speaking a passage of Scripture that you did not fully realize was living in your heart? Jesus said, "…He will cause you to recall (will remind you of, bring to your remembrance) everything I have told you" (John 14:26).

These words that Jesus spoke to His disciples apply to us today. The Holy Spirit is able to bring to our remembrance whatever we need whenever we need it. The Holy Spirit also will guide us to obey the instructions from the Word of God that live in our hearts. "…I will put my Spirit within you and cause you to walk in My statutes, and you shall heed My ordinances and do them" (Ezekiel 36:27).

The Holy Spirit causes the Bible to come alive to us. Some Christians find that the Bible is somewhat dry when they first begin to study it. The Word of God may seem to be dry *until* we begin to receive revelation from the Holy Spirit. This revelation will increase as we continue to meditate faithfully on the Word of God.

We cannot receive maximum revelation from the Word of God without the Holy Spirit. We cannot receive maximum revelation from the Holy Spirit without the Word of God. The Holy Spirit and the Word of God go together.

Our Father wants us to be so committed to studying and meditating on His Word that we continually receive fresh illumination and revelation. We should be like the psalmist who said, "Unless Your law had been my delight, I would have perished in my affliction. I will never forget Your precepts, [how can I?] for it is by them You have quickened me (granted me life)" (Psalm 119:92-93).

God "quickened" His Word to the psalmist because of his "delight" in the Word of God. He brought the psalmist safely through severe affliction because his mind and his heart were filled with the Word of God.

When the Holy Spirit quickens the Word of God to us, He causes it to come alive. Because of the illumination of the Holy Spirit, we will come to the point where we are absolutely certain that the promises from God we are meditating on are much greater and much more powerful than any circumstance we face.

Great spiritual truths that previously were hidden to us will be revealed to us as we constantly meditate on the Word of God. Jesus said, "...there is nothing hidden except to be revealed, nor is anything [temporarily] kept secret except in order that it may be made known. If any man has ears to hear, let him be listening and let him perceive and comprehend" (Mark 4:22-23).

We can only "perceive and comprehend" what the Holy Spirit is telling us if we constantly *listen* for His revelation. We determine how much revelation we will receive by the degree that we continually study and meditate on the Word of God. Jesus said, "...Be careful what you are hearing. The measure [of thought and study] you give [to the truth you hear] will be the measure [of virtue and knowledge] that comes back to you – and more [besides] will be given to you who hear" (Mark 4:24).

We should carefully select what we allow our ears to hear. The "measure of thought and study" we give to the truth of the Word of God will be the *same measure* of the revelation we will receive in return. A casual seeker cannot fully grasp the magnificent truths contained in the Word of God. Casual seekers cannot discern between the voice of the Holy Spirit, the voices of Satan's demons and the voices of other people they hear continually.

The Bible is our Book of Instructions. The Holy Spirit is our teacher. He is our guide. "...the Lord God has sent His Spirit in and with me. Thus says the Lord, your Redeemer, the Holy One of Israel: I am the Lord your God, Who teaches you to profit, Who leads you in the way that you should go" (Isaiah 48:16-17).

This Old Testament reference to the Spirit of God was confirmed by Jesus when He told His disciples what the Holy Spirit would do for them after He was crucified, rose from the dead and ascended into heaven. Jesus said, "...the Comforter (Counselor, Helper, Intercessor, Advocate, Strengthener, Standby), the Holy Spirit, Whom the Father will send in My name [in My place, to represent Me and act on My behalf], He will teach you all things…" (John 14:26).

The first part of this passage of Scripture explains many of the wonderful things the Holy Spirit can and will do for us. For now we want to focus on the words "He will teach you all things." If you have asked Jesus to be your Savior, the *same* Holy Spirit Who lived in the heart of Jesus during His earthly ministry lives in *your* heart today. The Holy Spirit will give you revelation, teach you everything you need to know and guide you in every aspect of your life. Jesus said, "…when He, the Spirit of Truth (the Truth-giving Spirit) comes, He will guide you into all the Truth (the whole, full Truth)…" (John 16:13).

Please highlight or underline the word "all" in this passage of Scripture. Please highlight or underline the words "whole, full" in the amplification of this passage of Scripture. These words leave no room for doubt. The Holy Spirit will give us complete guidance at all times if we faithfully obey God's instructions to continually fill our minds and our hearts with the Truth of His Word.

These words that Jesus spoke to His disciples shortly before He was crucified apply to each of us today. The Holy Spirit can and will guide us safely through the difficult problems we will face during the end times. God knows the way through every problem. "He delivers the afflicted in their affliction and opens their ears [to His voice] in adversity" (Job 36:15).

As we continually fill our hearts with the Word of God, the Holy Spirit will energize our faith in God. He will cause our faith in God to be dynamic and alive. The Holy Spirit can give us special faith when we face seemingly impossible circumstances. The Bible speaks of this supernatural gift of faith when it refers to "... [wonder-working] faith by the same [Holy] Spirit..." (I Corinthians 12:9).

We must not give up if we face a seemingly impossible situation. Nothing is impossible to God (see Matthew 19:26). The Holy Spirit will give us the faith to persevere when it seems as if there is absolutely no way out of the problems we face.

Chapter 28

Our Minds, Our Hearts and Our Mouths

The last eleven chapters have been devoted to the subject of increasing our faith in God by continually filling our *hearts* with the living Word of God. We have learned that we fill our minds with the Word of God by studying the holy Scriptures. We have learned that we fill our hearts with the Word of God by meditating on the holy Scriptures. We also have learned that continual meditation on the Word of God increases and improves the revelation we will receive from the Holy Spirit.

We now are ready to move on to the next scriptural step to increase our faith in God. The Bible teaches us that the Word of God should come up off the printed pages of the Bible into our minds, then drop down into our hearts and then flow continually out of our *mouths*. We now are ready to carefully study instructions from the holy Scriptures about the relationship between increasing our faith in God and the words we speak.

In the difficult times that lie ahead of us, we must learn how to be so yielded to the Holy Spirit and so immersed in the Word of God that we will boldly speak the Word of God whenever we face severe pressure. Many people will speak words of worry, fear, doubt and apprehension. Our Father has told us how to use our mouths to increase our faith in Him.

We saw in Joshua 1:8 that meditating on the Word of God and continually speaking God's Word go together. We saw that Joshua 1:8 says, "This Book of the Law *shall not depart out of your mouth…*" Our Father wants us to *speak* His Word continually regardless of the circumstances we face.

Many religious people do the best they can to live a good life, but they then *cancel* their good intentions by the words they speak. "If anyone thinks himself to be religious (piously observant of the external duties of his faith) and does not bridle his tongue but deludes his own heart, this person's religious service is worthless (futile, barren)" (James 1:26).

None of us want our Christian walk to be "worthless, futile and barren." We will be exactly what our Father wants us to be *if* we can learn to control all the words we speak. "…if anyone does not offend in speech [never says the wrong things], he is a fully developed character and a perfect man, able to control his whole body and to curb his entire nature" (James 3:2).

Would you like to become a "perfect" man (or woman) in God's sight? This passage of Scripture assures us that this goal *is* attainable. This magnificent goal can be achieved by learning how to control our God-given privilege to choose the words we allow to come out of our mouths.

Many of us have no comprehension of the tremendous spiritual power of the words we speak. "If we set bits in the horses' mouths to make them obey us, we can turn their whole bodies about. Likewise, look at the ships: though they are so great and are driven by rough winds, they are steered by a very small rudder wherever the impulse of the helmsman determines. Even so the tongue is a little member, and it can boast of great things. See how much wood or how great a forest a tiny spark can set ablaze!" (James 3:3-5).

A bit in the mouth of a horse is very small compared to the size of a horse. A rudder in a ship is very small compared to the size of a ship. However, a small bit in a horse's mouth and a small rudder on a ship are able to *turn* a large horse and a large ship.

The Word of God compares our tongues with a bit and a rudder. Our tongues are very small compared to the size of our bodies, but our tongues are *extremely powerful.* The words that we speak are able to direct our lives just as a small bit is able to direct a large horse and a small rudder is able to direct a large ship.

James 3:5 compares the power of our tongues to a "tiny spark" that is able to set a large forest on fire. Our tongues are spiritual "fire." They are so powerful that they can create tremendous havoc in our lives if we do not use them the way God intended them to be used. "…the tongue is a fire. [The tongue is a] world of wickedness set among our members, contaminating and depraving the whole body and setting on fire the wheel of birth (the cycle of man's nature), being itself ignited by hell (Gehenna)" (James 3:6).

Satan wants to control the words we speak. He wants us to use our tongues to speak words that deny the victory of Jesus. Satan's demons continually try to get into our minds hoping to influence the words we speak by the ungodly thoughts they attempt to put into our minds.

We are able to "contaminate" and "deprave" our bodies by the words we speak. We will "set ourselves on fire" spiritually if we allow our tongues to be "ignited by hell." This statement means that we can allow Satan's hellish demons to get into our minds to greatly influence the words we speak.

We cannot control our tongues through sheer will power. "...every kind of beast and bird, of reptile and sea animal, can be tamed and has been tamed by human genius (nature). But the human tongue can be tamed by no man. It is a restless (undisciplined, irreconcilable) evil, full of deadly poison" (James 3:7-8).

Even though we can train animals, birds, reptiles and creatures of the sea, we cannot train our tongues through will power. This passage of Scripture tells us that our tongues are "restless, undisciplined and irreconcilable." Our tongues are "evil and full of deadly poison."

These somber words show us that we can hurt ourselves severely by the words we speak. Some Christians praise the Lord and bless Him and then, with the same mouth that praises the Lord, they speak profanity. "With it we bless the Lord and Father, and with it we curse men who were made in God's likeness! Out of the same mouth come forth blessing and cursing. These things, my brethren, ought not to be so." (James 3: 9-10).

Our Father wants the words we speak to be *consistent*. He does not want us to speak like saints part of the time and sinners part of the time. Satan's demons will do everything they can to influence us to speak words that are an abomination to God.

Please stop for a moment to think carefully about the four passages of Scripture from the third chapter of James we have just studied. We *must* understand the vital importance of the words we speak and the tremendous effect these words can have on our lives.

We have learned that we cannot control our words through sheer will power. *How can we control these words?* We can begin the process of controlling the words we speak by obeying our Father's instructions to renew our minds continually in His Word. Renewed minds definitely have an effect on our words. "The mind of the wise instructs his mouth, and adds learning and persuasiveness to his lips" (Proverbs 16:23).

A similar statement is made in a subsequent chapter of Proverbs. "Listen (consent and submit) to the words of the wise, and apply your mind to my knowledge; for it will be pleasant if you keep them in your mind [believing them]; your lips will be accustomed to [confessing] them" (Proverbs 22:17-18).

Our minds have some influence on the words we speak, but I believe our *hearts* are the primary key to the words that come out of our mouths. We have learned that we must meditate continually on the holy Scriptures if we want our hearts to be filled with the supernatural power of the living Word of God. "…The Word (God's message in Christ) is near you, on your lips and in your heart…" (Romans 10:8).

The following passage of Scripture explains the relationship between what we believe in our hearts, what we confess in our mouths and receiving eternal salvation. "…if you acknowledge and confess with your lips that Jesus is Lord and in your heart believe (adhere to, trust in, and rely on the truth) that God raised Him from the dead, you will be saved. For with the heart a person believes (adheres to, trusts in, and relies on Christ) and so is justified (declared righteous, acceptable to God), and with the mouth he confesses (declares openly and speaks out freely his faith) and confirms [his] salvation" (Romans 10:9-10).

All Christians who ask Jesus to be their Savior must believe in their *hearts* that Jesus paid the full price for their sins when

He died on a cross at Calvary. We also must open our *mouths* to speak our assurance that God raised Jesus from the dead and that we trust Him completely for our eternal salvation (see the Appendix at the end of this book for more details on this great spiritual truth).

This *same* principle of believing in our hearts and speaking what we believe with our mouths that must occur before we are saved should *continue* throughout the remainder of our lives. We all will face many difficult circumstances in the last days before Jesus returns. We must learn how to prepare our hearts and minds to speak faith-filled words, regardless of the severity of the circumstances we face.

The *key* to the words we speak in a crisis situation is *what we truly believe in our hearts.* Our hearts are like a well. A bucket can only draw up as much water as the well contains. During a crisis, our mouths must be able to go down into our hearts to draw up an ample supply of the Word of God.

The following passage of Scripture is one of the most important passages of Scripture for Christians to learn and apply during these last days before Jesus returns. Jesus said, "…How can you speak good things when you are evil (wicked)? For out of the fullness (the overflow, the superabundance) of the heart the mouth speaks. The good man from his inner good treasure flings forth good things, and the evil man out of his inner evil storehouse flings forth evil things" (Matthew 12:34-35).

Jesus spoke these words to a group of Pharisees. He told them that they could not speak "good things" because their hearts were evil and wicked. Jesus then explained to them (and to each of us today) what we should do to fill our hearts with faith in God so that we will speak words of faith when we face a crisis situation. Sometimes we are able to control our words during good times through our minds, but our words in a crisis *always* will be determined by *whatever* we truly believe deep down in our hearts.

We *will* be able to "fling forth good things" with our mouths if we have stored up an "overflow" and "superabundance" of "good treasure" from the Word of God in our hearts. We store up this abundance in our hearts by obeying our Father's instructions to meditate continually on His Word. People whose hearts are not filled with the Word of God are likely to "fling forth evil things" when they face a crisis. The words that these people speak are likely to be evil because they do not have the power of the Word of God and they will be influenced by Satan's evil demons.

God's Word will pour out of our mouths when we face a sudden crisis *if* our hearts are filled with the Word of God. I like the word "fling" that is used twice in this passage of Scripture. When we fling something, we throw it. Hearts that are filled with the Word of God will continually throw out positive, faith-filled words through our mouths.

Chapter 29

Speak the Word of God with Unwavering Faith

We saw in Matthew 12:34-35 that we "fling forth" either good words or evil words with our mouths depending on the spiritual condition of our hearts. Jesus also said, "...whatever comes out of the mouth comes from the heart, and this is what makes a man unclean and defiles [him]. For out of the heart come evil thoughts (reasonings and disputings and designs) such as murder, adultery, sexual vice, theft, false witnessing, slander, and irreverent speech" (Matthew 15:18-19).

This passage of Scripture gives us information about the negative words that many people speak. Jesus said that our *hearts* are the key to any unclean and evil thoughts we express with our mouths. Some Christians who speak positive and uplifting words in good times will find the words that come out of their mouths during difficult times are not the words they would like to speak. We must prepare our hearts now for the difficult times we will face in the future. We cannot afford to speak words that deny the Word of God.

Sometimes Christians who have faithfully filled their hearts with the Word of God through continual Scripture meditation may be surprised by the words of faith that pour out of their mouths in a difficult situation. Other Christians who have not filled their hearts with God's Word may be surprised by the words of doubt and unbelief that come out of their mouths when they face a severe crisis.

If our hearts overflow with the Word of God, we will not have to make a conscious effort to speak faith-filled words. Faith-filled words will come out of our mouths spontaneously. Our faith in God should be so strong because of the abundance of His Word in our hearts that we continually will speak words of faith regardless of the circumstances we face.

The Hebrew word that is translated as "meditate" in Joshua 1:8 and Psalm 1:2 actually means to "murmur." We will prepare ourselves for the difficult times that are coming as we constantly speak the Word of God while meditating on it. The psalmist said, "My heart was hot within me. While I was musing, the fire burned; then I spoke with my tongue" (Psalm 39:3).

Several passages of Scripture emphasize how faithfully the psalmist David meditated on the Word of God. The Bible tells us that David was a man after God's own heart. David's heart became "hot" when he was "musing" on the Word of God. David then spoke the words that were welling up in his heart. We should follow David's example. Continual meditation on the Word of God will cause our hearts to be on fire.

Christians can release deep, strong and unwavering faith in God by constantly speaking words that line up with God's Word. These Christians receive supernatural results. When other Christians attempt to copy them by speaking similar words of faith and nothing happens, they wonder why they are not receiving results.

Our faith in God is *not* contingent only on the words we say. We cannot just mouth words of faith. Our faith in God can only be released when we *believe* the words we are speaking. The psalmist said, "I believed (trusted in, relied on, and clung to my God), and therefore have I spoken [even when I said], I am greatly afflicted" (Psalm 116:10).

The psalmist spoke words of faith when he was "greatly afflicted" with severe problems. He had so much faith in God that he "trusted, relied on and clung to God." The psalmist was able to speak genuine words of faith in a crisis because of his deep and strong faith in God.

The apostle Paul emphasized this same principle many years later. Paul quoted the psalmist when he said, "…we have the same spirit of faith as he had who wrote, I have believed, and therefore have I spoken. We too believe, and therefore we speak" (II Corinthians 4:13).

We will have to trust God completely in the difficult times that lie ahead of us. We will have to learn how to speak faith-filled words, regardless of the circumstances we face. We can *only* accomplish these goals if we have faithfully renewed our minds in the Word of God on a daily basis and if we have consistently meditated on the Word of God.

God often repeats Himself in the holy Scriptures for the purpose of *emphasis.* The repetition in this chapter that is based on repetition in the Word of God is used to emphasize *how vitally important it is for you* in these last days before Jesus returns to prepare yourself by constantly filling your mind and your heart with the supernatural power of the living Word of God.

The time that we invest to fill our minds and our hearts with the Word of God while we are on earth also will provide us with eternal benefits when we are in heaven. "…Train yourself toward godliness (piety), [keeping yourself spiritually fit]. For physical training is of some value (useful for a little), but godliness (spiritual training) is useful and of value in everything and in every way, for it holds promise for the present life and also for the life which is to come" (I Timothy 4:7-8).

Many people have placed great emphasis on physical fitness in recent years. There is no question that physical fitness is important. This passage of Scripture tells us that *spiritual fitness is even more important* because it will benefit us during our lives here on earth "and also for the life which is to come." We do not know how we will be blessed by this spiritual training when we are in heaven, but we do know that spiritual fitness will be "useful and of value" when we are in heaven.

We should exercise our bodies and eat wholesome food, but we must not stop there. We must "train ourselves toward godliness." We are emphasizing the importance of spiritual fitness throughout this book. This spiritual fitness *will* help us during difficult times. "The strong spirit of a man sustains him in bodily pain or trouble…" (Proverbs 18:14).

The spiritual process we have been studying in this book is a continual spiritual cycle. It consists of the Word of God flowing from our eyes and ears to our minds, our hearts and our mouths. This spiritual cycle is like riding a bicycle. A bicycle has to keep moving forward or it falls down. We cannot do what our Father wants us to do with our lives unless we keep moving forward. We must constantly fill our minds and our hearts with the holy Scriptures so that the Word of God will pour out of our mouths continually.

This process also can be compared to charging a battery in an automobile. We keep our spiritual batteries charged when we continually renew our minds in the Word of God, meditate on the Word of God and speak the Word of God. We must not allow our spiritual batteries to run down. We must keep them fully charged during these final days before Jesus returns.

Chapter 30

Our Words Are Powerful Spiritual Seeds

Many Christians have little or no understanding of what the Bible says about the power of the words that come out of their mouths. Some of us actually *block ourselves* from receiving blessings from our loving Father because many of our words contradict the Word of God.

God created us in such a way that speaking with our mouths enables His Word to go into our hearts and for His Word to come out of our hearts. We have seen that the Word of God goes into our hearts when we speak God's Word continually as we meditate on it. The Word of God flows out of our hearts to the degree that our hearts are filled with God's Word.

This book is filled with facts about the difficult times that lie ahead of us. The cumulative flow of the words we speak will bring us safely through the end times if we learn how to consistently speak the words our Father wants us to speak. "...wise men's lips preserve them" (Proverbs 14:3).

The words that we speak have the ability to "preserve" us. They can protect us from harm or damage. The average person speaks approximately thirty thousand words each day. A few people speak as many as one hundred thousand words each day. The cumulative effect of all of these words over a period of months and years is very powerful.

Most of us have heard the saying "Talk is cheap." This statement is true in regard to the idle words that many people speak continually. However, it does not apply to speaking the Word of God. Our talk is precious before God when we continually speak His Word with strong and unwavering faith.

When I was a little boy, children sometimes said, "Sticks and stones may break my bones, but words will never hurt me." This childish statement is not true. The Bible repeatedly teaches how damaging our words and the words of other people can be to us.

We can begin to understand the importance that God places on the words we speak if we will stop to think that, out of all the creatures God created, He only gave one species the ability to think and to express thoughts verbally. Our Father wants each of us to use this precious ability He has given us by obeying His specific instructions in this area.

Satan's demons know the importance of the spoken word. They constantly try to get into our minds in an attempt to influence us to speak destructive words that are the opposite of what God wants us to speak. Instead of speaking destructive words, we must continually speak words that clearly indicate our complete trust in God.

We each decide the words we will speak throughout every day of our lives. Unfortunately, some of us make our problems much worse by our words instead of using our words to walk in victory over these problems.

Our Father wants each of us to be humble and teachable. Proud and self-confident people who ignore God's instructions will *waste* the opportunity God has given each of us in regard to the words we speak. "The tongue of the wise utters knowledge rightly, but the mouth of the [self-confident] fool pours out folly" (Proverbs 15:2).

People who trust themselves instead of placing all of their trust in God speak words that "pour out folly." The words of proud and self-confident people inevitably bring problems into their lives. "A [self-confident] fool's lips bring contention, and his mouth invites a beating. A [self-confident] fool's mouth is his ruin, and his lips are a snare to himself" (Proverbs 18:6-7).

Our words can "snare" us and "invite a beating." We should do just the opposite. Our words should be a precious treasure before God. "The tongues of those who are upright and in right standing with God are as choice silver…" (Proverbs 10:20).

Our lives will be better and more enjoyable *if* we learn how to program our words by constantly filling our hearts with the Word of God. "…let him who wants to enjoy life and see good days [good – whether apparent or not] keep his tongue free from evil and his lips from guile (treachery, deceit)" (I Peter 3:10).

We will face many difficult problems in the days ahead. We still can "enjoy life and see good days" if we consistently speak the way our Father wants us to speak. Our words can bring us through adversity. "…the mouth of the upright shall deliver them…" (Proverbs 12:6).

Our words are spiritual seeds. Spiritual seeds produce spiritual fruit. We produce good fruit or bad fruit in our lives by the type of spiritual seeds we release with our mouths. Our words will produce *good fruit* in our lives if we continually plant the seed of God's supernatural Word in our hearts. "From the fruit of his words a man shall be satisfied with good…" (Proverbs 12:14).

Our words are *so powerful* that they actually are able to bring us into the marvelous spiritual refuge our Father has provided for us. "Lord, who shall dwell [temporarily] in Your tabernacle? Who shall dwell [permanently] on Your holy hill? He who walks and lives uprightly and blamelessly, who works rightness and justice and speaks and thinks the truth in his heart. He who does not slander with his tongue, nor does evil to his friend, nor takes up a reproach against his neighbor…" (Psalm 15:1-3).

We will "dwell in God's tabernacle" if we "speak and think the truth in our hearts." The Hebrew word "ohel" that is translated as "tabernacle" is "a covering, dwelling place, home." We will dwell in the covering that God provides for us if our hearts are filled with His Word and we continually speak God's Word with our mouths.

We can stay close to God and come into His presence based on the cumulative effect of the words we speak. Our hearts should be so filled with the Truth of God's Word that all of the words we speak will line up with God's Word. We must not use the ability to speak that God has given us to use our words to hurt other people.

Our words should be gracious and loving. We will receive "favor" from God when our words consistently line up with His Word. "The words of a wise man's mouth are gracious and win him favor…" (Ecclesiastes 10:12).

God's blessings are *voice-activated*. We will activate the wonderful blessings our Father wants to give us when we continually speak words that line up with His Word. One of the blessings our Father promises is healing. We must understand the relationship between the words we speak and receiving manifestation of healing from God. "There are those who speak rashly, like the piercing of a sword, but the tongue of the wise brings healing" (Proverbs 12:18).

Christians who "speak rashly" hurt other people with their words. Harsh words can be as detrimental in the spiritual realm as a sword is in the natural realm. If we consistently speak "wise" words, these words will "bring healing" to our situation. "A gentle tongue [with its healing power] is a tree of life, but willful contrariness in it breaks down the spirit" (Proverbs 15:4).

We are told that "a gentle tongue is a tree of life." The amplification of this passage of Scripture says that we release "healing power" when we speak gently. Our words will "break down our spirit" if we are contrary and willfully disobey our Father's instructions.

Once again we see that God emphasizes through repetition. Our Father emphasizes that our bodies *can and will be healed* if we continually speak words that line up with His Word. "Pleasant words are as a honeycomb, sweet to the mind and healing to the body" (Proverbs 16:24).

Our words are "pleasant" and "sweet" before God when they are positive and uplifting. These words have a definite effect on our minds and bodies. Do *you* need healing in your body? Please go back *now* and meditate on Proverbs 12:18, Proverbs 15:4 and Proverbs 16:24. There is no question that a definite relationship exists between the words we speak and receiving manifestation of healing from God.

If you would like to learn many scriptural facts pertaining to divine healing, you may want to purchase our Scripture Meditation Cards *Receive Healing from the Lord*. This set of Scripture cards contains approximately eighty Scripture references that will help you to understand what the Bible says about manifestation of healing from the Lord.

Our eighty-five minute cassette tape on this subject is filled with encouraging words from the Word of God. Some people have been healed by listening to this cassette tape. This tape explains many additional facts pertaining to divine healing that could not be included in the limited space contained on both sides of fifty-two two and a half by three and a half inch Scripture cards.

Do you want to live a long, full and healthy life? Of course you do. The Word of God explains the relationship between the words we speak and the length and quality of our lives. "What man is he who desires life and longs for many days, that he may see good? Keep your tongue from evil and your lips from speaking deceit" (Psalm 34:12-13).

One of the most important ingredients to living a long life and "seeing good" is to "keep our tongues free from evil and our lives from speaking deceit." *Many people die prematurely* because of the cumulative effect of the words they have spoken over a period of years.

Chapter 31

We Can Hurt Ourselves by the Words We Speak

Our Father has given us many specific instructions pertaining to the words we speak. We *cannot* repeatedly allow words to come out of our mouths that are contrary to these instructions and expect to receive blessings from God.

In these last days before Jesus returns, many people actually will be kept alive or put to death by the cumulative effect of their words. "A man's [moral] self shall be filled with the fruit of his mouth; and with the consequences of his words he must be satisfied [whether good or evil]. Death and life are in the power of the tongue, and they who indulge in it shall eat the fruit of it [for death or life]" (Proverbs 18:20-21).

The first part of this passage of Scripture speaks of our "moral self." Our moral self is what we really are deep down inside ourselves. What indicates what we really are like deep down inside of ourselves? The cumulative "fruit of our mouths" tells what we are like.

Two spiritual forces are at work in the world. The first five chapters of this book carefully explain the influence of Satan on the world. A great move of the Holy Spirit also is occurring during these last days before Jesus returns. We each decide whether we will allow Satan to obtain a foothold in our lives or whether we will walk closely with the Lord by what we allow into our minds and our hearts and by the words we speak.

We can live in the victory that Jesus won for us at Calvary or we can give Satan and his demons spiritual authority in our lives. Proverbs 18:20 says that we each "must be satisfied whether good or evil" by the consequences of our words.

Proverbs 18:21 says that "death and life are in the power of the tongue." I believe these words apply to spiritual life and death and also to physical life and death. We saw in the last chapter the relationship that exists between living a long life and the words we speak. There is no question that the words we speak affect physical death as well as spiritual death. We will be spiritually dead if we continually speak words that are contrary to God's Word. We will be spiritually alive if our words consistently line up with the Word of God that is "alive and full of power" (see Hebrews 4:12).

We bring many of the problems in our lives upon ourselves by the words we speak. Words that are aligned with the Word of God are good words. Words that deny the Word of God are bad words. Good words cause good things to happen. Bad words cause bad things to happen.

We each will be required to give an accounting in heaven for all the words we speak during our lives on earth. Jesus said, "...on the day of judgment men will have to give account for every idle (inoperative, nonworking) word they speak. For by your words you will be justified and acquitted, and by your words you will be condemned and sentenced" (Matthew 12:36-37).

Jesus does not want us to speak "idle words." The amplification in this passage of Scripture defines idle words as words that are "inoperative and nonworking." These words do not produce favorable results in the spiritual realm. We must not waste our precious God-given ability to choose the words we speak by constantly speaking spiritually dead words that have no spiritual power and no eternal significance.

The words we speak can imprison us or they can set us free. We can be "condemned and sentenced" by them or we can be "justified and acquitted." We have a tremendous opportunity to walk continually in the victory of Jesus if we fully understand and act on this principle. Some of us do just the opposite. "You are snared with the words of your lips, you are caught by the speech of your mouth" (Proverbs 6:2).

A "snare" is a type of trap that is set for animals. Satan's snares are subtle traps that his demons set for us. Satan's demons can tell whether or not they have caught us by the words they hear us speak. We also can be snared by our own carelessness.

Satan and his demons are very clever. They have had thousands of years of experience. They use many proven techniques in an attempt to trap people. Satan's demons are exhilarated when they hear us actually speaking words that were directly affected by their attempt to influence our thinking. They know that these words can block God from giving us the blessings He wants to give us.

Christians who continually fill their minds and their hearts with God's Word will have spiritual discernment. They will know what Satan's demons are trying to do to them. They will not fall into these traps. They will not speak words that are contrary to God's Word just because some demon is trying to influence their thoughts and the words they speak.

Some Christians live far below the privileges that have been given to us by the magnificent victory Jesus won for us at Calvary. Some of us negate this wonderful victory by our words. "…the lips of a fool consume him" (Ecclesiastes 10:12).

We are foolish if we fail to learn and obey God's instructions. We are foolish if our disobedience gives Satan a foothold in our lives. We will be "consumed" if we allow our words to be influenced by Satan instead of constantly speaking words that line up with the Word of God.

Some people give in to the temptation to talk constantly about the problems they face. Some of us tell other people many details about what we are going through because we want to receive their sympathy. We can pay a tremendous price in the spiritual realm because of our desire to receive a few sympathetic words in the natural realm. The more we talk about the problems we face, the worse they will be.

The Word of God repeatedly tells us that our Father will honor words of faith. Words of doubt and unbelief actually are able to *block the mighty power of God* from moving in our lives. We can see a clear illustration of this spiritual truth by reading about what took place when Jesus returned to His home town of Nazareth.

The people of Nazareth spoke words of doubt and unbelief after they heard Jesus teach in the synagogue. They said, "…Where did this Man acquire all this? What is the wisdom [the broad and full intelligence which has been] given to Him? What mighty works and exhibitions of power are wrought by His hands! Is not this the Carpenter, the son of Mary and the brother of James and Joses and Judas and Simon? And are not His sisters here among us? And they took offense at Him and were hurt [that is, they disapproved of Him, and it hindered them from acknowledging His authority] and they were caused to stumble and fall" (Mark 6:2-3).

These words of unbelief denied the power of Jesus. The people of Nazareth were "hurt" and "caused to stumble and fall" because of these words. "…Jesus said to them, A prophet is not without honor (deference, reverence) except in his [own] country and among [his] relatives and in his [own] house. And He was not able to do even one work of power there, except that He laid hands on a few sickly people [and] cured them. And He marveled because of their unbelief (their lack of faith in Him). And He went about among the surrounding villages and continued teaching" (Mark 6:4-6).

The people of Nazareth denied the mighty power of Jesus because of their familiarity with Him that developed during the many years He lived in Nazareth. Please note that Mark 6:5 does not say that Jesus did not choose to perform miracles in Nazareth. We are told that Jesus *was not able* to perform miracles there.

Unbelief can have a tremendous influence on our lives. The words of unbelief of the people in Nazareth were *so powerful* that they *blocked* the mighty power of Jesus. Words of unbelief can block His mighty power in *your* life today.

Jesus "marveled because of their unbelief and lack of faith in Him." *We must not make this mistake.* We must not allow words of doubt and unbelief to block Jesus from doing what He wants to do for us, in us and through us.

We do not have to let the problems that pull other people down to pull us down. Jesus wants us to continually speak of Him and His mighty power instead of talking about the problems we face. He can and will help us and protect us when our words and our actions consistently indicate our deep, strong, unwavering and unshakable faith in Him.

Chapter 32

We Should Follow God's Example

God showed us the power of the spoken word by the way He created the earth, everything on the earth and everyone on the earth. In the first chapter of the Bible we are repeatedly told that God created by *speaking words*:

- "And *God said*, Let there be light; and there was light" (Genesis 1:3).

- And *God said,* Let there be a firmament [the expanse of the sky] in the midst of the waters, and let it separate the waters [below] from the waters [above]. And God made the firmament [the expanse] and separated the waters which were under the expanse from the waters which were above the expanse. And it was so" (Genesis 1:6-7).

- "And *God said,* Let the waters under the heavens be collected into one place [of standing], and let the dry land appear. And it was so." (Genesis 1:9).

- "And *God said,* Let the earth put forth [tender] vegetation: plants yielding seed and fruit trees yielding fruit whose seed is in itself, each according to its kind, upon the earth. And it was so" (Genesis 1:11).

- "And *God said,* Let there be lights in the expanse of the heavens to separate the day from the night, and let them be signs and tokens [of God's provident care], and [to mark] seasons, days, and years, and let them be lights in the expanse of the sky to give light upon the earth. And it was so" (Genesis 1:14-15).

- "And *God said,* Let the earth bring forth living creatures according to their kinds: livestock, creeping things, and [wild] beasts of the earth according to their kinds. And it was so" (Genesis 1:24).

- "*God said,* Let Us [Father, Son, and Holy Spirit] make mankind in Our image, after Our likeness, and let them have complete authority over the fish of the sea, the birds of the air, the [tame] beasts, and over all of the earth, and over everything that creeps upon the earth. So God created man in His own image, in the image and likeness of God He created him; male and female He created them" (Genesis 1:26-27).

Each of these seven passages of Scripture begins with the words "God said." We have italicized these words to emphasize their importance. God *speaks* things into existence. Each of these passages of Scripture ends by explaining what God spoke into existence.

Genesis 1:26-27 tells us that God spoke the first man, Adam, into existence and that He created him "in His own image." If God used His words and His faith to accomplish His goals and if God created Adam and every person born after Adam in His image, we can be certain that He wants us to use our words and our faith in Him in the same way.

God *always* gets results when He speaks. "…as the rain and snow come down from the heavens, and return not there again, but water the earth and make it bring forth and sprout, that it may give seed to the sower and bread to the eater, so shall My word be that goes forth out of My mouth: it shall not return to Me void [without producing any effect, useless], but it shall accomplish that which I please and purpose, and it shall prosper in the thing for which I sent it" (Isaiah 55:10-11).

When God speaks He "accomplishes what He pleases and purposes." Our Father wants us to say what He says. He wants us to speak His Word continually. He wants us to have the same absolute certainty that we also will receive good results when we continually speak His Word. "…be imitators of God [copy Him and follow His example], as well-beloved children [imitate their father]" (Ephesians 5:1).

Our Father wants us to "imitate" Him. The amplification in this passage of Scripture says that we should "copy Him and follow His example." Jesus followed God's example. He released His faith in God throughout His earthly ministry by the words He spoke. If God released His faith with spoken words and if Jesus released His faith with spoken words, shouldn't we follow their example with the words that come out of our mouths?

Our Father has given each of us the ability to bring results that are invisible to our human eyesight into manifestation by consistently speaking faith-filled words that are anchored on His Word. Our Father wants us to speak into being what He has promised in His Word. We do not give God anything to work with if we fail to continually speak His Word.

Our loving Father *can* and *will* do mighty and powerful works for us, in us and through us when our hearts are filled with His Word and His Word continually pours out of our mouths. In a previous chapter we saw in James 3:6 that our tongues are "fire." We can release powerful spiritual fire when we speak

God's mighty and powerful Word. We release destructive spiritual fire with words of doubt and unbelief. "You conceive chaff, you bring forth stubble; your breath is a fire that consumes you" (Isaiah 33:11).

Many people waste their breath when they speak. The words "chaff" and "stubble" refer to the worthless leftovers in wheat, corn and other grain after they are threshed. The words of many people are worthless chaff and stubble. Their words do not release the power of God.

When we face seemingly impossible situations we should speak the Word of God again and again. Circumstances that seem impossible to us can and will be overcome by the supernatural spiritual power that is released when we boldly speak the Word of God with absolute and unwavering faith in God.

We mentioned previously that the Greek word "logos" refers to the *written* word of God. Logos is powerful, but "rhema" is more powerful. The Greek word "rhema" refers to the *living* Word of God. We give *spiritual life* to logos when we *speak* the Word of God with bold faith. We release the power of Almighty God when we speak from hearts that are filled with absolute certainty that God will honor His Word.

Our Father wants us to speak life, not death. We have repeatedly emphasized that the Word of God is alive and filled with the power of God (see Hebrews 4:12). Most people reading this book have heard many preachers, teachers or evangelists boldly speaking the Word of God. God causes His Word to *come alive* to us when it flows out of the mouths of His anointed servants. "The words of a [discreet and wise] man's mouth are like deep waters [plenteous and difficult to fathom], and the fountain of skillful and godly Wisdom is like a gushing stream [sparkling, fresh, pure, and life-giving]" (Proverbs 18:4).

The amplification of this passage of Scripture speaks of a "discreet and wise" man. If we are mature in the Lord, we will realize the immense power of our words. The words of a wise man are compared to a "gushing stream" that the amplification says is "sparkling, fresh, pure and life-giving." Our Father wants our words to be like a "fountain." He wants to hear words of faith that sparkle. The words that we speak should be just as the Word of God is – pure, fresh and alive.

The problems that the world will face during the end times will not be able to pull us down if we speak the Word of God continually. We have learned that our faith in God *will* increase if our ears continually hear our mouths speaking the Word of God (see Romans 10:17). The problems during the end times that will overcome many people will not be able to overcome us if we release God's power by constantly speaking His Word.

No problem on earth, no matter how severe it may seem, can stand up against a continual torrent of the Word of God flowing out of our mouths. The words that we consistently speak should show our absolute faith in the magnificent victory Jesus won for us at Calvary. "Inasmuch then as we have a great High Priest Who has [already] ascended and passed through the heavens, Jesus the Son of God, let us hold fast our confession [of faith in Him]" (Hebrews 4:14).

The victory that Jesus won when He rose from the dead belongs to every person who has asked Him to be his or her Savior. This victory will be automatic when we get to heaven, but this victory is *not* automatic here on earth. We must "hold fast our confession of faith" in Jesus to persevere during difficult times. A marvelous victory has been won for us by our "great High Priest Who has already ascended and passed through the heavens."

When we hold fast to something, we refuse to let go. Too many people "hold fast" to the problems they face by talking about them continually. These people are doing exactly what Satan wants them to do.

Jesus does *not* want us to focus on the problems we face. There is *no* place in the Word of God where we are told to focus on problems. We are tested whenever we face severe adversity. We pass or fail these spiritual tests by the words we speak when we are under severe pressure.

Will we allow the pressure we face to affect our words? Will we hold tightly to our faith in God without wavering? Will the words that we speak clearly indicate our deep, unwavering and unshakable faith in God?

In Chapter Eleven we studied many facts from the Bible about the faithfulness and reliability of Almighty God. Wouldn't we continually speak words of faith and absolutely refuse to give up *if* we know God intimately and trust Him completely?

Our Father does *not* want us to be swayed by circumstances. When we face adversity, He wants us to constantly say what His Word says. He does not want our trust in Him or our confession of our faith in Him to waver in the slightest.

Our Father wants us to continually acknowledge our absolute certainty that He *will* do exactly what His Word says He will do. He wants us to do this for as long as He requires. Sometimes God will require us to persevere in our faith for a long time. God wants us to trust His timing just as we trust Him in every other area.

Chapter 33

We Should Speak Boldly
to the Problems We Face

When we face a crisis we can panic by saying things like, "I'm scared. I'm worried. What am I going to do? How can I possibly get out of this situation?" Or we can choose to speak the Word of God continually out of a faith-filled heart.

Our *reaction* to the circumstances we face is much more important than the circumstances themselves. We can determine the outcome of a crisis situation by the words that come out of our mouths. Some Christians speak words of despair when they face severe adversity because their hearts have not been prepared by continually filling them with the supernatural power of the living Word of God.

We *cannot* dwell on problems if we continually speak the Word of God. We can push worried and fearful thoughts *out* of our minds and *keep them out* by continually speaking the Word of God with deep and unwavering faith in God.

When we hear bad news, we must not say what the world says. We must not dwell on what ABC, CBS, NBC, the cable television news networks, radio stations, newspapers and news magazines say. We must not say what Satan wants us to say. We should continually say what God says.

The word "confession" in the Bible refers to the words we speak. This word means "to agree with" or "to say the same thing as." We agree with Satan if we speak words that give manifestation to the thoughts that Satan's demons try to put into our minds. We should do exactly the opposite. Our words should be the same as God's Word.

God has a language of His own. His language is very different from the language of the world. The holy Scriptures are filled with God's language. We *will* speak God's language of faith continually if our hearts are filled with God's language of faith.

Our Father wants each of us to develop a vocabulary of success that is solidly anchored on His Word. Many people have a vocabulary of failure. Our faith in God can and will be measured by the cumulative total of the words we speak.

It is *much easier* to talk about difficult problems than to speak the Word of God. Jesus told us that we *should not speak* worried and anxious words. He said, "…do not worry and be anxious, saying, What are we going to have to eat? or, What are we going to have to drink? or, What are we going to have to wear?" (Matthew 6:31).

The word "saying" in this passage of Scripture is very important. The things we are tempted to be worried and anxious about will actually happen in our lives if we consistently allow worried and anxious words to come out of our mouths.

Many people will be paralyzed by the spirit of fear that will sweep through the world in the last days before Jesus returns. Their emotions will run rampant. They will make poor decisions. Many Christians who are not prepared for what is coming will join all of the unbelievers who will be pulled under by this spirit of fear.

Our Father wants us to have absolute faith that He will bring us through everything that is taking place in the world, no matter how dire these circumstances might seem. We should follow the example of the psalmist who said, "I sought (inquired of) the Lord and required Him [of necessity and on the authority of His Word], and He heard me, and delivered me from all my fears" (Psalm 34:4).

This verse says that the psalmist kept God first in his life. He persevered in faith until he heard from God. The amplification of this passage of Scripture says that we require the Lord "of necessity." We must understand that our relationship with God is a vital necessity in our lives. We must seek Him with every fiber of our being. The amplification in this passage of Scripture says that we should seek the Lord based on "the authority of His Word." *God's Word is the final authority.*

Please highlight or underline the word "all" in Psalm 34:4. Our precious Lord can and will deliver us from *all* of the fears we will be tempted to give in to during the difficult times that lie ahead. We *cannot afford* to harbor worried, anxious and fearful thoughts or to speak them. Jesus said, "…it shall be done for you as you have believed…" (Matthew 8:13).

We *will* speak the Word of God in the morning, we *will* speak the Word of God in the afternoon and we *will* speak the Word of God at night *if* we obey our Father's instructions to meditate on His Word throughout the day and night. Instead of focusing on problems, we should focus continually on God "Who does great things past finding out, yes, marvelous things without number" (Job 9:10).

There is no limit to what God can do except any limit *we set* through doubt and unbelief. Whenever we speak, our Father wants us to speak words that line up with His Word. "Whoever speaks, [let him do it as one who utters] oracles of God…" (I Peter 4:11).

The Greek word "logion" that is translated as "oracles" in this passage of Scripture means "an utterance of God." Whenever we face difficult circumstances, we should *boldly* say what God says. "…the [uncompromisingly] righteous are bold as a lion" (Proverbs 28:1).

All Christians are righteous before God because Jesus paid the full price for our sins. We must not compromise the victory Jesus won for us. We must not be timid when we face difficult circumstances. We should be "…bold to speak and publish fearlessly the Word of God [acting with more freedom and indifference to the consequences]… (Philippians 1:14).

The words that consistently come out of our mouths should be "bold" words. We should speak the Word of God "fearlessly." The amplification of this passage of Scripture says that we should be "indifferent to the consequences." We must not focus on the circumstances we face.

Our faith in God *will* soar *if* this process is repeated throughout each day and night over a period of months and years. We will not be able to explain it, but deep down inside of ourselves we will "know that we know that we know" that all of the Scripture we have been meditating on is filled with the supernatural power of Almighty God. We will be absolutely certain that God's promises are *much more powerful* than *any* circumstances we will ever face.

Jesus is our example in every area. The disciples woke Jesus up when He was asleep in a boat and the disciples were afraid of a violent storm. Jesus *spoke to the storm.* "He said to them, Why are you timid and afraid, O you of little faith? Then He got up and rebuked the winds and the sea, and thee was a great and wonderful calm (a perfect peaceableness)" (Matthew 8:26).

Jesus *spoke* to the wind and the sea when He "rebuked the winds and the sea." If you have asked Jesus to be your Savior, the same Jesus Who calmed this violent storm more than two thousand years ago *lives in your heart today* (see Galatians 2:20). Jesus can and will quiet the storms in our lives today if our words consistently indicate our deep, unwavering and unshakable faith in Him.

Jesus showed the power of the spoken word when He spoke to a fig tree. "…when they had come away from Bethany, He was hungry. And seeing in the distance a fig tree [covered] with leaves, He went to see if He could find any [fruit] on it [for in the fig tree the fruit appears at the same time as the leaves]. But when He came up to it, He found nothing but leaves, for the fig season had not yet come. And He said to it, No one ever again shall eat fruit from you. And His disciples were listening [to what He said]" (Mark 11:12-14).

That tree was changed forever. "In the morning, when they were passing along, they noticed that the fig tree was withered [completely] away to its roots. And Peter remembered and said to Him, Master, look! The fig tree which You doomed has withered away!" (Mark 11:20-21).

Jesus replied to Peter with words that will absolutely transform your life *if* you can comprehend this great spiritual truth. "…Jesus, replying, said to them, Have faith in God [constantly]. Truly I tell you, whoever says to this mountain, Be lifted up and thrown into the sea! and does not doubt at all in his heart but believes that what he says will take place, it will be done for him" (Mark 11:22-23).

Jesus wants each of us to "have faith in God constantly." We will *boldly speak to* the "mountains" in our lives if we have constant faith in God. Our spoken words that are solidly anchored on the Word of God are *much more powerful* than any "mountains" we will face, no matter how powerful these mountains may seem to be.

We can and should speak words of faith to the problems we face. We should speak to these problems in the name of Jesus. We should have such absolute faith in God that the words of faith we speak will bring victory to the crisis.

We are following God's example when we speak words of faith to the mountains in our lives. God told Abraham that he would be the father of many nations. He said that Abraham would speak "…of the nonexistent things that [He has foretold and promised] as if they [already] existed" (Romans 4:17).

Abraham spoke the truth of the Word of God that had not yet happened, knowing that it would happen. We can follow this same principle in our lives today. By faith we can speak of "nonexistent" promises in the Word of God as if the manifestation of these promises already existed.

We will be calm and quiet within ourselves if we absolutely refuse to dwell on the circumstances we face and, instead, continually speak the Word of God. Some of God's children allow their emotions to control them in a crisis situation because they have not obeyed their Father's instructions to continually fill their minds, their hearts and their mouths with the supernatural power of His living Word. Our Father wants our hearts to be so filled with His Word that our emotions will stay in the peace of God.

Chapter 34

We Can Fight Spiritual Battles with Our Words

In the next three chapters we will learn how to use the words we speak to engage in spiritual warfare against Satan and his demons. We also will learn how to use our mouths to activate mighty angels to help us and to help other people.

Some Christians are not knowledgeable about biblical instructions pertaining to Satan. They know that Satan exists, but they have little or no understanding about walking in victory in spiritual warfare against Satan and his demons. We *cannot* be victorious in spiritual warfare if we attempt to use human weapons. "…though we walk (live) in the flesh, we are not carrying on our warfare according to the flesh and using mere human weapons. For the weapons of our warfare are not physical [weapons of flesh and blood], but they are mighty before God for the overthrow and destruction of strongholds" (II Corinthians 10:3-4).

The purpose of this chapter is not to give a detailed scriptural explanation of how to fight spiritual warfare. Instead, we will focus on what the Bible says about using our *mouths* the way our Father wants us to use them. We cannot use guns, knives and fists to win spiritual battles. *We fight spiritual battles with the words that come out of our mouths.*

We *will* walk in the victory that Jesus won over Satan if we continually speak faith-filled words that pour out of hearts that overflow with the Word of God. We will be victorious if we keep speaking these words of faith for as long as the situation requires. We will lose these battles if words of doubt, unbelief, discouragement, defeat and despair take over.

God has made spiritual ammunition available to us. We must know how to use this ammunition. Our words are spiritual bullets. Our words contain immense spiritual power. Most people are very careful if they are near a loaded rifle or pistol. Unfortunately, many Christians do not realize that being careless about what they say can be *much more dangerous* than a loaded weapon.

Armies keep an ample supply of ammunition stored up so that it will be available when needed. In the spiritual realm our *hearts* are the storehouse for our spiritual ammunition. We cannot consistently walk in victory over Satan and his demons unless our hearts are filled to overflowing with the supernatural power of the living Word of God.

The Bible often speaks about the spiritual "swords" our Father has provided for us to use in spiritual warfare. The Word of God is a spiritual *sword* that the Holy Spirit can and will use in us and through us to win spiritual battles. The Bible speaks of "…the sword that the Spirit wields, which is the Word of God" (Ephesians 6:17).

We must understand that the sword of the Spirit is "wielded" by the Holy Spirit, *not* by us. The Holy Spirit will bring to our remembrance whatever Scripture we need from the vast array of spiritual ammunition we should have stored in our hearts. When we face a crisis situation, we can trust the Holy Spirit to provide the words we speak according to how we have yielded to Him and according to the amount of spiritual ammunition we have stored up inside of ourselves.

We resist Satan when the Word of God that is stored inside us flows out of our mouths. Whenever Satan comes at us, we can use specific passages of Scripture that have been stored in our hearts to boldly stick Satan with these spiritual swords. Satan will flee from us every time if we resist him effectively. "…be subject to God. Resist the devil [stand firm against him], and he will flee from you" (James 4:7).

We are instructed to "be subject to God" when we resist the devil. We are subject to God when we have a close relationship with Him, when we are humble and teachable, when we believe wholeheartedly in His Word that is stored up in our hearts and when we faithfully obey His instructions. We are subject to God when we fight spiritual battles by boldly speaking His Word with deep and unwavering faith instead of trying to fight spiritual battles with our inadequate human abilities.

Satan will "flee from us" when we stay close to God. Satan will flee from us when we continually live with unwavering faith in God. Satan will flee from us when we do our very best to live our lives at all times in obedience to the instructions in the Word of God.

Jesus is our example and the source of supernatural power in every area of our lives. Jesus released His power against Satan through the words He spoke. Matthew 4:4, Matthew 4:7 and Matthew 4:10 explain how Jesus spoke three times to Satan when He was engaged in a battle with Satan in the wilderness. Each time Jesus used the words, "It is written." Jesus spoke the Word of God against Satan. He effectively utilized the sword of the Spirit.

Our Father has given us another spiritual sword to use against Satan. We come at Satan with a very powerful spiritual sword when we praise God continually in the face of adversity. "Let the high praises of God be in their throats and a two-edged sword in their hands" (Psalm 149:6).

Satan and his demons cannot defeat us if we continually praise God and worship Him and thank Him for Who He is, even when everything seems to be going wrong. We are not thanking God *for* the situation. We are thanking God *in* the situation. We must understand the immense power of praising the Lord in the face of adversity. Satan will flee if we persistently and consistently praise the Lord, especially when there does not seem to be any logical reason to praise Him and thank Him.

We now will look again at a passage of Scripture we have studied previously. This time we will emphasize what it says about the Word of God being a sword. "...the Word that God speaks is alive and full of power [making it active, operative, energizing and effective]; it is sharper than any two-edged sword..." (Hebrews 4:12).

When the Bible was written, soldiers used two-edged swords that were honed to razor sharpness. *Are you* continually making effective use of the supernaturally alive and powerful razor sharp spiritual "sword" God has provided for you to use against Satan? Satan is a defeated foe. He cannot win spiritual battles *if* we know how to fight these battles effectively.

I want to repeat what I said previously – some Christians live far below the level of victory that Jesus has provided. One of the primary reasons for this failure is that they have not filled their hearts with the supernatural power of the living Word of God. They do not consistently confess who they are in Christ Jesus.

In these last days before Jesus returns, we cannot afford to live below the level of victory He has provided for us. We can talk ourselves into victory or we can talk ourselves into defeat. We have been given the ability to use our words to bring the victory of Jesus Christ into our lives. We can waste our God-given ability to choose the words we speak by allowing words to come out of our mouths that nullify the victory of Jesus.

When we are in a crisis situation, we all make the choice of whether we will say what Satan wants us to say or what God wants us to say. If our hearts are filled with God's Word, we will not allow ourselves to be defeated by fear, worry, apprehension, doubt or unbelief. We will not speak words that give spiritual leverage to Satan and his demons they cannot obtain in any other way. Our words will line up with God's Word. We will walk in the victory Jesus won for us regardless of the seeming severity of the problems we face.

We must be absolutely certain that the all-conquering, all-powerful Jesus Christ lives in our hearts. Jesus knows no limitations except any limitations *we set*. We limit Jesus when our words and our actions in a crisis situation clearly indicate that we do not trust Him. We have learned that we can block the mighty power of Jesus if we speak words of doubt, fear, worry and discouragement.

Satan is *not* omnipresent, omniscient or omnipotent. He can only be in one place at a time. God is omnipresent. He is everywhere at the same time. God also is omniscient – He knows all things. Satan only knows what we tell him or his demons. He cannot read our minds. Satan's demons *listen carefully* to what we say in order to learn everything they can about us.

Satan and his fallen angels and the Holy Spirit and God's angels are engaged in a continual battle for our minds, our hearts and our mouths. This battle will intensify in the last days before Jesus returns. Christians absolutely must learn how to walk in the victory that Jesus has won for us.

The last thing Satan's demons want to hear from us is words coming out of our mouths telling them with absolute certainty that we know the victorious Jesus lives in our hearts. Satan's demons cringe when they hear these great spiritual truths spoken with unwavering faith. They know they cannot deceive Christians whose minds and hearts are filled with the Word of God. They know they cannot defeat Christians who continually speak words of faith out of hearts that are filled to overflowing with the supernatural power of God's Word.

This chapter tells us how to use our words to walk in victory over Satan. We have found so many scriptural facts on this subject that they could not be contained in one chapter. The next chapter will give you additional encouraging information from the Word of God about walking in victory over Satan and his demons.

Chapter 35

Attack Satan with Bold and Unwavering Faith in God

Jesus won a total, complete and absolute victory over Satan. Satan and his demons do everything they can to keep us from walking in the victory Jesus won for us. Jesus said, "The thief comes only in order to steal and kill and destroy. I came that they may have and enjoy life, and have it in abundance (to the full, till it overflows" (John 10:10).

Satan is a "thief." The only way he can have his way with Christians is to attempt to "steal" the victory Jesus won for us at Calvary. Satan's goal is to "kill and destroy" us. We can be certain that Satan and his demons will turn up the pressure to do everything they can to steal from us, kill us and destroy us in these last days before Jesus returns.

We do *not* have to give in to the influence of Satan and his demons. By faith we *can* walk in the victory Jesus won for us. We can "enjoy life in abundance to the full until it overflows." Once again, this promise from Jesus does *not* have an asterisk saying that it is null and void during the last days before He returns.

We can and should walk in the victory Jesus won for us right up until the time He comes for us. Satan cannot get at us if we continually speak the Word of God boldly with unwavering faith in God. "...by the word of Your lips I have avoided the ways of the violent (the paths of the destroyer)" (Psalm 17:4).

Satan is the "destroyer." We have just seen that he wants to kill us and destroy us. He will *not* be able to destroy us if we constantly speak the Word of God with faith. We have seen that Satan wants to steal from us. The only way that Satan and his demons can steal from us is if our words and actions show that we do not have unwavering and unshakable faith in the total, complete and absolute victory Jesus has given to us.

Satan's demons want us to meditate continually on the problems we face and on the thoughts they try to put into our minds. Our Father wants us to meditate continually on His Word. We will clearly indicate what we have been meditating on by the words we speak when we face adversity.

We have been "redeemed" by Jesus Christ. Jesus has "delivered" us from Satan's ability to influence us. We should open our mouths to continually speak this great spiritual truth. "Let the redeemed of the Lord say so, whom He has delivered from the hand of the adversary" (Psalm 107:2).

Do you know the primary reason why Jesus came to earth? Jesus came to earth to *destroy* the works of Satan. "...The reason the Son of God was made manifest (visible) was to undo (destroy, loosen, and dissolve) the works the devil [has done]" (I John 3:8).

Satan and his demons know they are in big trouble if our words are in constant agreement with the Word of God. Satan and his demons know they cannot influence us to be worried, fearful or discouraged unless they somehow can influence us to stop these words of faith from pouring out of our mouths.

Too many Christians are saying what the devil wants them to say instead of constantly saying what God says. Too many Christians are repeating the thoughts that Satan's demons whisper into their ears instead of rejecting these thoughts and boldly speaking the Word of God instead.

We may not realize it but, in the spiritual realm, we actually invite Satan to influence us when we speak this way. We essentially are answering Satan's knock on the door of our lives by saying, "Come right in, Satan. Make yourself at home." None of us would think of openly inviting Satan into our lives, but this is exactly what some Christians do when they fail to renew their minds in God's Word each day and to meditate on the holy Scriptures throughout the day and night.

When we face a severe crisis, Satan's demons will hammer away at us trying to discourage us so we will give up and quit. They apply immense pressure to us when we face adversity. Satan's demons often try to fire a barrage of "What if?" questions into our minds in an attempt to discourage us.

Satan's demons want to influence us to worry about the future. They say things like, "What if this happens? What if that happens? What if the other thing happens?" Jesus does *not* want us to worry about the future. He wants us to live our lives one day at a time, trusting completely in Him to bring us through each day. Jesus said, "…do not worry or be anxious about tomorrow, for tomorrow will have worries and anxieties of its own. Sufficient for each day is its own trouble" (Matthew 6:34).

We must not allow Satan to put us on the defensive. Jesus has given us *everything we need* to stay on the offensive and to walk in victory over Satan and his demons. We do *not* have to allow Satan and his demons to hammer away at us. We can *hammer away at them* when the Word of God continually flows out of our mouths (see Jeremiah 23:29).

How have you been reacting to the crises you face? How much attacking are you doing? Are you often on the defensive? Do you boldly take the offensive? Do you continually open your mouth to speak faith-filled words in response to the thoughts that Satan's demons attempt to put into your mind?

Some Christians have a pity party when they face severe adversity. They grumble, gripe and complain. We play right into Satan's hands if we consistently speak words that deny God's Word. We block the mighty power of the Holy Spirit and the power of God's legions of angels from being released on our behalf if we speak words that deny the Word of God.

One of the most important times to yield to the Holy Spirit is when God does not seem to be answering our prayers. Satan's demons will try to get into our heads when nothing seems to be happening. They will tell us that God has forgotten us. They will tell us that God's promises are not working for us.

We must persevere in faith. We must not give up. We have seen that all of God's promises are *completely reliable*. Our Father does *not* tell us *when* He will give us manifestation of His promises. We must persevere in faith, no matter how long it takes. We must not let our words show Satan's demons that our faith is wavering in any way.

No matter what we face or how difficult the problems might seem, we can be certain that Jesus has given us a tremendous victory over those circumstances. "...amid all these things we are more than conquerors and gain a surpassing victory through Him Who loved us" (Romans 8:37).

The words "all these things" refer to the suffering, affliction, tribulation, calamity, distress, persecution, hunger, destitution and peril the apostle Paul spoke of in Romans 8:35. We are not just conquerors over the problems we face. Please highlight or underline the words "more than." Please highlight or underline the words "surpassing victory." Jesus has given us a victory that *surpasses any other victory* that ever has been won.

Jesus shed His precious blood on a cross at Calvary to give us this great victory. Our words in a crisis situation should always prove to Satan and his demons that we are absolutely certain we walk in victory over them. "...they have overcome (conquered) him by means of the blood of the Lamb and by the utterance of their testimony..." (Revelation 12:11).

The protection of the blood of Jesus provides a marvelous spiritual covering for every child of God. We will walk in victory and overcome Satan and his demons every time if our "testimony" consistently speaks of the protection we have been given by "the blood of the Lamb."

The last two chapters are filled with encouraging *facts* from the Word of God that tell us exactly how to walk in victory when we are engaged in spiritual warfare. In the next chapter we will look into the Word of God to learn many interesting facts about God's angels. They help us, protect us, minister to us and continually assist us in direct proportion to our words of faith.

Chapter 36

Angels are Activated by the Word of God

Some people have a misconception about angels. God's angels are not anything like the angels who often have been portrayed as little babies who hold a small bow and arrow. God's angels are awesome, mighty and powerful. II Kings 19:35 tells us that 185,000 people were slain by *one angel*.

I believe that God's angels have protected each of us many times when we were not aware of their protection. Our Father has provided angels to minister to each of His beloved children. "Are not the angels all ministering spirits (servants) sent out in the service [of God for the assistance] of those who are to inherit salvation?" (Hebrews 1:14).

This passage of Scripture says that these angels minister to, serve and assist "those who are to inherit salvation." Each person who has asked Jesus to be his or her Savior has inherited salvation. We inherit salvation if we believe in our hearts and confess with our mouths that we are sinners, if we repent of our sins, if we believe that Jesus has paid the full price for all of our sins and if we confess these truths we believe in our hearts with our mouths. If Jesus is your Savior, you can be certain that angels are in the atmosphere around you to minister to, serve and assist *you*.

Many people have become interested in angels in recent years. Many unbelievers are preoccupied with angels. Several books, newspaper articles, magazine articles and television programs have been devoted to angels. A great deal of what these people believe about angels does *not* line up with the Word of God. Angels follow God's directions. We can activate the power of these magnificent angels. This chapter will tell you how to activate these angels.

When Jesus was born in Bethlehem, an angel appeared at night before shepherds in a field. This angel suddenly was surrounded by many other angels. All of these angels praised God. "…suddenly there appeared with the angel an army of the troops of heaven (a heavenly knighthood), praising God and saying, Glory to God in the highest [heaven], and on earth peace among men with whom He is well pleased [men of goodwill, of His favor]" (Luke 2:13-14).

We should praise God at all times, regardless of the circumstances we face. Angels in the atmosphere around us pay careful attention to all of the words we speak to see if our words line up with God's Word. "…you His angels, you mighty ones who do His commandments, hearkening to the voice of His word" (Psalm 103:20).

This passage of Scripture emphasizes the great power of angels by referring to them as "mighty ones." These powerful angels "hearken" to the Word of God. The Hebrew word "shama" that is translated as "hearken" in this passage of Scripture means that angels listen carefully and take action on the spoken Word of God.

God's angels always are ready to do whatever God commands. Multitudes of mighty and powerful angels respond immediately whenever God speaks. "…the Lord utters His voice before His army, for His host is very great, and [they are] strong and powerful who execute [God's] word…" (Joel 2:11).

Christians can activate angels by speaking words that are consistent with the promises and instructions in God's Word. We can see that human beings can activate angels by the following words an angel spoke to the prophet Daniel. "…he said to me, Fear not, Daniel, for from the first day that you set your mind and heart to understand and to humble yourself before your God, your words were heard, and I have come as a consequence of [and in response to] your words" (Daniel 10:12).

We can block God's angels from helping us when we speak critical or angry words or when we gossip about other people. We can block God's angels when we grumble, gripe and complain and whenever we speak other words that do not line up with the Word of God.

We must not block God's mighty angels from working on our behalf. The Word of God tells us what we should do to activate the power of angels. "The Angel of the Lord encamps around those who fear Him [who revere and worship Him with awe] and each of them He delivers" (Psalm 34:7).

The amplification of this passage of Scripture describes fearing the Lord as "revering and worshipping Him with awe." When we fear the Lord, every aspect of our lives revolves around Him. We worship Him constantly. We study and meditate on His Word continually. We pray throughout the day and night. We spend precious quiet time each day fellowshipping with Him. "The Angel of the Lord encamps around us" when we do these things consistently.

The protection we read about in Psalm 34:7 is beautifully explained in the magnificent 91st Psalm that explains much more about the protection our Father has provided for us. "A thousand may fall at your side, and ten thousand at your right hand, but it shall not come near you" (Psalm 91:7).

Many testimonies have been given by people who were protected during warfare by their faith in God as they prayed Psalm 91. This promise will be vitally important in the difficult times that lie ahead of us. This passage of Scripture indicates that many people around us will fall, but *we can be protected.*

How does God determine who will receive this special protection? The Christians who will be protected are those of us who will *enter by faith* into a marvelous refuge that God has provided for us if we trust Him completely. "Only a spectator shall you be [yourself inaccessible in the secret place of the Most High] as you witness the reward of the wicked. Because you have made the Lord your refuge, and the Most High your dwelling place, there shall no evil befall you, nor any plague or calamity come near your tent" (Psalm 91:8-10).

This wonderful refuge that God has provided is referred to as "the secret place" because few people seek God earnestly enough to find it. This chapter is not intended to be a thorough explanation of the 91st Psalm. We hope to write an entire book on this subject in the future, but we are focusing on angels in this chapter. Psalm 91:1 says that we "remain stable and fixed under the shadow of the Almighty." When we are in God's presence, we are in His "shadow."

We *can* turn away from every circumstance in the world and cling to God in the secret place of the Most High. God keeps us safe. We begin to live more in the realm of God and turn from the realm of the world. We think clearly and we are wise in every situation because God is directing us. We will be "spectators" rather than victims of what will happen in the difficult days that lie ahead of us.

The amplification of Psalm 91:8 says that believers who are in the secret place of the Most High are "inaccessible." Satan and his demons and the difficult problems in the world will not be able to pull us down. "No evil" will be able to overcome us. No "plague or calamity" can come close to us.

God's angels are given the special assignment of protecting us when we live our lives in the secret place of the Most High. "...He will give His angels [especial] charge over you to accompany and defend and preserve you in all your ways [of obedience and service]. They shall bear you up on their hands, lest you dash your foot against a stone" (Psalm 91:11-12).

This passage of Scripture is extremely important to each of us during these final days before Jesus returns. God's angels will "accompany, defend and preserve" us in "all of our ways" *if* we seek God with every fiber of our being. Every aspect of our lives should revolve around a deep and sincere desire to obey God and to serve Him. This information ties together with Psalm 34:7 where we learned that God's Angel will "encamp" around us when we fear Him and revere Him.

Our loving Father has made full provision to protect each of His children. This chapter contains wonderful promises of angelic protection. These angels work on our behalf when we continually speak the Word of God with faith.

Angels helped Jesus after He completed forty very difficult days resisting Satan in the wilderness. Jesus refused to give in to the temptations of Satan. We have seen that Jesus *boldly spoke the Word of God* to Satan in the wilderness. Satan finally gave up and left. Angels ministered to Jesus at the end of this ordeal. "...the devil departed from Him, and behold, angels came and ministered to Him" (Matthew 4:11).

Angels are available to minister to *you* right now. Our Father wants us to constantly be aware of the supernatural protection He has provided for us from His angels. He wants us to constantly be aware of the relationship between our words and the protection and assistance we will receive from angels through the spoken Word of God.

We can negate God's provision for assistance from powerful angels by failing to continually worship God, praise God and boldly speak God's Word with deep and unwavering faith. No Christian should miss out on the protection from angels that our loving Father has provided for us.

Chapter 37

We Can Yield Our Tongues to the Holy Spirit

We have seen that we fight spiritual battles with our tongues. We have learned how to use our tongues to activate angels. In this chapter we will look into the Word of God to learn about the relationship between the Holy Spirit Who lives in the heart of every Christian and the words that come out of our mouths.

In these last days before Jesus returns, we often will find ourselves faced with difficult predicaments where we absolutely must receive guidance from the Holy Spirit. Jesus told His disciples about "…the Spirit of Truth, Whom the world cannot receive (welcome, take to its heart), because it does not see Him or know and recognize Him. But you know and recognize Him, for He lives with you [constantly] and will be in you" (John 14:17).

This great spiritual truth applies to us today. Unbelievers cannot experience the indwelling presence of the Holy Spirit. All Christians can enjoy a close and intimate relationship with the Holy Spirit. Please highlight or underline the word "you" in this passage of Scripture. If you have asked Jesus to be your

Savior, you can be certain that the Holy Spirit lives in *your heart*. He "lives with *you* constantly." He is "in *you*."

We must not make the mistake of living the way the world lives. We should have *so much faith* in God that we gladly will yield control of our lives to the Holy Spirit. "…you are not living the life of the flesh, you are living the life of the Spirit, if the [Holy] Spirit of God [really] dwells within you [directs and controls you]…" (Romans 8:9).

We make a tremendous mistake if we try to control our own lives. We will *not* have the answers we need for any of the difficult circumstances we will face in the end times. The Holy Spirit knows how to solve every problem. He can and will guide us *if* we trust Him so much that we truly do allow Him to "direct and control" our lives.

As we grow and mature as Christians, we should understand how inadequate we are. We should continually yield more control of our lives to the Holy Spirit. We should be enthusiastic about the magnificent opportunity we have been given to constantly receive guidance from the Holy Spirit. "…walk and live [habitually] in the [Holy] Spirit [responsive to and controlled and guided by the Spirit]…" (Galatians 5:16).

The amplification of this passage of Scripture uses the word "habitually." This word indicates that the Holy Spirit's control of our lives should be *constant*, not occasional. We should have such a close relationship with the Holy Spirit that we are continually "responsive to" Him.

We should constantly speak of our confidence in the mighty Holy Spirit. Throughout every day of our lives, our words should give clear evidence of our continual consciousness of the indwelling presence of the Holy Spirit. We should never be afraid of anything because we *know* that the mighty Holy Spirit is *with us* during every minute of every hour of every day of our lives.

If we yield control of our lives to the Holy Spirit, we obviously must yield control of our tongues to Him. He will speak through us on many occasions if we yield control of our tongues to Him with absolute faith.

Since these chapters are focused on the words we speak, the remainder of this chapter will focus on what the Bible says about God speaking through us. We see an excellent example of God speaking through humans in the life of Moses. Moses was a great man of God, but he knew that he was not eloquent. "…Moses said to the Lord, O Lord, I am not eloquent or a man of words, neither before nor since You have spoken to Your servant; for I am slow of speech and have a heavy and awkward tongue" (Exodus 4:10).

The Lord encouraged Moses. He told Moses that he would *not* have to depend on his human ability to speak. He said, "…go, and I will be with your mouth and will teach you what you shall say" (Exodus 4:12).

If we trust God completely, the Holy Spirit will do for us what God did for Moses. Our hearts will sing with joy if we completely trust the Holy Spirit to speak in us and through us. We will be very grateful for the continual guidance of the Holy Spirit whenever we hear ourselves saying things that we *know* did not come from us.

We will receive tremendous satisfaction and fulfillment when God gives us exactly the right words for a particular occasion and we know that these words came *through* us and not from us. We *can* trust God to give us the words we need to speak when we need to speak them. "The plans of the mind and orderly thinking belong to man, but from the Lord comes the [wise] answer of the tongue" (Proverbs 16:1).

Our Father does not want our lives to be guided by the logical and intellectual "orderly thinking" of the world. He wants us to have absolute faith that He will give us the "wise answer" we need just when we need it.

The psalmist David experienced God speaking through him on many occasions. David knew that God would speak in him and through him. "…the sweet psalmist of Israel, says, The Spirit of the Lord spoke in and by me, and His word was upon my tongue" (II Samuel 23:1-2).

We should *not* worry about our ability to speak the right words in a crisis situation. Jesus told His disciples that they would face powerful men who were opposed to God. Jesus told His disciples that they should not have any concern whatsoever about what to say. He said, "…when they deliver you up, do not be anxious about how or what you are to speak; for what you are to say will be given you in that very hour and moment, for it is not you who are speaking, but the Spirit of your Father speaking through you" (Matthew 10:19-20).

These powerful words apply to each of us today. We must "*not* be anxious about how or what we will speak." When our human ability seems completely inadequate, we should have complete confidence that the Spirit of God can and will speak through us. We should open our mouths with absolute faith that He will give us the words we have to have at "that very hour and moment."

I cannot tell you anything that is more exhilarating to me than to hear the Holy Spirit continually speaking through me. On thousands of occasions in my life I have marveled at what I hear myself saying. I know beyond the slightest shadow of a doubt that I am not the one who is speaking these words. I know that I do not have the ability to speak the words I often hear coming out of my mouth. I have learned over the years to trust completely in the Holy Spirit to speak through me.

On many occasions I have found myself in a position where I could not possibly say the words that must be said because of the limitations of my human intellect and understanding. As my faith in the Holy Spirit speaking through me has grown over many years, I have opened my mouth continually with complete trust that the Holy Spirit will fill it. He has never failed me. Yielding to the Holy Spirit is like a muscle that needs to be exercised – the more we use it, the stronger it becomes.

We must get ourselves out of the way. We were *not* meant to control our own lives. *Why* would any of us want to control our lives when the Holy Spirit lives within us? Why would we ever think we can speak the words that must be spoken in a crisis situation when the Holy Spirit promises to speak to us, in us and through us according to our surrender to God and our faith in Him?

Jesus told His disciples that they did not have to figure everything out before they opened their mouths to speak. Jesus said, "Resolve and settle it in your minds not to meditate and prepare beforehand how you are to make your defense and how you will answer. For I [Myself] will give you a mouth and such utterance and wisdom that all of your foes combined will be unable to stand against or refute" (Luke 21:14-15).

In this case Jesus was talking about His disciples defending themselves before government authorities. The words Jesus spoke here came shortly after the words He spoke about the last days in Luke 21:9-11 that we studied previously. Jesus lives inside of every Christian (see Galatians 2:20, Ephesians 3:17 and I John 3:24). When we face difficult problems during the end times, we can and should believe that He will give us such wisdom that no one will be able to dispute the words we speak.

The Holy Spirit is *not* pleased when we speak words that are not yielded to Him and do not line up with the Word of God. "Let no foul or polluting language, nor evil word nor unwholesome or worthless talk [ever] come out of your mouth, but only such [speech] as is good and beneficial to the spiritual progress of others, as is fitting to the need and the occasion, that it may be a blessing and give grace (God's favor) to those who hear it. And do not grieve the Holy Spirit of God [do not offend or vex or sadden Him]..." (Ephesians 4:29-30).

People who speak profanity are not controlled by the Holy Spirit. People who constantly speak trite and superficial words that have no eternal significance have not yielded control of their mouths to the Holy Spirit. Our words *will* be "good and beneficial to the spiritual progress of others" *if* the Holy Spirit truly is in control of our lives.

We will never speak unloving words toward other people if we truly do yield control of the words we speak to the Holy Spirit. The Holy Spirit wants us to lift others up, not cut them down. We "grieve the Holy Spirit" when "evil words" come out of our mouths.

Please review this chapter and carefully highlight or underline key passages of Scripture if you have not already done so. Meditate on them many times until they come alive inside of you. Open your mouth continually with absolute faith that the Holy Spirit can and will give *you* the words you will have to have when you need them.

Chapter 38

Final Instructions on the Words We Speak

In this final chapter pertaining to the words we speak we will learn many *basic* scriptural fundamentals. We saved these basic facts until last because we wanted you to have a deep and strong desire to improve your speech. This chapter will give you many facts that you will need *if* you now are highly motivated to improve the spiritual quality of the words you speak.

The psalmist understood the importance of carefully guarding the words he spoke. David prayed asking for God's help in this area. He said, "Set a guard, O Lord, before my mouth; keep watch at the door of my lips" (Psalm 141:3).

We should pray as David prayed whenever we are having a hard time controlling the words we speak. We should ask the Lord to help us to surrender to the Holy Spirit.

The Word of God repeatedly tells us that our words can bring us great blessings. Our words also can cause significant problems. "A good man eats good from the fruit of his mouth, but the desire of the treacherous is for violence. He who guards his mouth keeps his life, but he who opens wide his lips comes to ruin" (Proverbs 13:2-3).

Unbelievers often speak violent words because Jesus is not their Savior and their hearts are not filled with the Word of God. These words can cause these people to "come to ruin." We will live the way our Father wants us to live if we treat our words with the caution they deserve. "…he who restrains his lips is prudent" (Proverbs 10:19).

Some people speak without thinking. They will pay a significant price if they continue to knowingly or unknowingly disobey God's instructions in this area. "Do you see a man who is hasty in his words? There is more hope for a [self-confident] fool than for him" (Proverbs 29:20).

Some Christians talk when they should be listening. Our Father wants us to be good listeners. "…Let every man be quick to hear [a ready listener], slow to speak…" (James 1:19).

Our Father does not want us to use the His gift of speech to allow sinful words to come out of our mouths. "Let there be no filthiness (obscenity, indecency) nor foolish and sinful (silly and corrupt) talk, nor coarse jesting, which are not fitting or becoming; but instead voice your thankfulness [to God]" (Ephesians 5:4).

God is displeased if we speak "filthy, obscene and indecent words." Our Father also does not want us to speak "foolish, sinful, silly and corrupt" words. We should not be "coarse jesters." We should continually thank God and praise Him.

God gave us the ability to speak for a specific purpose. We should not waste this precious gift by speaking "empty" words that have no spiritual significance. "…avoid all empty (vain, useless, idle) talk, for it will lead people into more and more ungodliness" (II Timothy 2:16).

The amplification of this passage of Scripture warns us against speaking "vain, useless and idle" words that are not of

God. If we don't have anything important to say, we shouldn't say anything. "He who has knowledge spares his words, and a man of understanding has a cool spirit. Even a fool when he holds his peace is considered wise; when he closes his lips he is esteemed a man of understanding" (Proverbs 17:27-28).

We do not have to comment on everything that takes place. Mature Christians often close their mouths. Even immature people often will look wise and mature if they keep quiet instead of opening their mouths to reveal their immaturity.

We can learn from the example of Jesus. The prophet Isaiah prophesied that Jesus would not open His mouth to complain about the affliction He faced. "He was oppressed, [yet when] He was afflicted, He was submissive and opened not His mouth; like a lamb that is led to the slaughter, and as a sheep before her shearers is dumb, so He opened not His mouth" (Isaiah 53:7).

We have seen that God uses repetition for the purpose of emphasis. We are told twice in this one verse of Scripture that Jesus "opened not His mouth." In the book of Acts we see the fulfillment of Isaiah's prophesy pertaining to Jesus. "...Like a sheep He was led to the slaughter, and as a lamb before its shearer is dumb, so He opens not His mouth" (Acts 8:32).

Jesus repeatedly gave us the example of saying nothing. When Jesus was captured after Judas betrayed Him, He was taken to a hastily assembled meeting of the Sanhedrin which was the Jewish supreme court. The leaders of the Sanhedrin tried to find people to give false testimony against Jesus so they could give Him the death penalty as a result of this untruthful testimony.

Jesus said nothing when these men spoke against Him. "...the high priest stood up and said, Have You no answer to make? What about this that these men testify against You? But Jesus kept silent…" (Matthew 26:62-63).

The Jewish leaders then brought Jesus before the Roman governor, Pontius Pilate. Instead of responding to their false charges, Jesus again said nothing. "…when the charges were made against Him by the chief priests and elders, He made no answer" (Matthew 27:12).

Jesus kept His mouth closed when Pilate questioned Him. "…Pilate said to Him, Do You not hear how many and how serious are the things they are testifying against You? But He made no reply to him, not even to a single accusation, so that the governor marveled greatly" (Matthew 27:13-14).

When Pilate found out that Jesus was a Galilean, he sent Jesus to King Herod who had jurisdiction over Galilee. When King Herod tried to get Him to speak, Jesus again said nothing. "…when Herod saw Jesus, he was exceedingly glad, for he had eagerly desired to see Him for a long time because of what he had heard concerning Him, and he was hoping to witness some sign (some striking evidence or spectacular performance) done by Him. So he asked Him many questions, but He made no reply" (Luke 23:8-9).

Jesus did not speak on each of these occasions because He knew His Father did not want Him to speak. Sometimes we should do the same thing. Other times we should say only a few words. "Be not rash with your mouth, and let not your heart be hasty to utter a word before God. For God is in heaven, and you are on earth; therefore let your words be few. For a dream comes with much business and painful effort, and a fool's voice with many words" (Ecclesiastes 5:2-3).

Many foolish people talk and talk and talk. Mature Christians often restrain their words. When they speak, their words are meaningful. We have learned that we should yield our voices to the Holy Spirit. If we consistently yield our voices to the Holy Spirit, we can be sure the words that come out of our mouths will be words that God wants us to speak.

Ecclesiastes 5:2 tells us that we should "not be rash with our mouths." We should measure our words carefully. Christians who understand that words release spiritual power are always conscious that their words should line up with God's Word. If the Holy Spirit truly does control our words, we often will say less but these words will be much more significant and powerful than any words we could speak from our limited human understanding.

In the last chapter we learned that we grieve the Holy Spirit when we speak words He does not want us to speak. Gossip is one of the worst things we can do. People who gossip always end up hurting themselves. "The words of a whisperer or tale-bearer are as dainty morsels; they go down into the innermost parts of the body" (Proverbs 18:8).

We can hurt people badly with the words we speak. The Bible tells us that Job went through a great deal of suffering. On one occasion Job said to one of his accusers, "How long will you vex and torment me and break me in pieces with words?" (Job 19:2).

We must understand how badly we can hurt other human beings with the words we speak. We can inflict great pain and suffering. Job said that the words his accusers spoke "broke him into pieces."

Jesus warned us against judging and criticizing others. He said, "Do not judge and criticize and condemn others, so that you may not be judged and criticized and condemned yourselves. For just as you judge and criticize and condemn others, you will be judged and criticized and condemned, and in accordance with the measure you [use to] deal out to others, it will be dealt out again to you" (Matthew 7:1-2).

We will pay a severe penalty if we disobey these instructions from God. If we judge others, we sow spiritual seeds that will hurt us. "…be done with every trace of wickedness (depravity, malignity) and all deceit and insincerity (pretense, hypocrisy) and grudges (envy, jealousy) and slander and evil speaking of every kind" (I Peter 2:1).

Our Father also does not want us to complain about anything. The Israelites constantly grumbled and complained when they were in the wilderness. "…the people grumbled and deplored their hardships, which was evil in the ears of the Lord…" (Numbers 11:1).

The Israelites spent forty years in the wilderness on a journey to the Promised Land that should have taken only *eleven days*. One of the reasons they went through this prolonged ordeal was because they continually griped, grumbled, groaned and complained. They refused to obey God's instructions to live by faith.

We must not make this mistake today. Instead of complaining, we should focus constantly on God, on His indwelling presence and on His supernatural living Word. We will not complain if our hearts are filled with God's Word. We will speak the words God wants us to speak.

God can change any situation. God's presence and wisdom will prevail if we live in the Spirit. When we complain we actually speak words that "complain against God." "Do all things without grumbling and faultfinding and complaining [against God]…" (Philippians 2:14).

When I realize that I have spoken words that are displeasing to God, I repent and ask God to forgive me and to give me a fresh start. Our Father *will* forgive us whenever we humbly admit our sins, repent of these sins and ask for His forgiveness. "If we [freely] admit that we have sinned and confess our sins, He is faithful and just (true to His own nature and promises) and will forgive our sins [dismiss our lawlessness] and [continuously] cleanse us from all unrighteousness [everything not in conformity to His will in purpose, thought, and action]" (I John 1:9).

None of us will ever be perfect in regard to the words we speak. Sometimes we will fail to say what the Holy Spirit would have us say. Some people are unaware of how often they grieve God by the words they speak. We hope these chapters will give you the spiritual awareness you need so that you will realize when you have said what God does not want you to say and repent and ask your Father to forgive you.

We have seen that God will give us a clean slate if we repent and humbly ask His forgiveness. When God forgives, He also forgets. He will treat the words we ask forgiveness for as if they had not been spoken. "…their sins and their lawbreaking I will remember no more" (Hebrews 10:17).

Instead of speaking against others, we should use our God-given privilege of speaking to speak words that will "encourage" other people and lift them up. "…encourage (admonish, exhort) one another and edify (strengthen and build up) one another…" (I Thessalonians 5:11).

The biggest problem that some of us have is right under our nose. We must understand that we never will rise above the quality of the words we speak. You can make a significant change in the quality of your life if you will carefully study and meditate on the scriptural instructions contained in the past ven chapters. "The lips of the [uncompromisingly] righteous know [and therefore utter] what is acceptable…" (Proverbs 10:32).

Every person on earth lives with the consequences of all of the words he or she has spoken. We each can determine a great deal about the quality of our lives in the future by the words we speak from this day forward.

Our words are spiritual seeds. Most people sow *thousands* of seeds each day by the words they speak. God's laws of sowing and reaping tell us that we will reap whatever we continually sow. "…whatever a man sows, that and that only is what he will reap" (Galatians 6:7).

Farmers understand the power of seeds. They pay their bills and feed their families by choosing specific seeds and carefully cultivating these seeds to bring them to the best possible harvest. Farmers are careful about the seeds they buy. They are careful where they store these seeds and how they plant these seeds. We should be *even more careful* about the spiritual seeds we plant with our mouths. The continual flow of the words we speak ultimately will determine the harvest that will be produced in our lives.

Our faith in God will be reflected by the words we speak. We express our faith in God by our words and by our actions. Now that we have thoroughly studied the importance of the words we speak, we are ready to look carefully into the Word of God to learn how we can show our faith in God *by our actions.*

Chapter 39

The Importance of Obedience

We have seen that our Father wants His Word to enter continually into our eyes and our ears. We have learned how to fill our minds with God's Word, what to do to cause God's Word to drop from our minds down into our hearts and how we should speak the Word of God continually. Our Father tells us exactly what He wants us to do *after* we fill our minds, our hearts and our mouths with His Word. "...the word is very near you, in your mouth and in your mind and in your heart, so that you can do it" (Deuteronomy 30:14).

Our Father wants us to *do* what His Word instructs us to do. We have seen that Joshua 1:8 says that we will prosper, that we will be wise and that we will be successful *if* we meditate throughout the day and night on the Word of God and *if* we speak the Word of God continually. The third instruction for us in Joshua 1:8 is to "*observe* and *do* according to *all* that is written" in the Word of God.

In this chapter we will briefly study the subject of obedience to the instructions we have been given in the Bible. We will look at this subject from the perspective of the importance that obedience will be to each of us in these last days before Jesus returns.

Obedience is a very comprehensive topic. An entire book could be written on this subject. Because this book is about increasing our *faith* in God, we will devote only this chapter to a general study of obedience to God. We then will devote four additional chapters to a careful study of scriptural instructions pertaining to *doing* what the Word of God tells us to do by *stepping out in faith* on the promises our Father has given us.

The highest and best quality of life is the result of fearing God and obeying His instructions. "Blessed (happy, fortunate, to be envied) is everyone who fears, reveres, and worships the Lord, who walks in His ways and lives according to His commandments" (Psalm 128:1).

We should fear the Lord, revere the Lord, worship the Lord and obey His instructions. Obedience to God's instructions will be especially important during these final days before Jesus returns. If we continually fill our minds and our hearts with the Word of God, the scriptural facts that we learn will become embedded in our minds and our hearts. We will program ourselves to do exactly what our Father has instructed us to do.

God gave each of us a conscience when He created us. A definite relationship exists between a clear conscience and deep, strong, unwavering and unshakable faith in God. "…if our consciences (our hearts) do not accuse us [if they do not make us feel guilty and condemn us], we have confidence (complete assurance and boldness) before God. And we receive from Him whatever we ask, because we [watchfully] obey His orders [observe His suggestions and injunctions, follow His plan for us] and [habitually] practice what is pleasing to Him" (I John 3:21-22).

The amplification of this passage of Scripture explains that our conscience is in our hearts. God gave us a conscience to reveal to us anything we are thinking, saying or doing that is harmful to us. Our Father does not want our hearts to "accuse us and make us feel guilty."

Our faith in God will be much more effective if we have a clear conscience. This passage of Scripture says that we will "receive from God whatever we ask because we watchfully obey His orders." Once again, we can see the relationship between obeying our Father's instructions and receiving manifestation of His promises.

When we learn to listen to God, learn His Word and do what He instructs us to do, the result is a life that is above and beyond what we ever imagined possible. We set in motion God's plan and God's principles. They result in excellence.

Our Father promises to bless us if we live our lives in obedience to His Word. He will send blessings to "overtake" His children who consistently obey His instructions. "…all these blessings shall come upon you and overtake you if you heed the voice of the Lord your God" (Deuteronomy 28:2).

We now are ready to look into the Word of God to learn the relationship between righteousness and freedom from fear. We become righteous before God when we are saved. We live a righteous life by doing our very best to live according to the instructions in the Word of God and by yielding control of our lives to the guidance of the Holy Spirit. "You shall establish yourself in righteousness (rightness, in conformity with God's will and order): you shall be far from even the thought of oppression or destruction, for you shall not fear, and from terror, for it shall not come near you" (Isaiah 54:14).

This passage of Scripture says that we should "establish ourselves in righteousness." The Hebrew word "kuwn" that is translated as "establish" means "to be erect, to apply, to render sure, certainty, firmness, perfection and stability." We *will* "be far from even the thought of oppression or destruction" *if* we are established and if we live the way our Father has instructed us to live. We will *not* be afraid. Terror cannot enter hearts that are deeply rooted in God.

Isn't the last part of this passage of Scripture interesting? Do you see how it applies to the destruction and terrorism the world is facing now and will continue to face until Jesus comes for us? This passage of Scripture explains the relationship between living a righteous life and not being pulled down by oppression, fear and terror.

Unbelievers and children of God who do not obey God and are not under His covering may live in a state of panic during the end times. God's children who do their very best to obey their Father's instructions will live in a state of peace, regardless of what occurs.

Jesus explained the relationship between obeying His instructions and being able to persevere during difficult times. He said, "...everyone who hears these words of Mine and acts upon them [obeying them] will be like a sensible (prudent, practical, wise) man who built his house upon the rock. And the rain fell and the floods came and the winds blew and beat against that house; yet it did not fall, because it had been founded on the rock" (Matthew 7:24-25).

Please highlight or underline the word "everyone" in this passage of Scripture. Jesus is speaking to *you*. If you hear the Word of God and obey it, you will be like a man who built his house on a solid foundation of *rock*. When the storms of life come, you will *not* fall just as this house did not fall when the storms came because the house was founded on the rock.

Christians who hear the Word of God and *do not do* what it says will encounter difficult problems in the last days. Jesus said that "…everyone who hears these words of Mine and does not do them will be like a stupid (foolish) man who built his house upon the sand. And the rain fell and the floods came and the winds blew and beat against that house, and it fell – and great and complete was the fall of it" (Matthew 7:26-27).

Once again, we see the word "everyone" in this passage of Scripture. We are told that we will be "stupid" and "foolish" if we learn what the Word of God tells us to do and then disobey God. Our lives will not have a solid foundation. We will be like a house that was built on *sand* that could *not* withstand severe storms. We must learn what the Word of God tells us to do and then obey these instructions in order to survive during the difficult days that lie ahead of us.

Do you love Jesus? Please stop and ask yourself, *"Do I know how to show Jesus that I love Him?"* Many Christians do not know the scriptural answer to this question. Jesus gave us the answer when He said, "…If a person [really] loves Me, he will keep My word [obey My teaching]…" (John 14:23).

Many Christians attempt to show their love for God by doing things they believe will please Him. The Bible tells us that we show our love for God by *obeying* His instructions. "…the [true] love of God is this: that we do His commands [keep His ordinances and are mindful of His precepts and teaching]. And these orders of His are not irksome (burdensome, oppressive, or grievous)" (I John 5:3).

Sometimes people think that doing what the Word of God tells us to do is restrictive. This passage of Scripture tells us that doing what God instructs us to do is *not* "irksome, burdensome, oppressive or grievous." Just the opposite is true. Consistent Bible study and meditation place us in a position to receive the blessings our Father has promised when we learn and obey His instructions.

Children show their love for their parents by obeying them. Children who habitually disobey their parents show their lack of respect. This same principle applies to our relationship with our heavenly Father.

Fear will run rampant during the difficult times that lie ahead of us. We have learned that some people in the end times will be so afraid that their hearts will fail (see Luke 21:26). *How* can we escape the fear that will sweep through the world in the last days before Jesus returns? "There is no fear in love [dread does not exist], but full-grown (complete, perfect) love turns fear out of doors and expels every trace of terror! For fear brings with it the thought of punishment, and [so] he who is afraid has not reached the full maturity of love [is not yet grown into love's complete perfection]" (I John 4:18).

This passage of Scripture tells us that "perfect love turns fear out of doors and expels every trace of terror." We are told that "perfect love" is the key to overcoming fear. People who are afraid "have not reached the full maturity of love." They have "not yet grown into love's complete perfection."

Perfect love is vitally important if we are to be set free from fear. *How is our love perfected?* "…he who keeps (treasures) His Word [who bears in mind His precepts, who observes His message in its entirety], truly in him has the love of and for God been perfected (completed, reached maturity). By this we may perceive (know, recognize, and be sure) that we are in Him" (I John 2:5).

This passage of Scripture tells us that our love for God will be perfected if we "treasure His Word." Our love for God will be perfected if we "observe His message in its entirety." We can clearly see in this passage of Scripture that the perfect love we must have to overcome fear is directly tied into *doing* what God's Word tells us to do. For more information on this subject, we recommend our Scripture Meditation Cards and our cassette tape that are titled *Our Father's Wonderful Love*.

Isn't it remarkable to see how all of this Scripture fits together? The Word of God is awesome. Our loving Father has provided everything we will need to deal with the problems we face. We must do our very best to learn and obey His instructions, to learn and believe wholeheartedly in His promises and to spend more time each day becoming intimately acquainted with Him.

This chapter has explained the relationship between obedience and receiving the peace of God. In the next four chapters we will carefully study the Word of God to see what it says about *doing* what God tells us to do by stepping out on God's instructions and promises with unwavering faith.

Chapter 40

Action Completes the Cycle of Faith

We show our faith in God by what we *say* and what we *do* when we face adversity. Stepping out on our faith in God in a crisis situation is like the tests we took when we were in school. Students study and then take tests to see how much they have learned. This same principle applies to acting on our faith.

We will be able to step out on our faith in God *if* we have built a solid foundation. We build this foundation by constantly renewing our minds in God's Word, by continually meditating on the Word of God and by speaking the Word of God constantly. We will be able to step out on our faith in God if we have developed a close relationship with God Himself over a period of months and years.

We also should praise God and thank Him continually. We should draw closer to Him each day to develop an intimate relationship with Him. We will be able to step out confidently on our faith in God in the face of severe adversity *if* we do these things consistently.

We should obey the instructions that Jesus gave to His disciples in the upper room on the night before His death. Jesus told these men many great spiritual truths that night. He then said, "If you know these things, blessed and happy and to be envied are you if you practice them [if you act accordingly and really do them]" (John 13:17).

Jesus told His disciples to *act* on the truth He had given them. The disciples could do this because they enjoyed a close personal relationship with Jesus. They trusted Him completely. We need this same close relationship today to act on our faith. We do not have to actually *see* Jesus with our physical eyesight, as the disciples did, to enjoy a close relationship with Him. "Without having seen Him, you love Him; though you do not [even] now see Him, you believe in Him and exult and thrill with inexpressible and glorious (triumphant, heavenly) joy" (I Peter 1:8).

This passage of Scripture tells us that we should love Jesus even though we cannot see Him with our physical eyesight. As you faithfully obey all of the scriptural instructions in this book, you will develop a close relationship with Jesus. You will "believe in Him." Your heart will be filled with "inexpressible and glorious joy."

To believe in someone, you have to know that person intimately. Spend every day with Jesus, becoming closer and closer to Him. Refuse to allow *anything* to distract you from drawing closer to Jesus. "…let us run with patient endurance and steady and active persistence the appointed course of the race that is set before us, looking away [from all that will distract] to Jesus, Who is the Leader and the Source of our faith [giving the first incentive for our belief] and is also its Finisher [bringing it to maturity and perfection]. He, for the joy [of obtaining the prize] that was set before Him, endured the cross, despising and ignoring the shame, and is now seated at the right hand of the throne of God" (Hebrews 12:1-2).

The gospel of Jesus is the course set before each of us. There are two parts for us to complete. The first is our own walk with God. We must find our place in God's plan. Our Father has a specific plan for the lives of each of His children (see our book titled *God's Will For Our Lives* and our Scripture Meditation Cards and cassette tape titled *Find God's Will For Your Life*).

We can be certain that we will be required to endure persistently if we wholeheartedly seek to carry out God's will for our lives. We can accomplish this goal only by turning away from every distraction to focus consistently on Jesus Who is "the Leader and the Source of our faith."

This passage of Scripture tells us that Jesus also is the "Finisher" of our faith. The amplification says that Jesus brings our faith "to maturity and perfection." Jesus was our example with His persevering and enduring faith in God throughout His earthly ministry.

Jesus was so focused on doing what His Father called Him to do that He "endured" the cross. He "ignored the shame" of what He had to go through. He wants each of us to follow His example of persevering in faith to do what God has called us to do with our lives.

We have explained that Christians who do not continually study and meditate on the Word of God will not be any better off in the last days than unbelievers who do not understand the Word of God. These Christians will live eternally in heaven, but they will face the same battle against fear, worry, doubt and unbelief that unbelievers will face.

Christians who have disregarded God's specific instructions to meditate on His Word throughout the day and night will pay a severe price in the difficult times that lie ahead. They will be unable to say and do what God's Word tells us to say and to do when we face the severe problems that the entire world will face.

When people who are close to us give us their word that they will do something, we believe them because of our closeness to them. This same principle applies to stepping out on our faith in God. We will only act in faith under severe pressure *if* we have developed a close and intimate relationship with our loving Father.

Faith in God is comparable to love. We can tell other people that we love them, but we show our love by our words and our actions. If we truly have faith in God, we will express this faith by what we say and what we do.

If we are tempted to give in to doubt and unbelief, we must consistently draw closer to God to continue to increase our faith in Him. "…cleave unto and remain faithful to and devoted to the Lord with [resolute and steady] purpose of heart" (Acts 11:23).

The Greek word "proskollaeo" that is translated "cleave" in this passage of Scripture means "to glue to, to adhere." We stick to the Lord like glue when we cleave to Him. We refuse to be separated from Him. We hold tightly onto Him and absolutely refuse to let go.

On several occasions I have learned the hard way that my faith in God was not as deep and strong as I thought it was. I know of no other way to have deep, strong and unwavering faith in God than to faithfully and consistently obey the specific instructions from the holy Scriptures that are contained in this book.

Our faith in God never stands still. Our faith in God always is increasing or decreasing. We will *act* on our faith just as the disciples took action on their faith in Jesus *if* we continually develop a close personal relationship with God by setting aside precious time each day to draw closer to Him.

The Book of Acts is referred to as the Acts of the Apostles. This Book got its name because the disciples of Jesus *acted* on their faith in Jesus. The Book of Acts is filled with testimonies of simple men who stepped out on their faith in Jesus. He wants each of us to do the same.

Faith without action is like a bird that does not use its wings. A bird can hop around on the ground, but it cannot fly without opening its wings. We must step out on our faith in God if we want to "fly" in the spiritual realm.

Our faith in God can be compared to learning how to swim. Imagine a group of students in a swimming class. The instructor can carefully explain how to float and how to swim. The true test comes when the students put themselves in the water with absolute trust that the water will hold them up. We must trust our Father to hold us up when we do exactly what He has instructed us to do.

Chapter 41

The Power of God Is Released When We Step Out in Faith

Chapters Nine and Ten of this book are devoted to a thorough scriptural study of the supernatural power of the living Word of God. We receive manifestation of the supernatural power of God when we *take action* based on the promises and instructions in His Word. We *block* this supernatural power from working in our lives if we fail to take action on the Word of God.

We can understand something of the power of God by comparing it to power that we know here on earth. Electricity has tremendous power, but this power will be released only if we turn the switch that activates it. This same principle applies to an automobile. An automobile engine may be very powerful, but it will not start until we turn the key in the ignition.

We must know how to turn the switch on our faith. We do this by stepping out and taking action based on our faith in God. We will not take this step unless we have such a close and intimate relationship with God that we trust Him completely.

We cannot be all that God has planned for us without His presence and His anointing upon our lives. We cannot live our lives effectively when we are separated from God. We must be totally connected to Him and live and breathe in the very breath of God. We must be taking God in all of the time so that our lives clearly will be marked by His presence and His power.

Once we connect with God in this way, no other manner of living will ever satisfy us. Living in God's presence and power is so full of miracles and divine appointments that someone reading a book about our lives might question how these things could be true. Living for God is greater than any book or movie. The Bible speaks of "…the immeasurable and unlimited and surpassing greatness of His power in and for us who believe…" (Ephesians 1:19).

This passage of Scripture tells us that the power of God is "immeasurable and unlimited." God is *so powerful* that we cannot even remotely comprehend His mighty power with our limited human understanding. The "surpassing greatness" of God's power is much greater than anything we can understand. *How* do we receive manifestation of the immense power of God? This passage of Scripture tells us that God's mighty power is activated "in and for us *who believe.*"

If you are a Christian, the supernatural power of Almighty God already lives in your heart. You should have a continual consciousness that God's power is *in you.* God's power is available to *help you.* You will receive manifestation of God's mighty power if you step out on your absolute trust in Him with bold and unwavering faith.

The Book of James gives us several specific instructions on *doing* what the Word of God tells us to do. These passages of Scripture clearly show us the relationship between our faith in God and taking action on our faith. "What is the use (profit), my brethren, for anyone to profess to have faith if he has no [good] works [to show for it]? Can [such] faith save [his soul]?" (James 2:14).

This passage of Scripture tells us that we must do more than just "profess to have faith." We must have "good works to show" our faith in God. Professed faith that is not followed by action cannot receive manifestation of the power of God. "...faith, if it does not have works (deeds and actions of obedience to back it up), by itself is destitute of power (inoperative, dead)" (James 2:17).

This passage of Scripture tells us that faith that is not backed up by action is "destitute of power, inoperative and dead." Our Father is emphasizing the vital importance of doing what He says to do. His power will be "dead" in our lives if we fail to take action based on our faith in Him.

Faith and action go together. Faith without action is not faith at all. "...someone will say [to you then], You [say you] have faith, and I have [good] works. Now you show me your [alleged] faith apart from any [good] works [if you can], and I by [good] works [of obedience] will show you my faith" (James 2:18).

We can see that we must do more than just say we have faith. Our Father looks for "good works." Belief by itself is not enough. Satan's demons also believe in the power of God. "You believe that God is one; you do well. So do the demons believe and shudder [in terror and horror such as make a man's hair stand on end and contract the surface of his skin]!" (James 2:19).

Satan's demons "shudder in terror and horror" when they think of the mighty power of God being used against them. This supernatural power of God will empower us *if* we consistently *act* on our faith in Him. "Are you willing to be shown [proof], you foolish (unproductive, spiritually deficient) fellow, that faith apart from [good] works is inactive and ineffective and worthless?" (James 2:20).

Will you "show proof" of your faith in God? Will you step out on your faith in God so that this faith will not be "inactive, ineffective and worthless?" Some Christians who know what the Word of God tells us to do block the power of God because they do not do what God tells them to do.

We each should follow the example of Abraham who gave clear evidence of his faith in God by his actions. "Was not our forefather Abraham [shown to be] justified (made acceptable to God) by [his] works when he brought to the altar as an offering his [own] son Isaac?" (James 2:21).

Abraham was "justified to God by his work." This passage of Scripture refers to the offering Abraham made by his willingness to make a tremendous sacrifice that proved his faith in God. "[God] said, Take now your son, your only son, Isaac, whom you love, and go to the region of Moriah; and offer him there as a burnt offering upon one of the mountains of which I will tell you" (Genesis 22:2).

Isaac was the apple of Abraham's eye. Abraham had to wait until he was more than one hundred years old for Isaac to be born. God honored Abraham's faith by giving Abraham and Sarah a son when they were very old.

God tested Abraham's faith again when Isaac was a young man. He told Abraham to go up to a mountain to offer Isaac as a sacrifice. What did Abraham *do*? "…Abraham rose early in the morning, saddled his donkey, and took two of his young men with him and his son Isaac; and he split the wood for the burnt offering, and then began the trip to the place of which God had told him" (Genesis 22:3).

Abraham took the step of faith that God asked him to take. He took Isaac, two of his servants and a supply of split wood to the mountain for the burnt offering he was willing to make to God. "...Abraham said to his servants, Settle down and stay here with the donkey, and I and the young man will go yonder and worship and come again to you. Then Abraham took the wood for the burnt offering, and laid it on [the shoulders of] Isaac his son, and he took the fire (the firepot) in his own hand, and a knife; and the two of them went on together" (Genesis 22:5-6).

Abraham took the next step of faith after they arrived at the mountain. "When they came to the place of which God had told him, Abraham built an altar there; then he laid the wood in order and bound Isaac his son and laid him on the altar on the wood. And Abraham stretched forth his hand and took hold of the knife to slay his son" (Genesis 22:9-10).

Abraham loved Isaac with all of his heart. Nevertheless, he stepped out in faith to *do* what God told him to do. Abraham built an altar to God. He placed wood on the altar. He tied Isaac with rope to the altar. Abraham then "took hold of the knife to slay his son." This action is the epitome of faith in God.

God responded to Abraham's faith. "...the Angel of the Lord called to him from heaven and said, Abraham, Abraham! He answered, Here I am. And He said, Do not lay your hand on the lad or do anything to him; for now I know that you fear and revere God, since you have not held back from Me or begrudged giving Me your son, your only son" (Genesis 22:11-12).

God sent an angel from heaven to tell Abraham to stop. Abraham had passed this test of faith. "You see that [his] faith was cooperating with his works, and [his] faith was completed and reached its supreme expression [when he implemented it] by [good] works" (James 2:22).

Abraham's faith was "completed and reached its supreme expression when he implemented it by good works." Our Father wants each of us to do as Abraham did. He wants us to show by our *actions* that we *really do* believe in Him. "...a man is justified (pronounced righteous before God) through what he does and not alone through faith [through works of obedience as well as by what he believes]" (James 2:24).

This passage of Scripture emphasizes that faith is not sufficient by itself. We each need to follow Abraham's example and take action upon our faith in God. "...as the human body apart from the spirit is lifeless, so faith apart from [its] works of obedience is also dead" (James 2:26).

Have you ever seen a dead person in a casket in a funeral home? Morticians embalm dead people in an attempt to make them look normal, but their success is limited because the spirit of the dead person has departed. The dead person is not alive, no matter what the mortician does. Our faith in God is not alive unless we take action on our faith.

When a person dies, the body remains but "the spirit is lifeless." Our faith in God "is also dead" if we fail to step out on our faith. Our Father wants us to continually develop our faith so that we always will trust Him enough to take action based on this faith.

Significant changes are coming in the world. We cannot continue to live the way that many of us are living. We must learn what the Word of God tells us to do to increase our faith in God. Then we must do what God's Word instructs us to do. Now is the time to faithfully do what our Father has told us to do so that our unwavering faith in Him will bring His mighty power into manifestation.

The story of David and Goliath gives us an excellent example of a person who *took action* based on his faith in God. David was a teenager who watched over his father's sheep. David's three brothers were Israeli soldiers who were camped in a valley in preparation for a battle against the Philistines. David's father sent him to bring bread and cheese to his brothers.

When David arrived, he heard the champion of the Philistines speaking boldly. This man, Goliath, was a giant who was almost ten feet tall. He challenged the Israelites to send a man to do battle with him on a winner take all basis.

Goliath's body was covered with heavy armor. He wore a large protective helmet on his head. All of the Israelites were "terrified" by Goliath. "…all the men of Israel, when they saw the man, fled from him, terrified" (I Samuel 17:24).

David was not afraid. He boldly spoke up and offered to fight Goliath. "David said to Saul, Let no man's heart fail because of this Philistine; your servant will go out and fight with him" (I Samuel 17:32).

David previously had acted on his faith in God when he faced a lion and also a bear. David said to Saul, "Your servant killed both the lion and the bear; and this uncircumcised Philistine shall be like one of them, for he has defied the armies of the living God! David said, The Lord Who delivered me out of the paw of the lion and out of the paw of the bear, He will deliver me out of the hand of this Philistine…" (I Samuel 17:36-37).

Saul attempted to put armor on David and to give him a sword. David refused the armor and the sword. He went to battle against Goliath armed with his sling, five stones he found in a brook and his faith in God.

When the giant Goliath saw this teenager, he ridiculed him and cursed him. "…when the Philistine looked around and saw David, he scorned and despised him, for he was but an adolescent, with a healthy reddish color and a fair face" (I Samuel 17:42).

David then showed how much faith he had in God. He *acted* on his faith by actually *running toward Goliath*. "When the Philistine came forward to meet David, David ran quickly toward the battle line to meet the Philistine" (I Samuel 17:48).

God honored David's faith. David fired a stone with his sling and hit Goliath in the forehead. Goliath fell down as a result of this blow. David did not have a sword, so he took Goliath's sword and killed him.

David running *toward* Goliath is one of the greatest stories in the Bible of someone *acting* on faith in God. When we face difficult problems in our lives, we should have so much faith in God that we will face these problems boldly. We should run toward the problems instead of running away from them.

Our Father does not want us to have a "Plan B" in case He fails to come through. He wants us to be in a position where we have to depend totally, completely and absolutely on Him. We turn away from all human security when we take the step of faith our Father wants us to take. Our faith must be strong when we are in a position where God must do what has to be done or we will fail.

Chapter 42

Human Reason and Logic Often Inhibit Our Faith in God

Some Christians are inhibited from stepping out on their faith in God because God's ways and the ways of the world are very different. God's ways do not make sense to human logic and reason. We must not limit God because of our lack of understanding. "As you know not what is the way of the wind, or how the spirit comes to the bones in the womb of a pregnant woman, even so you know not the work of God, Who does all" (Ecclesiastes 11:5).

We cannot understand everything about why and how the wind blows. We cannot explain every detail of how God can create a child in the womb of a woman. Human logic and reason cannot possibly "know the work of God Who does all."

Many Christians look at seemingly unsolvable problems and give up when they cannot see any possible solution. They hesitate to act on their faith in God because acting on this faith makes no sense to their human logic and reason. Following God's way is more natural than man's way once a person experiences the faithfulness of God. God's way becomes the only way.

We do not have to understand how or why something works in order to act in faith. We often will come to a time when we are at the end of our human understanding. *We must not stop there.* Faith in God goes far beyond what we can understand and explain. God is not limited by human reasoning. We face the same limitations as unbelievers if we think we have to figure everything out logically. "...Has not God shown up the nonsense and the folly of this world's wisdom?" (I Corinthians 1:20).

Unbelievers have no alternative. They do not have the Word of God as their Book of Instructions. They do not know what the Bible tells us to do to increase our faith in God. They do not have the Holy Spirit to teach them, guide them, help them and strengthen them. They can only depend on "the nonsense and the folly of this world's wisdom."

Our Father has made provision to give us *everything we need* (see Psalm 34:10, Matthew 6:26, Romans 8:32 and Philippians 4:19). The problems in the end times will be so severe that there will not seem to be any solution. We must seek God to ask for His wisdom and His provision.

We become Christians in the first place by turning away from intellectual reasoning to ask Jesus to be our Savior. We make this decision with simple childlike faith. Human logic cannot explain how the Son of God could come down from heaven to earth to be born out of the womb of a virgin.

Every person who has received Jesus as his or her Savior has believed this scriptural truth. Receiving eternal salvation through Jesus does not make any sense from the limitation of human logic and reason. "...the story and message of the cross is sheer absurdity and folly to those who are perishing and on their way to perdition…" (I Corinthians 1:18).

Faith in God and human logic and reason often are opposed. If our faith in God is very strong, we often will say and do things we never would consider saying or doing based on the limitations of human logic and reason. Doubt and unbelief will prevail when human logic and reason prevail.

Some Christians spend far too much time trying to figure things out with their limited intellectual capabilities. We must not make the mistake of trying to use human logic and reason to solve problems that only can be solved by God. "If then you have died with Christ to material ways of looking at things and have escaped from the world's crude and elemental notions and teachings of externalism, why do you live as if you still belong to the world?…" (Colossians 2:20).

Faith in God means trusting God based on what His Word says, even though human logic and reason may say that what we are preparing to do is absolutely impossible. We have to *break through* the barriers of doubt and unbelief before we can really trust God and take action because of our faith in Him. We must be able to move on when human logic and reason say "No" and the Word of God says "Yes." We must step out with unwavering faith in the absolute reliability of Almighty God Who stands one hundred percent behind *every* promise in His Word.

Our Father wants us to do more than just read the Bible and listen to the Bible. We have learned that He wants us to meditate on His Word continually until our hearts are so full of His Word that we will *do* what His Word tells us to do. "…be doers of the Word [obey the message], and not merely listeners to it, betraying yourselves [into deception by reasoning contrary to the Truth]…" (James 1:22).

I believe that "betraying ourselves into deception" speaks of allowing Satan's demons to deceive us. How do we do this? We permit this deception "by reasoning contrary to the Truth." Satan's ways and the ways of the world are contrary to God's instructions. We must not make the mistake of doing something just because it "seems right" to us. "There is a way which seems right to a man and appears straight before him, but at the end of it is the way of death" (Proverbs 14:12).

We can and will lead ourselves to spiritual death and ultimately to premature physical death if we constantly make decisions based only on what "seems right" to our limited human understanding. We see a good example of this principle in the story of Noah and the ark. Noah did not give in to his limited understanding when God told him to build an ark.

God regretted creating humans because of the wickedness He saw prevailing throughout the earth (see Genesis 6:12). God told Noah that He intended to wipe out all mankind. He told Noah to build a 450 foot ark. He told Noah to bring his family and a male and female of every species into the ark. He told Noah to bring food into the ark because He was about to destroy all living things with a flood (see Genesis 6:13-22 and Genesis 7:1-4).

Noah would not have acted on God's instructions if he had reacted based on his limited human logic and understanding. Noah had *no* concept of what a flood was. He had never seen rain. "…the Lord God had not [yet] caused it to rain upon the earth…" (Genesis 2:5).

Noah needed great faith to act on God's instructions. What God told him to do did not make any sense at all, but Noah *acted in faith*. "…Noah did all that the Lord commanded him" (Genesis 7:5).

Noah spent many years building the ark. People must have ridiculed him constantly, but Noah persevered because of his faith in God. "[Prompted] by faith Noah, being forewarned by God concerning events of which as yet there was no visible sign, took heed and diligently and reverently constructed and prepared an ark for the deliverance of his own family…" (Hebrews 11:7).

Noah took action because of his faith in God even though what he was doing did not make *any sense whatsoever* to his human understanding. Our Father wants us to do the same. He wants us to take action on what He tells us in His Word whether or not these instructions and promises make logical sense.

In the last days before Jesus comes for us, we will face circumstances that seem to have no possible solution. Instead of focusing on these difficult circumstances, we should immerse ourselves continually in the supernatural living Word of God so that we will know what to do. Then we must act on our faith in God instead of reacting with fear.

The Bible is filled with many stories that defy logic. How could Moses lead millions of Israelites to the edge of the Red Sea with high mountains on each side and the Egyptian army behind them and come safely through this seemingly impossible situation? Human logic says there is no way that Moses could stretch forth a rod in his hand and part the waters of the Red Sea so the Israelites could walk safely through to the other side. Exodus 14:1-31 tells us that this great miracle of God actually took place.

God performed such a miracle that the Israelites actually walked on dry land even though the ground had been very muddy just a few moments before (see Exodus 14:21). The story of the Israelites walking through the Red Sea is an excellent example of the manifestation of the supernatural power of God in response to the faith and obedience of a believer.

Human logic would not think it likely that Jesus could miraculously turn large amounts of water into wine. John 2:7-11 tells us about this first of many miracles that Jesus performed.

Human logic tells us that people cannot step out of a boat and walk on top of the water. Matthew 14:24-29 tells us that Jesus walked on water as He approached the disciples' boat. Peter acted on his faith in Jesus to walk on the water himself (see Matthew 14:28-29).

Human logic says that it is impossible to feed four thousand men and their wives and children with seven loaves of bread and a few small fish. Matthew 15:29-39 tells us that this miracle was performed by Jesus.

Human logic says that Jesus could not tell Peter to throw a hook into water and that the money to pay their taxes would be in the mouth of the first fish he caught. Matthew 17:24-27 tells us that Jesus received money for His taxes in this manner.

Human logic says that it is impossible to raise a man from the dead four days after he had died. John 11:1-45 tells us that Jesus raised a decaying and smelly Lazarus from the dead four days after he died.

Jesus did not look in the classified ads of a Jerusalem newspaper to find a room to rent for His final meal on the night before He was betrayed. Jesus told Peter and John to walk into the city where a man carrying a pitcher of water would meet them. Jesus told them to tell this man that He wanted to use his large upstairs room for the Passover dinner with His disciples. Jesus told Peter and John that this man would show them a room that already was prepared for the Passover meal (see Luke 22:7-13).

The preceding examples are just a few of hundreds of instances in the Bible that defy human logic and reason. In the difficult times that lie ahead of us, we often will be called on to act on our faith in God, even though this action will not make logical sense because of the severity of the circumstances we will face. "…the mind of the flesh [which is sense and reason without the Holy Spirit] is death [death that comprises all the miseries arising from sin, both here and hereafter]. But the mind of the [Holy] Spirit is life and [soul] peace [both now and forever]" (Romans 8:6).

The amplification in this passage of Scripture speaks of "sense and reason without the Holy Spirit." Thinking without the Holy Spirit will lead us to spiritual death. We are told that "the mind of the Holy Spirit is life and soul peace both now and forever."

The Holy Spirit does *not* operate based on the limitations of human logic and reason. We will experience His supernatural peace in the midst of a seeming crisis if we really do yield control of our lives to Him and trust completely in Him. We will be able to take action based on our faith in the guidance we are certain He will give us. As we have more and more past history of God's faithfulness, our trust in God increases.

We have learned that we will be able to hear the Holy Spirit speaking to us if we consistently obey God's instructions to fill our hearts with His Word. We will not be limited by human logic and understanding. "If we live by the [Holy] Spirit, let us also walk by the Spirit. [If by the Holy Spirit we have our life in God, let us go forward walking in line, our conduct controlled by the Spirit.]" (Galatians 5:25).

Human logic and reason say that we should control our decisions. The Word of God says that we should "go forward walking in line with *our conduct controlled by the Spirit.*" The Holy

Spirit will tell us exactly what to do when we turn away from the limitations of human understanding because we trust completely in Him. "…your ears will hear a word behind you, saying, This is the way; walk in it, when you turn to the right hand and when you turn to the left" (Isaiah 30:21).

This Old Testament passage of Scripture refers to hearing a word "behind" us. The New Testament tells us that the Holy Spirit lives in our hearts. He can and will speak to us continually. We can hear His voice in our hearts. We must turn away from the limitations of human logic and reason and fill our hearts to overflowing with the supernatural power of the living Word of God.

Our Father looks for His children who come to Him daily and enjoy Him. He is a relationship God. Our Father is looking for humble, teachable and trusting Christians who will obey Him. He is looking for His children who will speak His Word continually and do exactly what His Word says to do even if this act of faith is contrary to the limitations of human logic and reason.

Our Father wants us to *trust Him so much* that we will turn completely away from the limitations of our understanding. "Lean on, trust in, and be confident in the Lord with all your heart and mind and do not rely on your own insight or understanding. In all your ways know, recognize, and acknowledge Him, and He will direct and make straight and plain your paths. Be not wise in your own eyes; reverently fear and worship the Lord and turn [entirely] away from evil" (Proverbs 3:5-7).

Please highlight or underline the words "do not rely on your own insight or understanding." The Word of God instructs us to turn away from the limitations of our human understanding. We are instructed to "lean on, trust in and be confident in the Lord with all of our hearts and minds." Everything we do should "recognize and acknowledge" God. God "will direct and make straight and plain our paths" if we obey these instructions.

We must "not be wise in our own eyes." We should not rely on the limitations of human wisdom (see I Corinthians 3:19-20). We will "turn entirely away from evil" if we fear the Lord and hold Him in reverent awe at all times.

Chapter 43

Take the Next Step by Faith

We are very secure when we are in our comfort zone. Everything is a known quantity. We are in familiar territory. That is why we feel so comfortable. Our Father often requires us to step out in faith beyond this comfort zone. He requires us to take this step when we cannot see anything beyond it. Our Father wants us to have complete trust that He will show us the next step *after* we have stepped out on our faith in Him.

The Word of God instructs us to live our lives one day at a time (see Matthew 6:34). This one at a time principle also applies to taking one step at a time. We saw in the last chapter that we often are required to step out in faith without trying to figure everything out. "Man's steps are ordered by the Lord. How then can a man understand his way?" (Proverbs 20:24).

We must not limit the Lord by our lack of understanding. A small step of faith is a big step the first time we take it. Each time we take a step of faith, our faith will increase as we receive answers from God that we could not have received otherwise.

Sometimes Christians who have a great deal of God-given human ability find security in their own talents. Our Father does not want us to insist on directing our lives no matter how talented we may be. "...I know that [the determination of] the way of a man is not in himself; it is not in man [even in a strong man or in a man at his best] to direct his [own] steps" (Jeremiah 10:23).

God should be in charge of our lives. God knows exactly where He wants us to go when He requires us to step out on our faith in Him. Job said, "Does not [God] see my ways and count all my steps?" (Job 31:4).

God is omniscient. He knows everything that is taking place in the life of every one of the billions of people in the world. He can and will help each of us when we take a step of faith in Him. "The steps of a [good] man are directed and established by the Lord when He delights in his way [and He busies Himself with his every step]. Though he falls, he shall not be utterly cast down, for the Lord grasps his hand in support and upholds him" (Psalm 37: 23-24).

This passage of Scripture speaks of "a good man." I believe a good man from a New Testament perspective is a person who has received Jesus as his or her Savior. This person studies and meditates on the Word of God continually and attempts to obey all of God's instructions and willingly yields control of his (or her) life to the Holy Spirit. God directs the steps of these humble, obedient and trusting believers.

Our Father delights to see us obey Him and walk by faith in Him. He guides our every step as we trust in Him. We do not have to stay down if we fall down. Our Father will help us to get up. He will hold us up if He has to.

We learned in the last chapter that human logic and reason are insufficient. Sometimes the Lord will direct our steps in an entirely different direction from where we think we should go.

"A man's mind plans his way, but the Lord directs his steps and makes them sure" (Proverbs 16:9).

We will face many very difficult circumstances in the last days before Jesus comes for us. We often will be required to take a step of faith in God even though conditions do not seem to be favorable. "He who observes the wind [and waits for all conditions to be favorable] will not sow, and he who regards the clouds will not reap" (Ecclesiastes 11:4).

This passage of Scripture tells us to take our eyes off the wind and the clouds – the external circumstances in our lives. We must *not* focus on the storms in our lives. We often will not be able to "wait for all conditions to be favorable" before we act.

We will have to step out into the unknown many times if we live the life of faith our Father has called us to live. Unbelievers sometimes say such things as "Seeing is believing" and "I'll believe it when I see it." *God says just the opposite.* He says, "Believe and *then* you will see."

Jesus revealed Himself to Mary Magdalene and many of His disciples when He rose from the dead three days after He was crucified. One of His disciples, Thomas, was not with the other disciples when they saw Jesus. When Thomas heard that Jesus had risen from the dead "…he said to them, Unless I see in His hands the marks made by the nails and put my finger into the nail prints, and put my hand into His side, I will never believe [it]" (John 20:25).

This statement explains why Thomas often is referred to as "doubting Thomas." Thomas would not believe until he could see. "Eight days later, His disciples were again in the house, and Thomas was with them. Jesus came, though they were behind closed doors, and stood among them and said,

Peace to you! Then He said to Thomas, Reach out your finger here, and see My hands; and put out your hand and place [it] in My side. Do not be faithless and incredulous, but [stop your unbelief and] believe! Thomas answered Him, My Lord and my God!" (John 20:26-28).

Jesus graciously allowed Thomas to see Him even though Thomas was very skeptical. Jesus told Thomas to "stop his unbelief and believe." Jesus said, "…Because you have seen Me, Thomas, do you now believe (trust, have faith)? Blessed and happy and to be envied are those who have never seen Me and yet have believed and adhered to and trusted and relied on Me" (John 20:29).

We must learn this important lesson in these last days before Jesus returns. Jesus *will* bless us even though we cannot see Him *if* we "believe, adhere to and rely on Him." Our natural inclination is to walk by sight, not by faith. Our Father wants us to do just the opposite. "…we walk by faith [we regulate our lives and conduct ourselves by our conviction or belief respecting man's relationship to God and divine things, with trust and holy fervor; thus we walk] not by sight or appearance" (II Corinthians 5:7).

This passage of Scripture tells us to "regulate our lives and conduct ourselves" by our faith in God, "*not* by sight or appearance." We do *not* have to see where we are stepping. We would be walking by sight and not by faith if we always could see where we were going. We need to see with eyes of faith before we will see with our natural eyesight the manifestation of what we are believing God for.

We have seen that we *can do all things* through the strength of Jesus (see Philippians 4:13). "All things" include the step of faith that is very difficult for many people to take when they cannot see where they are headed. We must have absolute faith that Jesus will give us the strength that is required to take this step.

This book repeatedly emphasizes the scriptural importance of renewing our minds in the Word of God each day and meditating on the Word of God throughout the day and night. We must realize that our faith in God will not increase just from studying and meditating on the Word of God. We must apply the principles we have learned. We often will be required to step out on our faith in God if we want our faith to continue to grow and mature.

We need to act on the faith we have so that we will develop more faith. Our faith in God will become deeper, stronger, unwavering and unshakable as days, weeks, months and years go by. Our faith in God is similar to the muscles in our bodies. Our muscles become weak if we do not use them. Our faith in God will become weaker if we do not exercise this faith continually.

Many people lift weights to strengthen their muscles. We must use our muscles against strong opposing forces if we want them to become stronger. We must act on our faith in God against strong opposition if we want this faith to grow.

We have learned that the Word of God instructs us to *live by faith*. We cannot live by faith unless we continually take steps into areas where we cannot see where we are headed. From God's perspective, the very best place any of us can be is in a place where we have to place all of our trust in Him.

Conclusion

You now have completed a detailed study of more than four hundred Scripture references that tell you how to increase your faith in God. This book is filled with scriptural instructions that will help you to come safely through the remaining time before Jesus comes for us. These practical principles can be implemented in your life immediately.

We would like to summarize the contents of this book so that you can see in one place *why* we need to increase our faith in God and *how* we can increase our faith in God:

- We have seen many factual indications that we live in the *last days* before Jesus returns. Because of this certainty, we should be determined to increase our faith in God.

- We *cannot please God* unless we have faith in Him. Our Father has given us the Bible to provide us a solid foundation for our faith.

- We have learned that the Word of God is filled with the supernatural power of Almighty God. We can be assured that this power of God is *much greater* than any problem we will face, no matter how difficult this problem may seem to us.

- One chapter of this book is filled with facts to show you that God is *completely faithful.* We can and should place total and absolute trust in Him.

- We have learned that our Father wants us to *renew our minds* in His Word on a daily basis. We must learn to think more and more the way God thinks so that we will be able to see the end times from His perspective.

- We have learned that we get the Word of God from our minds into our *hearts* by continually *meditating* on the holy Scriptures. Any reader who knows and believes exactly what our Father has said about meditating on His Word should have a deep and a strong desire to meditate on the Word of God on a daily basis.

- Eleven chapters of this book are dedicated to a thorough and detailed scriptural explanation of the significant importance of *the words that come out of our mouths.* We have learned that the only way we can control the words we speak in a crisis situation is by having our hearts so full of the Word of God that the abundance of God's Word in our hearts will continually pour out of our mouths.

- We have learned the importance of *doing* what the Word of God instructs us to do. Our Father wants us to obey His instructions. He wants us to believe His promises. Stepping out in faith on God's promises completes the cycle of faith and causes the mighty power of God to be released.

Our Father has given us many warnings of what lies ahead. We should have a sense of urgency that will motivate us to work diligently at increasing our faith in God. Many Christians in the United States and other relatively prosperous countries are complacent. They have not paid the price to steadily increase their faith in God. They do not see the need for paying this price. They soon will see this need.

Athletes go into training before they participate in a major athletic contest. We have a major "spiritual contest" on the horizon. Our faith in God will be tested as it never has been tested before. We need to "go into training" now.

Many people who have been Christians for a long time need to go back to the basics. Just because we have been a Christian for a certain number of years does not automatically mean that our faith in God is strong. Many times people who have been Christians for many years need to admit that their faith in God is not what it should be.

We must not allow anything to deter us from continually strengthening our faith in God. During the difficult times that lie ahead, we often will be in a position where we have no other choice but to trust God. Although this may seem to be an undesirable position from a worldly perspective, we could not be in a better place from a Christian perspective.

We can trust God no matter what the future holds. The Word of God tells us that we *can* walk in victory over whatever is taking place in the world through our faith in God. "…whatever is born of God is victorious over the world; and this is the victory that conquers the world, even our faith" (I John 5:4).

This book is filled to overflowing with specific instructions from God telling us *exactly* what He wants us to do to increase our faith in Him. Our Father has done His part. We must do our part.

We urge you to make the commitment *now* to get into the Word of God and to get the Word of God into you. Do not try to *find time* to do this. You must *make time* for the Lord every day.

We urge you to put your time with the Lord in first place and to keep it there (see Matthew 6:33). Refuse to let anything or anyone come ahead of your resolve to draw closer to the Lord. Nothing is more important.

This book is not a book just to be read. This book must be *studied*. We urge you to highlight or underline the scriptural facts in this book. You then can go back over the material you have highlighted or underlined as you go through this book a second time. Many of our readers study the scriptural contents three or more times. Repeated readings of this book will be very beneficial to you if you use this book as a detailed scriptural study guide to help you to increase your faith in God.

As I finish this book, I know how much I still have to learn. The first thing I will do when I receive my copy of the book from the printer is to begin a thorough study of the scriptural contents of this book so that my mind, my heart and my mouth will be filled to overflowing with facts on increasing my faith in God. "…you who teach others, do you not teach yourself?…" (Romans 2:21).

We invite you to share this book with others. Many of your friends and loved ones *must understand* that we live in the last days before Jesus returns. You know many people who need to learn exactly and specifically how to increase their faith in God. Do not hesitate to give this book to unbelievers. Many people have asked Jesus to be their Savior as a result of the salvation message that is contained in each of our books.

This book contains a strong "wake up call." If you are close to someone who does not have strong faith in God, ask this person to read the first five chapters of this book with an open mind. He or she then can decide whether to read further.

You will see from the order forms at the end of this book that we offer a substantial quantity discount on our publications. We have offered this discount from the beginning of our ministry so our readers to *share* the scriptural contents of our publications with as *many* people as possible.

Please look at the following list of topics and our publications on these topics to see if you are interested in our other publications. All of our books and Scripture Meditation Cards are solidly anchored on the Word of God.

Increase your faith in God
Book: *Unshakable Faith in Almighty God*
Scripture cards and cassette tape: *Continually Increasing Faith in God*

Overcome worry and fear
Book: *Conquering Fear*
Scripture cards and cassette tape: *Freedom from Worry and Fear*

Find God's will for your life
Book: *God's Will for Your Life*
Scripture cards and cassette tape: *Finding God's Will for Your Life*

Receive healing from sickness
Scripture cards and cassette tape: *Receive Healing from the Lord.*

Divine health
Book: *Increased Energy and Vitality.*

Financial success

Book: *Trust God for Your Finances*

Scripture cards and cassette tape: *Financial Instructions from God*

Assurance of God's indwelling presence

Scripture cards and cassette tape: *God is Always with You.*

Peace with God and the peace of God

Book: *Exchange Your Worries for God's Perfect Peace*

Scripture cards and cassette tape: *Enjoy God's Wonderful Peace*

Calm confidence in a crisis

Book: *Quiet Confidence in the Lord*

Your Father's love for you

Scripture cards and cassette tape: *Our Father's Wonderful Love*

A closer relationship with the Lord

Scripture cards and cassette tape: *A Closer Relationship with the Lord*

Increased patience and perseverance

Book: *Never, Never Give Up*

A Christian's eternal home in heaven

Book: *What Will Heaven be Like?*

Overcoming adversity

Book: *Soaring Above the Problems of Life*

Scripture cards and cassette tape: *Receive God's Blessing in Adversity*

Effective Bible study

Book: *How to Study the Bible*

Eternal salvation

Book: *100 Years from Today*

Please take a few moments to read the following comments from people all over the world whose lives have been changed by our books. As you read these comments, please ask yourself which publications that are commented upon contain an explanation of Scripture on a topic that could help you or someone you know.

We prayed for the readers of this book as we wrote it. We pray that this book pertaining to faith in God has blessed you abundantly. We pray that your faith in God will increase steadily from now until the day Jesus comes for us. We would be so pleased to hear from you. You will bless us and others by sending us your comments about the changes that have resulted in your life through reading this book. We love you and we bless you in Jesus' name for His glory and your joy.

Comments on our Books

We have devoted thousands of hours during the past twenty-one years writing sixteen Christian books and ten sets of Scripture Meditation Cards. We believe that our publications can help you if you are determined to increase your faith in God. Please take full advantage of the hours of labor we have put in to help *you* increase your faith in God.

You already have read comments on our Scripture Meditation Cards. The following are just a few of the more than one thousand comments we have received on our books. Please take a few minutes to read these comments to see if any of these books can be a benefit to you:

- "I originally made a goal to read one chapter of the book on wisdom every day as part of my daily meditation and fellowship with God. However, sometimes I get to the point where even one page is more than enough for me. Sometimes even just one Scripture is enough. I stop and meditate on that Scripture throughout the day. This book is tremendous. It is just overwhelming. Sometimes I can only take very small bites of it because it is way too much if I try to read it too quickly." (Wisconsin)

- "*Exchange Your Worries for God's Perfect Peace* is a masterpiece. I have read hundreds of Christian books and nothing has revolutionized my life or my ministry like this book. I am reading this book to the people here in the Philippines. I saw tears flowing down their faces as I read them parts of this book. I must get this book translated into their language. I am reading this book for the second time. After thirty years in the ministry I finally have learned how to turn my worries over to God. I have learned more from this book in the last few months than I have ever learned in my life. I will not allow my copy of this book to leave my presence. I thank God for you." (Philippines)

- "You did a fantastic job on *God's Wisdom is Available to You*. This book is an encyclopedia on God's wisdom. The writing style is just great. Many books don't bring the reader through the subject the way this book does. I'm very impressed with that. You have made it a real joy for me to study and re-digest Scripture. This book has been very good for me." (North Carolina)

- "Thank you very much for many dynamic blessings coming from your books, tapes and meditation cards. Your publications are very unique, very rich, full of life and very real. I have never been to Bible college. Your publications are my Bible college. Brother Hartman, you have been so instrumental in my life and in the church I am pastoring. All of our church leaders and myself are being greatly blessed. We don't know how to thank you. God richly bless you." (Zambia)

- "As I write, I am in a prison cell in South Africa awaiting trial. I want to thank Mr. Jack Hartman for his book *Soaring Above the Problems of Life*. I really do not know what I would have done without it. As I read through the pages, light dawned on me and I got comforted and understood why it is necessary that we go through a season of adversity." (Zimbabwe)

- "The free books and Scripture cards you sent me were so much more than I expected. I was moved almost to tears. May our Lord bless you one thousand times over for your generosity. I now have four of your books in my library. I dedicated my life to the Lord in part to your book *100 Years From Today.* I have loaned this book to five other men here in prison. Four of these men also have turned their lives over to the Lord. Hallelujah!" (Florida)

- Rev. Jack, two times I read your book *Trust God for Your Finances.* This book is wonderful, great! This book brings people close to God. I praise God in heaven for the Lord Jesus Christ. This book is very much needed in Russia. We need to have more books like this that will touch a soul, heart, spirit and mind. God bless you." (Russia)

- "I am incarcerated at this time in a prison in Georgia. I thank you very much for your book *How to Study the Bible.* I fell in love with this book. I read it over three times before I put it down. This book has been such a positive factor in my spiritual life that I really feel super close to my God and my Lord Jesus Christ." (Georgia)

- "God sent me your book *Never, Never Give Up.* I praise God for using you to write and publish that book. Doing time in prison, especially here because I'm locked down 23 hours a day, 5 days a week and 24 hours on the weekend, has really taught me patience, endurance and perseverance living as a Christian and an inmate. I'm giving this book to the chaplain to put in the

Chaplain's prison library so that it will be a blessing to other inmates." (Oklahoma)

- "When I received your book, *Never, Never Give Up,* all was well in my life. I was supposed to be married when I graduated from the Higher Institution of Learning, but this marriage never materialized. The lady I loved so much suffered from migraine headaches and eye pain. She suffered in great pain for almost a year and then she died. In all of this journey of suffering I read your book three times. The contents were meaningful to me and built a good strong character in me. Though my fiancée died and went to be with the Lord, God saw me through that problem. *Never, Never Give Up* was a timely book. It is written simply and is easy to understand. I pray that the Lord will continue to use your ministry to help people who are going through tough times." (Zambia)

- "I would like permission to translate *Trust God for Your Finances.* This book is badly needed by the people of Turkey. Your books and your Scripture cards have been very helpful to my wife and myself. Thank you for your help." (Turkey)

- "I had my baby one and a half months early. I've been in the clinic for five nights. The baby weighs only four pounds. It was a bit frustrating when the baby was ready to deliver and there was no doctor. I've been reading *Conquering Fear* while here. It has been very helpful." (Peru)

- "We find your material to be so readable and upbuilding. Your writing communicates a clear and fatherly concern for the edification of the believer. *Trust God for Your Finances* is a tremendous book. Your book by far is the most thorough and systematic work I have read to date. The church here in Greece has a great need for this book." (Greece)

- "Thank you for the free books you sent me. I read *What Will Heaven be Like?* and I became a Christian immediately. Jesus Christ is now my Savior. I have started preaching to others who need Christ. God bless you and your family and all of your ministry workers." (Ghana)

- "I have just finished your book, *Soaring Above the Problems of Life,* and I am so excited. Each chapter ministered to me so much. My husband is an alcoholic. This book has prepared me for what I am struggling with now. It could not have come at a better time. God bless you." (Colorado)

- "It's a miracle. I read your book *Soaring Above the Problems of Life* with the idea of underlining all the good parts. I have underlined it all! It is wonderful that you went through all of that trouble to be a blessing to others." (Florida)

- "I've looked at several books on heaven and bought some, but none had the depth of the Holy Spirit in them as your book on heaven. I want to express my appreciation for the way the Spirit wrote through you." (Kentucky)

- "Your book, *What Will Heaven be Like?*, moved me deeply and made me even more anxious to join my husband in that wonderful eternal home. You will rejoice with me that one person to whom I gave your book has been saved as a result of reading it. The Holy Spirit is working through you." (New York)

- "I lost my brother, father-in-law, brother-in-law and our family dog of fifteen years in six months. Two years later, I lost my Mom. I suffered deep depression. Your book on heaven was a lifesaver. It lifted my spirits so much. It meant so much in my life that I ordered several to have on hand for friends. Thank you for writing it." (Missouri)

- "I am the Youth Director of our church and I'm leading a group of high school students in a Bible study of your book on heaven. We all respect your opinions and have found your book to be an excellent springboard for discussion. It is thought provoking and informative. This book has much substance and is well organized." (California)

- "Your book *How to Study the Bible* is terrific. At last we have a method to help on this important task. My wife and I just love it." (Nebraska)

- "Your book, *How to Study the Bible,* has helped me and opened my eyes. Because of this book I accepted the Lord Jesus Christ as my personal Lord and Savior. Now I am a Baptist preacher. Please help me to help others. Bless you in His Name." (Ghana)

- "I must tell you how much your book, *Trust God for Your Finances,* has meant to me. I wish I had read it ten years ago when I first began my dental practice. It would have saved me much financial woe." (Mississippi)

- "Your book *Trust God for Your Finances* is absolutely terrific! You wrote it so clearly and in such a relaxed manner that anyone at any level can certainly understand it. Praise God!" (Minnesota)

- "My wife and I feel that *Trust God for Your Finances* is one of the most significant books of the last few decades. It is balanced, scriptural and corrective. Many will be encouraged to step out now that a mature word has been spoken in the midst of some confusion and imbalance. I predict an astonishing fruitfulness for this book." (Washington)

- "Your book *Trust God for Your Finances* is tremendous and has helped me very, very much. I found your book so interesting and knowledgeable and it excited me so that I found myself reading too fast just to find out what was ahead. The second reading of your wonderful book has helped me tremendously. Jack Hartman, you are gifted from God. I think that every Christian should have a copy of this book. God bless you." (Illinois)

- "Your book Trust *God for Your Finances* is so 'loaded' that it takes awhile to digest. God is opening my eyes to truths I haven't understood in the past. This book gives me fresh courage and faith." (Virginia)

- "I do not even have my G.E.D., but *Trust God for Your Finances* is so simple in detail that I am excited about understanding it." (Texas)

Appendix

This book contains comprehensive biblical instructions that explain how to increase your faith in God. These instructions are given to God's children - those human beings who have entered into His kingdom. We ask each person reading this book, "Have *you* entered into the kingdom of God?"

We do not enter into the kingdom of God by church attendance, baptism, confirmation, teaching Sunday school or living a good life. We *only* can enter into the kingdom of God if we have been "born again." Jesus said, "...I assure you, most solemnly I tell you, that unless a person is born again (anew, from above), he cannot ever see (know, be acquainted with, and experience) the kingdom of God" (John 3:3).

Some people are so caught up with their religious denomination and their personal beliefs that they completely miss God's instructions on how to enter His kingdom. This process begins by admitting that we are sinners. We then must repent of these sins. Jesus said, "...unless you repent (change your mind for the better and heartily amend your ways, with abhorrence of your past sins), you will all likewise perish and be lost eternally" (Luke 13:5).

Many people miss out on eternal life in heaven because they are trusting in the goodness of their lives to get them to heaven. With the exception of Jesus, *every* person who has ever lived is a sinner. "…None is righteous, just and truthful and upright and conscientious, no, not one" (Romans 3:10). We *all* are sinners. "…all have sinned and are falling short of the honor and glory which God bestows and receives" (Romans 3:23).

God does not have degrees of sin. If we have committed one sin, we are just as guilty before God as someone who has committed many sins. "For whosoever keeps the Law [as a] whole but stumbles and offends in one [single instance] has become guilty of [breaking] all of it" (James 2:10).

In addition to acknowledging our sins and repenting of them, we must take one additional step. "…if you acknowledge and confess with your lips that Jesus is Lord and in your heart believe (adhere to, trust in, and rely on the truth) that God raised Him from the dead, you will be saved. For with the heart a person believes (adheres to, trusts in, and relies on Christ) and so is justified (declared righteous, acceptable to God), and with the mouth he confesses (declares openly and speaks out freely his faith) and confirms [his] salvation" (Romans 10:9-10).

We must do more than just pay mental assent to the crucifixion of Jesus to receive eternal salvation. We must admit that we are sinners. We must repent of our sins. We must turn away from our sins and go the other way. Repent means to change.

We must believe deep down in our *hearts* that Jesus has paid the full price for all of our sins by taking our place on the cross at Calvary. We must believe that Jesus died for us and that He has risen from the dead. We must believe totally, completely and absolutely that we will live eternally in heaven *only* because of the price Jesus paid for us.

If we really believe these spiritual truths in our hearts, we will speak them with our *mouths*. We may feel timid about doing this at first, but speaking of Jesus increases our faith and draws others to Him. We should tell other people that we have been born again, that we are Christians and that we trust completely in Jesus for our eternal salvation.

All of us were born physically on the day our mothers gave birth to us. We must have a *second birth* to be born spiritually. "You have been regenerated (born again), not from a mortal origin (seed, sperm), but from one that is immortal by the ever living and lasting Word of God" (I Peter 1:23).

Why do we have to be born of the Spirit? We are born into the world with a body and a mind. The spirit of man was separated from God when Adam and Eve sinned. We live our lives only in the body and mind until the Spirit of God plants Himself in our hearts. At that moment, we are born of the Spirit. We are born again.

Jesus became a man and lived a sinless life to become the required sacrifice for our sins. Jesus is our bridge back to God. God sees us as righteous not because we are good, but because we are in Christ Jesus. The blood of Jesus, the sinless sacrifice, was required to enable us to come into God's holy presence.

God does not reveal Himself to us through our intellect. He reveals Himself through our hearts. We may be adults in the natural realm, but we need to start all over again as children in the spiritual realm. We must have childlike faith. Jesus said, "…unless you repent (change, turn about) and become like little children [trusting, lowly, loving, forgiving], you can never enter the kingdom of heaven [at all]" (Matthew 18:3).

The following prayer will result in your spiritual birth if you truly believe these words in your heart and if you boldly confess them to others with your mouth. "Dear Father God I come to You in the name of Jesus Christ. I admit that I am a sinner. I am genuinely sorry for my sins. I want to change my ways. Please help me. Please forgive me. I believe in my heart that Jesus is Your Son and that He died on the cross to pay for my sins. I believe that You raised Him from the dead and that He is alive today sitting at Your right hand. I trust completely in Jesus as my only way of receiving eternal salvation. Thank You, dear Lord Jesus. Thank You, dear Father. Amen."

You have been born again if you prayed this prayer from your heart and if you confessed these heartfelt beliefs with your mouth. You have been given a fresh new start "…if any person is [ingrafted] in Christ (the Messiah) he is a new creation (a new creature altogether); the old [previous moral and spiritual condition] has passed away. Behold, the fresh and new has come!" (II Corinthians 5:17).

You now have entered into the most precious relationship of all. Your previous spiritual condition changed when you were born into Christ Jesus. You are not the same person you were before. You are a child of Father God.

Begin to talk with your Father each day. Pray to Him continually. Study the Bible daily. Meditate on the Word of God continually. Praise God and thank Him each day.

Find other Christians who love God. Fellowship with them. Speak to others of your relationship with God. This new relationship that began when you asked Jesus to be your Savior will grow and grow and your new life will be a very wonderful life where you constantly will draw closer to God.

Please contact us and let us know that you have become a child of God. We would like to pray for you and welcome you as our new brother or sister in Christ Jesus. We love you and bless you in the name of our Lord Jesus Christ. We would be so pleased to hear from you.

Biblical Health in a Nutshell

by Judy Hartman

I can't spend all of this time with you in our book without sharing with you what I believe may save your life. I am sixty-five years old and have been studying health, fitness, and nutrition since I was twenty-one. I have lived what I have learned. I am healthier today that I have ever been in my life. I feel better each day that I ever have before. I am stronger and more limber, more flexible than I have ever been. My mind is clear and alert.

I pray the same for you, dear friend. Whatever your age, the time is now to take responsibility for your own health. Begin your long-term care now yourself so that you can carry out God's specific plan for your life with joy, clarity, vigor and vitality.

First, let's search the Bible for what keeps some people from being open to the statistics on health today. God tells us in Romans 14:2 that "One [man's faith permits him to believe he may eat anything, while a weaker one [limits his] eating to vegetables."

I am in the group who can eat everything. God has given us the liberty to eat whatever we choose to eat. Based on my study and experience, my body does best on a plant-based died. It fact, it thrives on a plant-based diet.

We know that Jesus ate fish with the disciples when He returned to earth after His resurrection. In John 21, Jesus provided the fish and ate bread and fish with the disciples. We know that most, if not all, fish today caught in the seas, oceans, lakes, and streams contain mercury, a very harmful toxin.

I do not make a biblical doctrine of my eating. I continually find instructions in the Bible that clearly tell me what to do as I read through the Bible again and again.

I have a passion to share what I have learned about health. I teach a monthly class at our church, Christ Church in Palm Harbor, Florida. We are seeing remarkable changes in people's lives as a result of making simple changes in their lives.

The reason that I teach health to those who want to learn about it is found in Romans 14: "For it is written, As I live, says the Lord, every knee shall bow to Me and every tongue shall confess to God [acknowledge Him to His honor and to His praise."

Our focus in life is to keep ourselves in Christ Jesus and to be instruments of God's message for others to have ears to hear the gospel. Every single person will bow his or her knee to God. Our hearts break with the thought that some will bow their knees from a place that will result in eternal separation from God. Many lives are cut short because of the SAD, the Standard American Diet.

"Father, help us to show the way of salvation to others in a way that their hearts can receive You. Holy Spirit, empower us to be instruments of the gospel while there is still time. In Jesus' name, we pray. Amen."

I want to be healthy in order to go on the mission trips to countries where our books have been translated into the local language, to meet and encourage the Christian leaders and bless them in every way that I can. Teaching simple health principles will enable others to fulfill the plan that God has for their lives.

I am now taking this message of health to the nations. As this book is being prepared for printing, I am traveling to India with Laura Lee Ryan to teach simple health and fitness principles. I will be traveling to Zambia and Ghana with the same message. I want to present what I have learned and lived to the nations who are embarking on the Standard American Diet believing it is equal to prosperity, not knowing that it brings a painful, compromised life and early death.

I do not judge anyone for the way he or she chooses to worship God or the way he or she chooses to eat. I will not allow eating to create a division. I explain that I have chosen to eat this way for my own health and I am clear not to judge others by what they eat.

God is very specific about the care of the temple in the Old Testament. He is just as specific about the care of the temple in the New Testament. That temple is the body where the Holy Spirit takes residence the moment we acknowledge Jesus as our Messiah. Over 90% of all disease is directly related to an unclean temple or tabernacle, an unclean body. The two major causes of disease are toxicity and malnutrition. I choose to eliminate toxins as much as I can and to provide optimal nutrients to feed every cell in my body.

I have made changes to reduce toxins in our home. The Consumer Product Safety Commission reports that "150 chemicals commonly found in homes have been linked to allergies, birth defects, cancer, and psychological abnormalities."

In a 15-year study, women who worked at home had a 54% higher death rate from cancer than did women who worked away from home. The study concluded that the increased death rate was because of daily exposure to toxic chemicals in household products. Formaldehyde is found in household cleaners, disinfectants, carpet, permanent press fabrics, many personal care products, medicines, antiseptics, and many other products used in the home.

I choose to wear only 100% cotton, 100% silk or linen, or 100% wool (stays packed for trips to the cold north). I use a vegetable-based laundry soap for washing our clothes. Much toxicity remains in clothes washed with the chemicals of laundry soaps and clothes drier sheets. These chemicals are against the body and can enter through the skin or the nostrils.

Here is a health equation provided by Hallelujah Acres where I have been a Health Minister since 1997. A person's level of health equals nutrition plus exercise, minus toxins and stress.

Please understand that what I am sharing is not biblical doctrine. I am presenting facts that today present a SAD picture of health in the United States and in every country that adopts our fast foods and our animal-based diet. SAD means Standard American Diet.

I would like to present the principle of eating to live, not living to eat. In Proverbs we are warned to "take a knife to our throat if we are given to appetite." God warns that gluttony is a sin. If I have extra fat on my body, I have eaten more than my body requires to live and to operate optimally.

The United States is the most overfed and undernourished nation in the world. I choose to select nutrient dense food. I eat only when I am hungry. Each of the trillions of cells in my body was created by God to process live food. The best live food would be just picked from the tree or bush or from under the ground.

The next best is organic produce. When necessary, I purchase produce from the produce section of the grocery store. More and more stores in our area are carrying organic produce. Statistics show that organic produce is more nutrient dense than its toxin-filled, fertilized, poison-spayed counterparts found in the produce section of the grocery store. Yet these veggies and fruit are better for my health than cooked food. I allow myself some cooked food at the end of the day after I have fed my cells lots of nutrients through freshly squeezed vegetable juices and the green powder of barley leaves and fresh fruit.

I clean veggies and fruit by spraying them first with straight hydrogen peroxide and let them sit for ten minutes. Then I spray them with white or cider vinegar and let them sit for another ten minutes. Then I rinse them, prepare the veggies for the week, and then put them all in the refrigerator. I try to do this as soon as I arrive home from purchasing my produce.

Immediately I prepare the greens for the week. I dry them and cut with scissors lettuce, kale, parsley, cilantro, and any other greens. I use as many different greens as I can find. I cut just a little of each of the tougher ones and more of the different kinds of lettuce. I place them in quart-sized plastic bags in the refrigerator.

Raw greens are the major source of protein for many species of animals. Where does the cow get protein? When do the elephant and giraffe get protein? The greens lose a little of the nutrients through being cut, but having salads and veggies all ready for many dishes is worth the slight loss of nutrients. When I go for a physical exam, I see that my protein levels are exactly where they should be.

Then I take other vegetables that are not juicy, such as broccoli, cauliflower, carrots, zucchini, green beans, snap peas, and other. I place these in the Cuisinart food processor with the blade. I pulse the machine on and off until the veggies are the size I want, about bite-sized. I place these in quart plastic bags in the refrigerator.

Now I have fast food salads all ready. I just slice some tomatoes. I make salad dressings with avocados, sunflower seeds, flax seeds, pumpkin seeds, sesame seeds, plus lemon or lime juice, natural apple cider vinegar, or a fresh juice such as orange or tomato. I add flavorings from the garden, such as dill or basil, or use dried herbs.

I also have veggies ready to stir-fry in vegetable stock or a sweet and sour veggie dish with pineapple and dried grated coconut (from the health food store) over brown basmati rice.

I have much information about meat-based diets being the cause of heart disease. Dr. Caldwell Esselstyne of the world-famous Cleveland Clinic Foundation spoke to our Health Minister Reunion in 2004. He has a plan of eating that virtually eliminates the heart disease that was not listed in the medical journals before the 1900s. Dr. Esselstyne reports that heart disease is the result of the increase of meat in the diet in the United States and other countries that adopt the SAD (Standard American Diet) when our fast food businesses arrive in their countries.

In Nigeria, Ghana, and West Africa, there is a noticeable absence of men older than 40, a health crisis has occurred because the meat-eating men are dying of heart attacks at an early age. The influx of the Western style of meat eating, fast foods, and the belief that meat-eating equals prosperity are killing the men of these nations.

The incidence of heart disease in Japan was very low before the SAD diet arrived in their country. They also had almost no lung cancer until smoking arrived in their culture.

Eating meat creates an odor in humans. Remember that the Indians would not eat meat before they went to hunt. They knew that the animals could smell the meat in their bodies. Vegetarians usually do not have body odor and do not need deodorants.

I do not use deodorants that contain aluminum. In fact, I do not use deodorants at all. The lymph system is right at the point where the deodorant is placed. A large majority of breast cancer is at the upper outside corner of the breast where deodorant is placed year after year. There is a strong possibility that aluminum has a part in the onset of Alzheimer's disease as well as breast cancer.

Any chemicals that I place on my skin can enter my body through the pores. I no longer use chemical-laden sunscreen. I purchase sunscreen at the health food store but never over the number 15. I do not use perfumes, creams, shampoos, conditioners, hair dyes, or any other chemical that would poison my body. I know that in time the accumulation of toxins in the brain or skin will cause disease in my body. I use chemical-free products for personal care and for maintaining my home.

I am not presenting a biblical doctrine. I prefer to live the Genesis 1:29 plan that God gave to Adam and Eve. It is so full of delicious food that I do not want to eat anything else. There are many sources for recipes, but I am very creative and love to make up my own. Please contact me if you would like to receive my recipes and ideas for taking responsibility for your own health.

I have seven keys to health that I do my best to follow. They are Salvation, Oxygen, Sunshine, Nutrition, Exercise, Water, and Scripture.

#1 – Salvation: We have presented God's plan to redeem every person back to Himself. Redeem means to exchange something for something else. Jesus exchanged His life and His blood for each of us. He stood in our place before God as if He were a sinner. He took all of our sin upon Himself as He stood before His Father and our God. We each have a choice to redeem our lives or to forever be separated from God. We redeem our lives by acknowledging Jesus as our Messiah, the King of Kings and Lord of Lords. We believe that the time in which this decision can still be made is short. We plead with every reader to be certain that your name is written in heaven. Please see our Appendix for instructions to be certain that you are part of the family of God through Jesus.

#2 – Oxygen: Deep breathe like a baby, from your diaphragm. As you walk, breathe in to the count of four and breathe out to the count of four. All during the day, do deep breathing by breathing in to the count of four, holding to the count of four, exhaling to the count of four, and then holding to the count of four. As you inhale, exaggerate the intake. As you exhale, exaggerate the exhale. Clean out your windpipes! As you exhale the air, exhale all the negative thoughts and worries as well.

#3 – Sunshine: Try to be out in the sunshine for at least fifteen minutes each day. The sun provides nutrients, especially Vitamin D, for our physical health as well as the beauty of light for our mental health. We know that plants do not create chlorophyll without light. Our bodies require light for optimum health.

#4 – Nutrition: Living food was designed for the human body: living food. I try to consume 85% raw and 15% cooked food, with the cooked food at the end of the day. I use the Green Power and Champion juicers, a VitaMix blender, a Cuisinart food processor, and an Excalibur food dehydrator.

Drinking freshly extracted vegetable juices is an essential part of my nutrition. The extra nutrients enable my body to tackle unfinished business, all old wounds and anything left over from every sickness I ever had. My body cleans house and sends workers to the areas where there was a weakness and corrects the imbalance. God made the body to heal itself if it is given the right tools.

Protein and calcium are the major issues that people bring up about a plant-based diet. Fresh greens are loaded with protein and calcium. Ask the zebra, the buffalo or the gazelle.

I carry fruit with me and a small packet of nuts and seeds for snacks. I carry apples and carrots for my horse and for my grandchildren and me as well!

#5 – Exercise: Muscles do not age. I fit aerobics, weight training, and stretching into my life through T-Tapp, the wellness workout that works. Walking is the very best exercise. I aim for a mile in fifteen minutes. My goal is a 45-minute three-mile walk or walk-jog.

I combine walking with the rebounder mini-trampoline which was created by NASA for the astronauts. It combines acceleration, deceleration, and gravity which clean the lymphatic system by exercising every cell with every bounce. The lymphatic system has no pump of its own. An inexpensive rebounder may damage your back. I purchase only Needak rebounders.

#6 – Water: Drink pure water equal to at least half of your weight, but measure in ounces instead of pounds. Drink two glasses of water when you first awaken. Sip pure water all day long. The brain especially needs pure water to function properly. The eyes need water, as does the entire body.

#7 – Scripture: The Bible is God's message to me. God gives me instructions, loves me, and blesses me every day in His Word. I have a plan to read through the Bible. As I read it, I note verses on specific subjects. I am interested in so many subjects that I have many lists! I keep these verses together so I can create a message on a specific topic. I also carry verses and a chapter with me to be writing on my heart. God keeps me in His love, walking in forgiveness. I choose to "pre-forgive" whatever may happen each day that might hurt or offend me. Forgiveness is a major key to health.

My heart breaks when I see the lack of health in the body of Christ. We should be the shining examples of health for others. They should come running to our churches because they want to be as healthy as we are!

The good news is that the miraculous, self-healing body can reverse the most severe of diseases if given the proper tools. God's nature is to heal. We pray for the sick and trust in the power of God to heal. The person healed must then learn what caused the sickness and make changes to prevent the sickness from returning through toxicity or malnutrition, poison or a lack of nutrients.

I like to bring together the natural and the supernatural. I pray that we can keep our bodies fit for the King as we complete the assignment He has given us which includes feeding the poor and praying for the sick as we take the gospel to every nation.

If I can help you in any way, please contact me.

You can write me at PO Box 1307, Dunedin FL 34697.

You can call me at 1-800-733-8467.

My email address is lamplight@lamplight.net.

Study Guide

What Did You Learn From This Book?

The questions in this Study Guide are carefully arranged to show *you* how strong your faith in God is and how ready you are to deal with severe adversity. We have prayerfully compiled this Study Guide so that anyone who does well on this test *will* have confidence that he or she will be able to deal with the difficult times that are coming.

We have not included questions on every Scripture reference in the book. This is not an academic test. The sole purpose of the following questions is to help you receive help from God according to your faith in Him.

Page reference

1. Why are many of God's people destroyed by adversity? Why did the Israelites fail to escape from the wilderness many years ago? Why must we avoid making the same mistake today? (Hosea 4:6, Galatians 3:26 and Hebrews 12:25) 9-11

2. Why are Satan and his demons so fervent in their attempt to significantly influence the apathy, complacency and moral decay that exists today? (Revelation 12:12) 11-12

68. We must not confuse the Bible with books written by men and women. The Bible truly is the

A few words about Lamplight Ministries

Lamplight Ministries, Inc. originally began in 1983 as Lamplight Publications. After ten years as a publishing firm with a goal of selling Christian books, Lamplight Ministries was founded in 1993. Jack and Judy Hartman founded Lamplight Ministries with a mission of continuing to sell their publications and also to *give* large numbers of these publications free of charge to needy people all over the world.

Lamplight Ministries was created to allow people who have been blessed by our publications to share in financing the translation, printing and distribution of our books into other languages and also to distribute our publications free of charge to jails and prisons. Over the years many partners of Lamplight Ministries have shared Jack and Judy's vision. As the years have gone by Lamplight Ministries' giving has increased with each passing year. Tens of thousands of people in jails and prisons and in Third World countries have received our publications free of charge.

Our books and Scripture Meditation Cards have been translated into eleven foreign languages – Armenian, Danish, Greek, Hebrew, German, Korean, Norwegian, Portuguese, Russian, Spanish and the Tamil dialect in India. The translations in these languages are not available from Lamplight Ministries in the United States. These translations can only be obtained in the countries where they have been printed.

The pastors of many churches in Third World countries have written to say that they consistently preach sermons in their churches based on the scriptural contents of our publications. We believe that, on any given Sunday, people in several churches in many different countries hear sermons that are based on the scriptural contents of our publications. Praise the Lord!

Jack Hartman was the sole author of twelve Christian books. After co-authoring one book with Judy, Jack and Judy co-authored ten sets of Scripture Meditation Cards. Judy's contributions to *God's Wisdom Is Available To You*, *Exchange Your Worries for God's Perfect Peace* and *Unshakable Faith in Almighty God* were so significant that she is the co-author of these books. Jack and Judy currently are working on several other books that they believe the Lord is leading them to write as co-authors.

We invite you to request our newsletters to stay in touch with us, to learn of our latest publications and to read comments from people all over the world. Please write, fax, call or email us. You are very special to us. We love you and thank God for you. Our heart is to take the gospel to the world and for our books to be available in every known language. Hallelujah!

Lamplight Ministries, Inc.,
PO Box 1307
Dunedin, Florida, 34697.
USA
Phone: 1-800-540-1597 • Fax: 1-727-784-2980 • website: lamplight.net • email: gospel@tampabay.rr.com

We offer you a substantial quantity discount

From the beginning of our ministry we have been led of the Lord to offer the same quantity discount to individuals that we offer to Christian bookstores. Each individual has a sphere of influence with a specific group of people. We believe that you know many people who need to learn the scriptural contents of our publications.

The Word of God encourages us to give freely to others. We encourage you to give selected copies of these publications to people you know who need help in the specific areas that are covered by our publications. See our order form for specific information on the quantity discounts of 40% to 50% that we make available to you so that you can share our books and cassette tapes with others.

A request to our readers

If this book has helped you, we would like to receive your comments so that we can share them with others. Your comments can encourage other people to study our publications to learn from the scriptural contents of these publications.

When we receive a letter containing comments on any of our books, cassette tapes or Scripture Meditation Cards, we prayerfully take out excerpts from these letters. These selected excerpts are included in our newsletters and occasionally in our advertising and promotional materials.

If any of our publications have been a blessing to you, please share your comments with us so that we can share them with others. Tell us in your own words what a specific publication has meant to you and why you would recommend it to others. Please give as much specific information as possible.

We will need your written permission to use all or any part of your comments. We will never print your name or street address. We simply use the state or country you live in (Illinois).

Thank you for taking a few minutes of your time to encourage other people to learn from the scripture references in our publications.

Books by Jack and Judy Hartman

Exchange Your Worries for God's Perfect Peace—Our Father does not want His children to worry. He wants each of us to be absolutely certain that He has provided for all of our needs, that He lives in our hearts, that He is with us at all times and that He will help us if we have faith in Him. This books contains over 400 Scripture references that explain exactly what we should do to be set free from worry and fear and exactly what we should do to receive God's perfect peace that has been provided for us.

God's Wisdom Is Available To You explains from more than 500 Scripture references how to receive the wisdom our Father has promised to give to us. God looks at the wisdom of the world as "foolishness" (see I Corinthians 3:19). You will learn how to receive the revelation knowledge, guidance and wisdom from God that bypasses sense knowledge.

Trust God for Your Finances is currently in its nineteenth printing with more than 150,000 copies in print. This book which has been translated into nine foreign languages contains over 200 Scripture references that explain in a simple, straightforward and easy-to-understand style what the Word of God says about our Father's instructions and promises pertaining to our finances.

Never, Never Give Up devotes the first five chapters to a scriptural explanation of patience and the remaining thirteen chapters to scriptural instruction pertaining to the subject of perseverance. This book is based on almost 300 Scripture references that will help you to learn exactly what our loving Father instructs us to do to increase our patience and perseverance.

Quiet Confidence in the Lord is solidly anchored on more than 400 Scripture references that explain how to remain calm and quiet in a crisis situation. You will learn from the Word of God how to control your emotions when you are faced with severe problems and how to increase your confidence in the Lord by spending precious quiet time alone with Him each day.

What Will Heaven Be Like? explains from more than 200 Scripture references what the Bible tells us about what heaven will be like. Many people have written to tell us how much this book comforted them after they lost a loved one. We have received many other letters from terminally ill Christians who were comforted by scriptural facts about where they would be going in the near future.

Soaring Above the Problems of Life has helped many people who were going through severe trials. This practical "hands on" book is filled with facts from the Word of God. Our Father has given each of us specific and exact instructions telling us how He wants us to deal with adversity. This book is written in a clear and easy-to-understand style that will help you to learn to deal with the adversity that we all must face in our lives.

How to Study the Bible. Many Christians attempt to study the Bible and give up because they are unable to find a fruitful method of Bible study. This book explains in detail the method that Jack Hartman uses to study the Bible. This practical, step-by-step technique will give you a definite, specific and precise system for studying the Word of God. Any person who sincerely wants to study the Bible effectively can be helped by this book and our two cassette tapes on this subject.

Increased Energy and Vitality. Jack and Judy Hartman are senior citizens who are determined to be in the best possible physical condition to serve the Lord during the remainder of their lives. They have spent many hours of study and practical trial and error to learn how to increase their energy and vitality. This book is based on more than 200 Scripture references that will help you to increase your energy and vitality so that you can serve the Lord more effectively.

Nuggets of Faith – Jack Hartman has written over 100,000 spiritual meditations. This book contains some of his early meditations on the subject of increasing our faith in God. It contains 78 "nuggets" (average length of three paragraphs) to help you to increase your faith in God.

100 Years from Today tells exactly where each of us will be one hundred years from now if Jesus is our Savior and where we will be if Jesus is not our Savior. This simple and easy-to-understand book has helped many unbelievers to receive Jesus as their Savior. This book leads the reader through the decision to eternal salvation. The book closes by asking the reader to make a decision for Jesus and to make this decision now.

Conquering Fear – Many people in the world today are afraid because they see that various forms of worldly security are disappearing. Our Father does not want us to be afraid. He has told us 366 times in His Word that we should not be afraid. This book is filled with scriptural references that explain the source of fear and how to overcome fear.

God's Will For Our Lives teaches from the holy Scriptures why we are here on earth, what our Father wants us to do with our lives and how to experience the meaning and fulfillment we can only experience when we are carrying out God's will. God had a specific plan for each of our lives before we were born. He has given each of us abilities and talents to carry out the assignment He has given to us.

Scripture Meditation Cards and Cassette Tapes by Jack and Judy Hartman

Each set of Scripture Meditation Cards consists of 52 2-1/2 inch by 3-1/2 inch cards that can easily be carried in a pocket or a purse. Each set of Scripture cards includes approximately 75 Scripture references and is accompanied by an 85-minute cassette tape that explains every passage of Scripture in detail.

Freedom From Worry and Fear

The holy Scriptures tell us repeatedly that our Father does not want us to be worried or afraid. There is no question that God doesn't want us to be worried or afraid, but what exactly should we do if we have a sincere desire to overcome worry and fear? You will learn to overcome worry and fear from specific factual instructions from the Word of God. You will learn how to have a peaceful mind that is free from fear. You'll learn to live one day at a time forgetting the past and not worrying about the future. You'll learn how to trust God completely instead of allowing worry and fear to get into your mind and into your heart.

Enjoy God's Wonderful Peace

Peace with God is available to us because of the sacrifice that Jesus made for us at Calvary. In addition to peace with God, Jesus also has given us the opportunity to enjoy the peace of God. You will learn how to enter into God's rest to receive God's perfect peace that will enable you to remain calm and quiet deep down inside of yourself regardless of the circumstances you face. You will learn exactly what to do to experience God's peace that is so great that it surpasses human understanding. The Holy Spirit is always calm and peaceful. We can experience His wonderful peace if we learn how to yield control of our lives to Him.

Find God's Will for Your Life

The Bible tells us that God had a specific plan for every day of our lives before we were born. Our Father will not reveal His will for our lives to us if we seek His will passively. He wants us to hunger and thirst with a deep desire to live our lives according to His will. God's plan for our lives is far over and above anything we can comprehend with our limited human comprehension. We cannot experience deep meaning, fulfillment and satisfaction in our lives without seeking, finding and carrying out God's will for our lives.

Receive God's Blessings in Adversity

The Lord is with us when we are in trouble. He wants to help us and He will help us according to our faith in Him. He wants us to focus continually on Him instead of dwelling on the problems we face. We must not give up hope. Our Father will never let us down. He has made provision to give us His strength in exchange for our weakness. Our Father wants us to learn, grow and mature by facing the problems in our lives according to the instructions He has given us in His Word. We must persevere in faith to walk in the magnificent victory that Jesus won for us.

Financial Instructions from God

Our loving Father wants His children to be financially successful just as loving parents here on earth want their children to be successful. God's ways are much higher and very different from the ways of the world. Our Father doesn't want us to follow the world's system for financial prosperity. He wants us to learn and obey His instructions pertaining to our finances. You will learn how to renew your mind in the Word of God so that you will be able to see your finances in a completely different light than you see them from a worldly perspective. You will be given step-by-step instructions to follow to receive financial prosperity from God.

Receive Healing from the Lord

Many people are confused by the different teachings about whether God heals today. Are you sick? Would you like to see for yourself exactly what the Bible says about divine healing? Study the Word of God on this important subject. Draw your own conclusion based on facts from the holy Scriptures. You will learn that Jesus has provided for your healing just as surely as He has provided for your eternal salvation. You will learn exactly what the Word of God instructs you to do to increase your faith that God will heal you.

A Closer Relationship with the Lord

Because of the price that Jesus paid at Calvary all Christians have been given the awe-inspiring opportunity to come into the presence of Almighty God. These Scripture cards clearly explain the secret of enjoying a sweet and satisfying relationship with the Lord. Many Christians know about the Lord, but He wants us to know Him personally. We should have a deep desire to enjoy a close personal relationship with our precious Lord. He has promised to come close to us if we sincerely desire a close relationship with Him.

Our Father's Wonderful Love

God showed His love for us by sending His beloved Son to earth to die for our sins. Jesus showed His love for us by taking the sins of the entire world upon Himself on the cross at Calvary. The same love and compassion that was demonstrated during the earthly ministry of Jesus is available to us today. Because of the sacrifice of Jesus all Christians are the beloved sons and daughters of Almighty God. God is our loving Father. Our Father doesn't want us to seek security from external sources. He wants us to be completely secure in His love for us. You will learn from the Word of God exactly how faith works by love and how to overcome fear through love.

God is Always with You

God is not far away. He lives in our hearts. We must not neglect the gift that is in us. We are filled with the Godhead -- Father, Son and Holy Spirit. Why would we ever be afraid of anything or anyone if we are absolutely certain that God is always with us? God's power and might are much greater than we can comprehend. He watches over us at all times. He wants to help us. He wants us to walk in close fellowship with Him. His wisdom and knowledge are available to us. He wants to guide us throughout every day of our lives.

Continually Increasing Faith in God

We all are given the same amount of faith to enable us to become children of God. Our Father wants the faith that He gave us to grow continually. We live in the last days before Jesus returns. We must learn how to develop deeply rooted faith in God. You will learn how to walk in the authority and power you have been given over Satan and his demons. You can walk in victory over the circumstances in your life. You will learn exactly what the holy Scriptures tell us to do to receive manifestation of God's mighty strength and power. You will learn the vital importance of the words you speak. You will learn that there is only one way to control the words you speak when you are under severe pressure in a crisis situation.

Why you cannot combine orders for quantity discounts for Scripture Meditation Cards with other products

We desire to make the purchase of our products as *simple* as possible. However, we are unable to combine orders for our Scripture Meditation Cards with orders for our other products.

The reason for this decision is that the cost of printing and packaging Scripture Meditation Cards is much higher in proportion to the purchase price than the price of printing books. If we wanted to offer the same percentage quantity discount that we offer with our books, the cost for one set of Scripture Meditation Cards would have to be $7. This price was unacceptable to us.

We decided to offer each individual set of Scripture Meditation Cards for a reasonable price of $5 including postage. In order to keep this price for individual sets of Scripture Meditation Cards this low we had to develop an entirely different price structure for quantity discounts. Please see the enclosed order form for information on these discounts.

Cassette Tapes
by Jack Hartman

01H How to Study the Bible (Part 1) – 21 scriptural reasons why it is important to study the Bible

02H How to Study the Bible (Part 2) – A detailed explanation of a proven, effective system for studying the Bible

03H Enter Into God's Rest – Don't struggle with loads that are too heavy for you. Learn what God's Word teaches about relaxing under pressure.

04H Freedom From Worry – A comprehensive scriptural explanation of how to become free from worry

05H God's Strength, Our Weakness – God's strength is available if we can admit our human weakness and trust instead in His unlimited strength.

06H How to Transform Our Lives – A scriptural study of how we can change our lives through a spiritual renewal of our minds.

07H The Greatest Power in the Universe (Part 1) – The greatest power in the universe is love. This tape explains our Father's love for us.

08H The Greatest Power in the Universe (Part 2) – A scriptural explanation of our love for God and for each other, and how to overcome fear through love.

09H How Well Do You Know Jesus Christ? – An Easter Sunday message that will show you Jesus as you never knew Him before.

10H God's Perfect Peace – In a world of unrest, many people search for inner peace. Learn from God's Word how to obtain His perfect peace.

11H Freedom Through Surrender – Many people try to find freedom by "doing their own thing." God's Word says that freedom comes from surrendering our lives to Jesus.

12H Overcoming Anger – When is anger is permissible and when is it a sin? Learn from the Bible how to overcome the sinful effects of anger.

13H Taking Possession of Our Souls – God's Word teaches that patience is the key to the possession of our souls. Learn from the Word of God how to increase your patience and endurance.

14H Staying Young in the Lord – Some people try to cover up the aging process with makeup, hair coloring and hairpieces. Learn from the Bible how you can offset the aging process.

15H Two Different Worlds – Specific instructions from the Word of God to help you enter into and stay in the presence of God.

16H Trust God For Your Finances – This tape is a summary of the highlights of Jack's best-selling book, *Trust God For Your Finances*.

17H   The Joy of the Lord – Learn how to experience the joy of the Lord regardless of the external circumstances in your life.

18H   Let Go and Let God – Our Father wants us to give our problems to Him and leave them with Him because we have complete faith in Him..

19H   Guidance, Power, Comfort and Wisdom – Learn the specific work of the Holy Spirit Who will guide us, empower us, comfort us and give us wisdom.

20H   Go With God – This tape is based on 35 Scripture references that explain why and how to witness to the unsaved.

21H   One Day at a Time – Our Father doesn't want us to dwell on the past nor worry about the future. Learn how to follow biblical instructions to live your life one day at a time.

22H   Never, Never Give Up – Endurance and perseverance are often added to our faith as we wait on the Lord, releasing our will to His.

23H   The Christ-Centered Life – Some Christians are still on the throne of their lives pursuing personal goals. Learn how to center every aspect of your life around the Lord Jesus Christ.

24H   Fear Must Disappear – The spirit of fear cannot stand up against perfect love. Learn what perfect love is and how to attain it.

25H   Internal Security – Some Christians look for security from external sources. In this tape, Jack shares his belief that difficult times are ahead of us and the only security in these times will be from the Spirit of God and the Word of God living in our hearts.

26H Continually Increasing Faith – Romans 12:3 tells us that all Christians start out with a specific amount of faith. In these last days before Jesus returns, we will all need a stronger faith than just the minimum. This tape offers many specific suggestions on what to do to continually strengthen our faith.

27H Why Does God Allow Adversity? – Several Scripture references are used in this tape to explain the development of strong faith through adversity.

28H Faith Works by Love – Galatians 5:6 tells us that faith works by love. Christians wondering why their faith doesn't seem to be working may find an answer in this message. A life centered around the love of the Lord for us and our love for others is absolutely necessary to strong faith.

29H There Are No Hopeless Situations – Satan wants us to feel hopeless. He wants us to give up hope and quit. This tape explains the difference between hope and faith. It tells how we set our goals through hope and bring them into manifestation through strong, unwavering faith.

30H Walk By Faith, Not By Sight – When we're faced with seemingly unsolvable problems, it's easy to focus our attention on the problems instead of on the Word of God and the Spirit of God. In this tape, Jack gives many personal examples of difficult situations in his life and how the Lord honored his faith and the faith of others who prayed for him.

31H Stay Close to the Lord – Our faith is only as strong as its source. A close relationship with the Lord is essential to strong faith. In this tape, Jack explores God's Word to give a thorough explanation of how to develop a closer relationship with the Lord.

32H   Quiet Faith – When we're faced with very difficult problems, the hardest thing to do is to be still. The Holy Spirit, however, wants us to remain quiet and calm because of our faith in Him. This message carefully examines the Word of God for an explanation of how we can do this.

33H   When Human Logic is Insufficient – Human logic and reason often miss God. This message explains why some Christians block the Lord because they're unable to bypass their intellects and place their trust completely in Him.

34H   The Good Fight of Faith – In this message, Jack compares the "good fight of faith" with the "bad" fight of faith. He explains who we fight against, where the battle is fought, and how it is won.

ORDER FORM FOR BOOKS AND CASSETTE TAPES

Book Title	Quantity	Total
Unshakable Faith in Almighty God ($12.00)	_____	_____
Exchange Your Worries for God's Perfect Peace ($12.00)	_____	_____
God's Wisdom is Available to You ($12.00)	_____	_____
Increased Energy and Vitality ($10.00)	_____	_____
Quiet Confidence in the Lord ($9.00)	_____	_____
Never, Never Give Up ($8.00)	_____	_____
Trust God For Your Finances ($8.00)	_____	_____
What Will Heaven Be Like? ($8.00)	_____	_____
Conquering Fear ($8.00)	_____	_____
Soaring Above the Problems of Life ($8.00)	_____	_____
God's Will For Our Lives ($8.00)	_____	_____
How to Study the Bible ($5.00)	_____	_____
Nuggets of Faith ($5.00)	_____	_____
100 Years From Today ($5.00)	_____	_____

Cassette Tapes (please indicate quantity being ordered) • *$5 each*

____01H ____02H ____03H ____04H ____05H ____06H ____07H
____08H ____09H ____10H ____11H ____12H ____13H ____14H
____15H ____16H ____17H ____18H ____19H ____20H ____21H
____22H ____23H ____24H ____25H ____26H ____27H ____28H
____29H ____30H ____31H ____32H ____33H ____34H

Price of books and tapes	_____
Minus 40% discount for 5-9 items	_____
Minus 50% discount for 10 or more items	_____
Net price of order	_____
Add 15% **before discount** for shipping and handling	_____
(Maximum of $50 for any size order)	
Florida residents only, add 7% sales tax	_____
Tax deductible contribution to Lamplight Ministries, Inc.	_____
Enclosed check or money order (do not send cash)	_____

(Please make check payable to Lamplight Ministries, Inc. and mail to: PO Box 1307, Dunedin, FL 34697)

MC____ Visa____ AmEx____ Disc.____ Card # _____

Exp Date _____ Signature _____

Name _____

Address _____

City _____

State or Province _____ Zip or Postal Code _____

(Foreign orders must be submitted in U.S. dollars.)

ORDER FORM FOR BOOKS AND CASSETTE TAPES

Book Title	Quantity	Total
Unshakable Faith in Almighty God ($12.00)	_____	_____
Exchange Your Worries for God's Perfect Peace ($12.00)	_____	_____
God's Wisdom is Available to You ($12.00)	_____	_____
Increased Energy and Vitality ($10.00)	_____	_____
Quiet Confidence in the Lord ($9.00)	_____	_____
Never, Never Give Up ($8.00)	_____	_____
Trust God For Your Finances ($8.00)	_____	_____
What Will Heaven Be Like? ($8.00)	_____	_____
Conquering Fear ($8.00)	_____	_____
Soaring Above the Problems of Life ($8.00)	_____	_____
God's Will For Our Lives ($8.00)	_____	_____
How to Study the Bible ($5.00)	_____	_____
Nuggets of Faith ($5.00)	_____	_____
100 Years From Today ($5.00)	_____	_____

Cassette Tapes (please indicate quantity being ordered) • *$5 each*

_____01H _____02H _____03H _____04H _____05H _____06H _____07H
_____08H _____09H _____10H _____11H _____12H _____13H _____14H
_____15H _____16H _____17H _____18H _____19H _____20H _____21H
_____22H _____23H _____24H _____25H _____26H _____27H _____28H
_____29H _____30H _____31H _____32H _____33H _____34H

Price of books and tapes	_____
Minus 40% discount for 5-9 items	_____
Minus 50% discount for 10 or more items	_____
Net price of order	_____
Add 15% **before discount** for shipping and handling	_____
(*Maximum of $50 for any size order*)	
Florida residents only, add 7% sales tax	_____
Tax deductible contribution to Lamplight Ministries, Inc.	_____
Enclosed check or money order (do not send cash)	_____

(Please make check payable to Lamplight Ministries, Inc. and mail to: PO Box 1307, Dunedin, FL 34697)

MC____ Visa____ AmEx____ Disc.____ Card # _____

Exp Date _____ Signature _____

Name _____

Address _____

City _____

State or Province _____ Zip or Postal Code _____

(Foreign orders must be submitted in U.S. dollars.)

ORDER FORM FOR SCRIPTURE MEDITATION CARDS AND CASSETTE TAPES

Due to completely different price structure for the production of Scripture Meditation Cards and 85-minute cassette tapes, we offer a different quantity discount which cannot be combined with our other quantity discounts. The following prices *include shipping and handling*. $5 per card deck or cassette tape; $4 for 5-9 card decks or cassette tapes; $3 for 10 or more card decks or cassette tapes.

SCRIPTURE MEDITATION CARDS	QUANTITY	PRICE
Find God's Will for Your Life	_____	_____
Financial Instructions from God	_____	_____
Freedom from Worry and Fear	_____	_____
A Closer Relationship with the Lord	_____	_____
Our Father's Wonderful Love	_____	_____
Receive Healing from the Lord	_____	_____
Receive God's Blessing in Adversity	_____	_____
Enjoy God's Wonderful Peace	_____	_____
God is Always with You	_____	_____
Continually Increasing Faith in God	_____	_____

CASSETTE TAPES		
Find God's Will for Your Life	_____	_____
Financial Instructions from God	_____	_____
Freedom from Worry and Fear	_____	_____
A Closer Relationship with the Lord	_____	_____
Our Father's Wonderful Love	_____	_____
Receive Healing from the Lord	_____	_____
Receive God's Blessing in Adversity	_____	_____
Enjoy God's Wonderful Peace	_____	_____
God is Always with You	_____	_____
Continually Increasing Faith in God	_____	_____

TOTAL PRICE _____

Florida residents only, add 7% sales tax _____

Tax deductible contribution to Lamplight Ministries, Inc. _____

Enclosed check or money order (do not send cash) _____

Please make check payable to Lamplight Ministries, Inc. and mail to: PO Box 1307, Dunedin, FL 34697

MC____ Visa____ AmEx____ Disc.____ Card # _____

Exp Date _____ Signature _____

Name _____

Address _____

City _____

State or Province _____ Zip or Postal Code _____

(Foreign orders must be submitted in U.S. dollars.)

ORDER FORM FOR SCRIPTURE MEDITATION CARDS AND CASSETTE TAPES

Due to completely different price structure for the production of Scripture Meditation Cards and 85-minute cassette tapes, we offer a different quantity discount which cannot be combined with our other quantity discounts. The following prices *include shipping and handling.* $5 per card deck or cassette tape; $4 for 5-9 card decks or cassette tapes; $3 for 10 or more card decks or cassette tapes.

SCRIPTURE   MEDITATION   CARDS   QUANTITY   PRICE

Find God's Will for Your Life   _____   _____
Financial Instructions from God   _____   _____
Freedom from Worry and Fear   _____   _____
A Closer Relationship with the Lord   _____   _____
Our Father's Wonderful Love   _____   _____
Receive Healing from the Lord   _____   _____
Receive God's Blessing in Adversity   _____   _____
Enjoy God's Wonderful Peace   _____   _____
God is Always with You   _____   _____
Continually Increasing Faith in God   _____   _____

CASSETTE   TAPES

Find God's Will for Your Life   _____   _____
Financial Instructions from God   _____   _____
Freedom from Worry and Fear   _____   _____
A Closer Relationship with the Lord   _____   _____
Our Father's Wonderful Love   _____   _____
Receive Healing from the Lord   _____   _____
Receive God's Blessing in Adversity   _____   _____
Enjoy God's Wonderful Peace   _____   _____
God is Always with You   _____   _____
Continually Increasing Faith in God   _____   _____

TOTAL   PRICE   _____

Florida residents only, add 7% sales tax   _____

Tax deductible contribution to Lamplight Ministries, Inc.   _____

Enclosed check or money order (do not send cash)   _____

Please make check payable to Lamplight Ministries, Inc. and mail to:
PO Box 1307, Dunedin, FL 34697

MC____ Visa____ AmEx____ Disc.____ Card # _____

Exp Date _____ Signature _____

Name _____

Address _____

City _____

State or Province _____ Zip or Postal Code _____

(Foreign orders must be submitted in U.S. dollars.)

The Vision of Lamplight Ministries

Lamplight Ministries, Inc. is founded upon Psalm 119:105 which says, "Your word is a lamp to my feet and a light to my path." We are so grateful to our loving Father for His precious Word that clearly shows us the path He wants us to follow throughout every day of our lives.

From the beginning of our ministry God has used us to reach people in many different countries. Our vision is to share the instructions and promises in the Word of God with multitudes of people in many different countries throughout the world.

We are believing God for the finances to provide the translation of our publications into many different foreign languages. We desire to give our publications free of charge to needy people all over the world who cannot afford to purchase them.

We are believing God for many partners in our ministry who will share our vision of distributing our publications which are solidly anchored upon the Word of God. It is our desire to provide these publications in every foreign language that we possibly can.

We yearn to share the Word of God with large numbers of people in Third World countries. We yearn to share the Word of God with large numbers of people in prisons and jails. These people desperately need to learn and obey God's instructions and to learn and believe in God's promises.

Please pray and ask the Lord if He would have you help us to help needy people all over the world. Thank you and God bless you.